WRITING THROUGH REPRESSION

WRITING

THROUGH

REPRESSION

Literature, Censorship, Psychoanalysis

Michael G. Levine

The Johns Hopkins University Press
Baltimore and London

This book has been brought to publication with the generous
assistance of the Frederick W. Hilles Publications Fund of
Yale University.

The Johns Hopkins University Press
2715 North Charles Street
Baltimore, Maryland 21218-4319
The Johns Hopkins Press Ltd., London

Library of Congress Cataloging-in-Publication Data

Levine, Michael G.
Writing through repression : literature, censorship,
psychoanalysis / Michael G. Levine.
p.   cm.
Includes bibliographical references and index.
ISBN 0-8018-4835-0
1. Authorship—Psychological aspects.   2. Psychoanalysis and
literature.   3. Censorship.   I. Title.
PN151.L44   1994
808'.02'019—dc20   94-15385

A catalog record for this book is available from the British Library.

To the memory of my grandparents
To my parents

CONTENTS

ACKNOWLEDGMENTS

Many people have helped me as I worked on this book, and I want here to express my gratitude and appreciation. The early stages of my research were carried out at the Center for Advanced Study at the University of Virginia and were supported by a grant from the Andrew Mellon Foundation. For their advice, criticism, and encouragement I would like to thank my friends in the German Department at Virginia: Renate Voris, Walter Sokel, Volker Kaiser, and Benjamin Bennett. Colleagues and students at Yale University commented on various stages of the manuscript; I owe much to Cathy Caruth, Lynn Enterline, Shoshana Felman, Michael Holquist, Jeffrey Sammons, Annette Schwarz, Mark Wollaeger, Henry Pickford, and Ulrich Baer for their careful readings and thoughtful suggestions. I learned a great deal from conversations with friends at Columbia University and am grateful to Dorothea von Mücke, Mark Anderson, John Archer, and Mark Petrini for their insights and support. I owe a special debt of gratitude to John Michael, Neil Saccamano, Neil Hertz, Samuel Weber, and Rainer Nägele, who have been such generous interlocutors over the years. I also wish to thank my editors at the Johns Hopkins University Press: Eric Halpern, for his judicious advice, and Carol Ehrlich, for her sensitive copyediting of the manuscript; the book is much improved thanks to their efforts. I am particularly grateful to Juliann Garey for her sharp editorial eye, her luminous wit, and her lovely smile.

The completion of the manuscript was funded in part by a grant from the A. Whitney Griswold Fund.

WRITING THROUGH REPRESSION

The Other Hand

Censorship and the Question
of Style

Ihr Krückstock, der einmal,
einmal . . . durchs Stumme hindurchspricht

Paul Celan

When the German governments responded to the revolutions of 1848 by rescinding the censorship laws, the exiled poet Heinrich Heine exclaimed, "Ach! I can't write anymore. How can I write when there's no longer any censorship? How should a man who's always lived with censorship suddenly be able to write without it? All style will cease, the whole grammar, the good habits!"[1]

The irony of these remarks is obvious to anyone familiar with Heine's lifelong struggle with German censorship. To write with the censor in mind was for him akin to living with a sword suspended by a thread over his head. Haunted by threats both real and imagined, he described censorship as a hand that stroked his brow only to wipe his thoughts away or as a pair of scissors that did to the "best part" of his body what they usually did to the choicest passages of his texts. "Why it's enough to drive you insane!" he confided to his publisher, Campe, in 1836.

While Heine undoubtedly experienced the administration of censorship as a process of textual, physical, and spiritual mutilation, he was also well aware that this Damoclean sword—like his own ironic words—tended to cut two ways. Indeed, as the remarks cited above suggest, the anticipated intervention of censorship not only exerted an inhibitory pressure on his writing, it also exercised a direct formative influence on the style of his texts.[2] There is thus a more difficult and embarrassing question that emerges through Heine's evident sarcasm, a question that may perhaps be raised only in an ironic and half-joking manner: namely, what kind of writing, what style and grammar, what habits of collaboration and co-dependency does the imposition of censorship and, more particularly, its *self-imposition* make possible?

In other words, if one is prepared to acknowledge that censorship functions, on the one hand, as a debilitating impediment and, on the other, as an impetus to stylistic innovation, the question that imposes itself, and that I seek to address in this book, is: What kind of interaction joins these two hands? What does it mean to view censorship as a condition of writing that is at once crippling and enabling? In contrast to more traditional philological approaches to the question, which seek primarily to identify specific textual elisions and imposed alterations in the hope of eventually restoring a work to its original, uncensored form, my study seeks to come to grips with a more unstable and collaborative mode of textual (de)composition. Whereas the term "collaboration" usually implies active, conscious cooperation with an enemy or at least some form of collective action, I would like to use it to describe a style of writing in which opposing forces are bound to each other in a relationship of conflictual interdependence. "Writing *through* repression" in the twofold sense that concerns us here involves an attempt to understand the ways in which censorship functions as an obstacle that *cannot* and yet *must* be overcome, as an impediment whose very resistance makes another, more equivocal and double-edged style of writing possible. Treating censorship not simply as a process of distortion and deletion but rather as a mode of double incision, the following chapters attend to the radically different kind of wound such incisions open: a wound that is not simply textual, corporeal, psychical, or political, but rather a crosscutting intersection of these spaces—the opening of an unstable, conflictual interspace in which writing and repression cut into and through each other.

Before proceeding let me say explicitly that I do not believe that censorship should always be treated as a double-edged sanction. Such an assertion would be irresponsible, not only because it threatens to universalize a problem that must be examined on a case-by-case basis as a particular interaction of competing forces, but also because it risks making a virtue of what is often a very painful and debilitating necessity.[3] My own interest in a more compromised and compromising notion of censorship has developed gradually out of a sense of frustration with more familiar scholarly approaches to the problem. Indeed, what I discovered in the course of my research into the question of self-censorship in Heine, which is the focus of Chapter 3, is a propensity among philologists to divide this question in two; that is, they tend to deal with it either as a strategy devised by the writer to smuggle contraband intellectual goods "into the harbor of the public sphere" or as a debilitating internalization of the power relations the author seeks to circumvent.[4] While it seems obvious that the two sides of the question are intimately related, it is less clear how one might begin to document this interaction.

If scholars—and particularly those involved in the preparation of a new historical-critical edition of Heine's work—have tended to shy away from such questions, I believe they have done so for two related reasons: first, because a double-edged notion of self-censorship tends to confuse the borders of a text rather than clarify them; second, because such a conception forces one to raise more basic questions about the very definition of authorship and the limits of textual integrity.[5] In attempting to work in the margins of traditional approaches to the question, I seek to document the ways in which a more pervasive interaction of writing and repression tailors a very different kind of textual fabric. Chapter 3, for example, is a reading of a relatively obscure fragment by Heine structured by a series of narrative interruptions. Rather than simply breaking off the narrative movement, these ruptures tend to transform it into a generalized mode of stuttering whose self-interruptions not only rehearse a kind of standoff between an urge to speak and a need to censor what is said, but in doing so also give voice to a tangle of *interirruptive* relationships in the text. In Heine's fragmentary narrative there is no speech that is not broken speech, no voice that does not crack in breaking through the fissures of another.

In attempting to link this painfully broken speech to a more dynamic notion of self-censorship, I seek both to reopen a question that has often been shunted to the periphery of Heine scholarship and to treat that question itself as a kind of crossing at which psychological, political, and textual questions intersect in such a thoroughgoing manner that each may be approached only via the mediation of the others. Such an approach, I would submit, has important implications for a reading of Freud—especially when one considers the pivotal role played by the metaphor of censorship in his thinking about dreams. "The kernel of my theory," he remarks in *The Interpretation of Dreams,* "lies in my derivation of dream distortion from the censorship."[6] While readers of this seminal work are usually quick to point out the general contribution made by a censoring instance in the formation of dreams, few have actually explored the specific nature of the interaction of the dreamwork with the dream censorship. Ignoring Freud's own suggestion that "censorship" be treated merely as a "serviceable term for describing a *dynamic relation*" (*S.E.*15, 140), critics have until now tended to view it merely as a negative obstacle, as a hindrance that can be circumvented and outwitted by the unconscious mechanisms of condensation, displacement, considerations of representability, and secondary revision. In opposition to this view, I argue (Chapter 2) that any attempt to come to terms with the dynamic instability of the Freudian notion of censorship must work through the double bind that ties it to the processes of the dreamwork. In short, I seek to explore the ways in which these seemingly opposed forces are at once more intimately connected and more intensely at odds with themselves than has heretofore been appreciated.

Beginning with my reading of *The Interpretation of Dreams* and continuing throughout the book, I attempt to develop some of the implications of a claim made by Derrida in an early essay on Freud in which he asserts that "writing is unthinkable without repression." I take this to mean three things: first, that the relationship between these operations, as it has traditionally been conceived, needs to be radically rethought; second, that writing needs to be thought first and foremost through its relation to repression; and third, that the texts of Freud constitute a privileged scene in which this hitherto unthinkable kind of relationship is unthinkingly— that is, unconsciously—thought through. In other words, I construe Derrida's remark (read in the context of his more general argument) to suggest that a different way of thinking about the relationship of writing and repression is legible in Freud's texts, but it is to be read there on the level of a certain pantomimic "gesture" and not on the level of the text's theoretical content; that is, it is to be read as a conflict that is silently acted out in Freud's writing and not simply as a relationship directly described by him.[7] In short, Derrida entitles his essay "Freud and the Scene of Writing" in order to stress the way in which a different kind of relationship between writing and repression is staged as an unresolved and perhaps unsolvable problem that not only haunts the Freudian corpus but also structures and impels it.

As a spectator interested in the dumbshow performance of Freud's text, Derrida turns from what is written there to the gestural language of the hand that writes. Or to be more precise, he focuses on the movement of the two hands at work in Freud's texts, one of which writes while the other erases, one of which registers impressions while the other fends them off. As I note at several points in the following chapters, the movement of these two hands and the figure of ambidextrous writing in general is used by Derrida to describe a relationship between writing and repression that can no longer be conceived of in the alternating, oppositional logic of "on the one hand, on the other."[8] Instead, such figures gesture toward the contradictory functioning of a writing process as much at odds with itself as with a repressive or censorial other to which it is more obviously opposed.

It is no accident that Derrida's essay stands literally under the sign of Freud's comments about the early psychoanalytic notion of "breaching": *"Worin die Bahnung sonst besteht bleibt dahingestellt* (In what pathbreaking consists remains undetermined)" (*Project for a Scientific Psychology,* 1895). Taking this remark as its epigraph, Derrida's text is itself an attempt to break open new paths of investigation guided by hitherto unsuspected continuities and unconsciously insisting problems (like that of "breaching" itself) in the Freudian corpus. In focusing on those aspects of Freud's text which are never quite assimilated *or* excluded, Derrida draws attention both to the very limits of Freud's thinking and to those overdetermined points of intersection where psychoanalysis is crosscut and traversed by other related discourses. At these points of intersection, the self-subversive potential of Freudian discourse — its constitutive otherness-to-itself — actively and incisively opens within it the possibility of a different kind of encounter with other fields of investigation. The point is worth emphasizing, since what is at stake here is the difference between more traditional modes of *applied* reading, which all too often treat psychoanalysis as a positive body of knowledge used to interpret literary and social texts, and an approach Shoshana Felman has referred to as a process of "interimplication," in which "psychoanalytic theory and the literary text mutually inform — and displace — each other."[9]

It is this sense of interimplication and mutual displacement that I develop in the following chapters through readings of texts by Heine, Freud, Benjamin, Baudelaire, Ovid, and Kafka. Rather than seeking to extract a particular notion of censorship from Freud in order to apply it elsewhere, I contend that it is more instructive to examine the difficulties he has in coming to terms with this notion. As I argue in Chapter 2, it is only by paying attention to the trouble spots in his text that one may begin to grasp the instability of "censorship" and the dynamic interaction of the competing forces that inhabit and dislocate it. In short, what is of interest here is the way censorship, viewed as a creative problem, shapes the style of Heine's and Freud's texts in particular. Furthermore, it is precisely through the problem of censorship that the writings of these two exceptional stylists may be seen to intersect and unthinkingly communicate with each other in ways that unsettle and enrich our understanding of both. As was suggested earlier, such intersections also imply that the problem of censorship itself is one that may remain beyond the grasp of any one particular field of study or critical jargon. In other words, if censorship inevitably raises questions about discursive boundaries and their transgression, in order to address this issue it may in turn be necessary to work at the intersection of a number of discursive and disciplinary fields, reading the language of one through the filter of another.

The subtitle, *Literature, Censorship, Psychoanalysis,* alludes to the necessity of this interdisciplinary approach. Yet, it also suggests that the relationship between literature and psychoanalysis might itself be more effectively explored by replacing the apparently neutral and transparent coordinating conjunction "and" linking these fields with a term suggesting a more agonistic, obstructed, and equivocal kind of connection. As was noted earlier, such an approach is closely related to what Felman advocates in the name of a more dynamic "interimplication" of literature and psychoanalysis. In order to situate my own project in the context of current debates about the possibilities and risks of collaboration between these disciplines, it may be useful at this point to examine in some detail Felman's introduction to *Literature and Psychoanalysis: The Question of Reading: Otherwise,* which has helped to define the terms of that debate. There she remarks:

> Although "and" is grammatically defined as a "coordinate conjunction," in the context of the relationship between "literature and psychoanalysis" it is usually interpreted, paradoxically enough, as implying not so much a relation of coordination as one of *subordination,* a relation in which literature is submitted to the authority, to the prestige of psychoanalysis. While literature is considered as a body of *language*—to be *interpreted*—psychoanalysis is considered as a body of *knowledge,* whose competence is called upon *to interpret.* Psychoanalysis, in other words, occupies the place of a subject, literature that of an object.[10]

Thus, according to Felman, the seeming neutrality of the "coordinate conjunction" effectively dissimulates a relation of power in which one of the terms brought together by the "and" enjoys an implicit privilege over the other.[11] "It is usually felt," she adds, "that psychoanalysis has much or all to teach us about literature, whereas literature has little or nothing to teach us about psychoanalysis" (7). Given the stylized symmetry of these and other remarks in her essay, one might be led to assume that what is needed then is simply a more balanced, reciprocal kind of rapport—a "real *dialogue,*" as she says, and not just a "unilateral monologue of psychoanalysis *about* literature" (6). Such appearances, however, are misleading, for Felman's ultimate aim, as I see it, is not so much to place literature on a more equal footing with psychoanalysis as to *displace* the very terms and structure of their relationship.

In Felman this displacement proceeds along two related lines: first, she suggests that literature, far from being merely a contiguous field of external verification in which psychoanalysis can test its hypotheses, is a body of language which has always already inhabited psychoanalysis and provided it with the very terms it uses to speak of itself—terms such as the Oedipus complex and Narcissism (derived from fictional characters) or masochism and sadism (based on the names of authors). Here one begins to sense that the possibility of a "real *dialogue*" between literature and psychoanalysis, as envisaged by Felman, ultimately depends less on the mutual recognition of two parties struggling to comprehend each other than on the acknowledgment of an internal splitting of the speaking subject—an acknowledgment, that is, of the ways in which the voice of psychoanalysis has from the very beginning been inhabited and even ventriloquized by that of its purported interlocutor. A "real *dialogue*" would thus involve a relationship in which literature and psychoanalysis not only speak *to* but also *through* one another.

As was noted earlier, the second kind of displacement proposed by Felman involves a shift from traditional methods of applied reading—be they psychoanalytic *or* literary—to a "radically different notion of *implication*"; it is for this reason that her volume *Literature and Psychoanalysis* bears the subtitle *The Question of Reading: Otherwise*. Indeed, to read "differently" for Felman means "bringing analytical questions to bear upon literary questions, *involving* psychoanalysis in the scene of literary analysis" (8–9).

> The interpreter's role would here be, not to *apply* to the text an acquired science, a preconceived knowledge, but to act as a go-between, to *generate implications* between literature and psychoanalysis—to explore, bring to light and articulate the various (indirect) ways in which the two domains do indeed *implicate each other,* each one finding itself enlightened, informed, but also affected, displaced, by the other.

Ironically, one of the implications generated by Felman's remarks concerns the very question of their own applicability. For in advocating an interpretive practice whose watchword is "read otherwise," Felman enjoins her reader "to re-invent the 'and'" and to displace the relationship between literature and psychoanalysis *each time one reads.* Her notion of implication, in other words, cannot be understood simply as a new method of reading—another interpretive grid to be imposed upon a text. If anything, it is an antimethodology in the sense that it challenges those who would follow her to run the risk of improvisation—to dare to be inventive in exposing themselves to the chance of an unpredictable, singular, and transformative encounter with that which remains opaque and unassimilable in any given text. A "real *dialogue*" between literature and psychoanalysis would thus depend not only on a constitutive splitting of the speaking subject but also on a different mode of receptivity: a way of "listening with the third ear," to be sure, but also, to paraphrase Lacan, an opening of the sender to— and by—that which he *receives from the receiver:* namely, his own (potentially self-subversive) message ironically turned back on it-self, *re*turned in an unfamiliar and inverted form.[12]

It is important to note here that in moving from a rather static sense of the seemingly separate identities of literature and psycho-analysis toward a more dynamic notion of their mutual implica-tion, Felman also proposes a different way of describing the con-flicts embroiling them. In order to gauge this difference, it may be useful to compare her remarks to those of Françoise Meltzer. As Meltzer's polemical introduction to *The Trial(s) of Psychoanalysis* makes clear, so long as it is a question of the relative identities of literature and psychoanalysis, so long, that is, as the attempt is made to determine their proper place with respect to one another ("psychoanalysis is on trial," she says, "in order to be put back into its place—or, at least, into *a* place"), a language of invasion, colonization, and expropriation will generally be used to describe their struggles.[13] By contrast, Felman rejects the language of bor-der disputes in favor of figures that give the sense of a more perva-sive enfolding of literature and psychoanalysis within and through each other. Rather than neutralizing conflict, this twisting move-ment of mutual implication tends, if anything, to intensify it, and in so doing, obliges one to speak in terms of a more compromis-ingly equivocal collaboration between psychoanalysis and its liter-ary Other:

> Each is thus a potential threat to the interiority of the other, since each is contained in the other as its *otherness-to-itself,* its *uncon-scious.* As the unconscious traverses consciousness, a theoretical body of thought always is traversed by its own unconscious, its own "unthought," of which it is not aware, but which it contains in itself as the very conditions of its disruption, as the possibility of its own self-subversion. . . . in the same way that psychoanalysis points to the unconscious of literature, *literature, in its turn, is the uncon-scious of psychoanalysis;* . . . the unthought-out shadow in psycho-analytic *theory* is precisely its own involvement with literature; . . . literature *in* psychoanalysis functions precisely as its "*unthought*":

> as the condition of possibility *and* the self-subversive blind spot of
> psychoanalytic *thought*. (10)

If relations between literature and psychoanalysis have often shown signs of struggle and strain, Felman's remarks enable one to view these tensions not merely as indications of antagonism and blockage, but also as signs of the emergence of a different, more complex and unstable topology of mutual implication. What remains to be seen is how these entanglements may function like the knotting of the dream navel in Freud as another kind of communicating link, as a "point of contact with the unknown" (*S.E.*4, 111).[14]

■   ■   ■

> With my burned hand I write about the nature of fire
>
> Ingeborg Bachmann

While literary critics like Meltzer have objected to what they perceive to be the colonial ambitions of psychoanalysis, in the past two decades practicing analysts have in their turn been faced with an increasing number of "literary-critical" studies of Freud in which "content," to cite Stanley Coen, "is subordinated to process, style, and what transpires between author and reader."[15] "Raising questions, problematizing the reading of Freud's texts," he adds, "now supersedes finding answers from Freud" (484). Thus, while literary critics are often exasperated by analysts who appear to have all the answers, analysts in their turn are troubled by critics who seem to have nothing but questions. As Coen observes, "This is currently a popular mode in literary criticism (as elsewhere): raising questions rather than finding answers; studying the process of reading a text; what happens to the reader as he reads. Literary critics then may use the psychoanalytic process as further justification for reading texts as an interactional process between author, text, and reader" (484).

In general, Coen's essay "How to Read Freud: A Critique of Recent Freud Scholarship" manifests an interesting ambivalence with regard to the so-called literary reading. For while the author is largely sympathetic to the ambitions of writers like Patrick Mahoney, Shoshana Felman, and Samuel Weber, he also seems to feel that the latter two in particular sometimes go too far. In an effort to clarify some of the stakes of the literary reading and to address certain reservations often voiced about it, I would like to take up a number of issues raised by Coen.

While the passage cited above seems to suggest that there is nothing more at stake for critics and analysts in the current return to the letter of Freud's text than simply raising questions and studying the reading process, elsewhere Coen draws attention to the very concrete ways in which this return has altered our understanding of James Strachey's English translation of Freud. The *Standard Edition* is unquestionably a work of tremendous patience, dedication, and erudition. Yet, as has often been suggested, its terminological consistency and uniformity of style—the very qualities that make it such a reliable research tool—also at times deny the Anglophone reader access to other, less familiar dimensions of Freud's thought. Some critics have even claimed that Strachey's translation has a tendency to do to Freud's German what the mechanism of secondary revision described in the *Traumdeutung* does to the material of dreams. For just as secondary revision is said to reduce the dream's apparent absurdity and incoherence by filling in its gaps and reorganizing its material into a more intelligible whole, Strachey's translation is felt to paper over seeming inconsistencies and idiosyncrasies in Freud's language and style.

Thus, for example, as Coen, following Roustang, observes, the story told through Freud's syntax, word placement, and linguistic repetitions is often rewritten and obliterated by Strachey in his effort to render the overall meaning of a passage. Similarly, Freud's use of the present tense, which gives the impression of fictional immediacy and evokes the time frame of joke telling and dreaming, is often rendered in the more distant past or present perfect tense. As Bettelheim, Ornston, and Mahoney note, Strachey's translation is also overly formal and stiff in contrast to Freud's more flexible and forceful colloquial, Viennese style.[16] It has also been observed that the *Standard Edition* generally tends to make the writing simpler, less affectively charged, less open-ended, and less complex. Furthermore, as Bettelheim and others have noted, Strachey's substitution of Latin terms (such as *ego* and *id*) for familiar German words (*ich* and *es*) with intensely personal meanings has the effect of distancing the language from the realm of daily experience while making it sound more like the specialized jargon of scientific discourse. Critics attentive to the stylistic and linguistic nuances of the German have also been able to detect a subtle transformation of Freud's hypothetical, subjunctive images into fixed statements in the English as well as a reduction of connotative associations in the translation's privileging of denotative meanings.

If, early on, Freud himself describes repression as a "failure of translation [*Versagung der Übersetzung*],"[17] it is certainly time we paid closer attention to particular shortcomings of the standard English translation of his work currently in use.[18] As was noted above, Strachey's translation not only tends to distort Freud's text but, like the secondary revision of dreams, also distorts its distortions by producing a façade of "false and misleading plenitude" (*S.E.*5, 490). In reading Strachey's translation as a kind of secondary revision of Freud, it is important to bear in mind that what is at stake here are not only the specific errors committed by a particular translator, but also and above all the ways in which the symptomatic "failures" of this translation raise larger questions about the status of psychoanalytic thought in general. Indeed, as Samuel Weber observes in *The Legend of Freud*, "if such self-dissimulating distortions have long been recognized as the privileged object of Freudian psychoanalysis, it is only recently that this domain has been extended to encompass the workings of psychoanalytic discourse itself."[19]

Citing the writings of Derrida and Lacan as the pioneering works in this return to the symptom as both *object and operation* of the Freudian text, Weber stresses that such work seeks not merely to perform yet another psychoanalysis of the founding father but, more radically, to ask whether psychoanalytic thinking itself can escape the effects of what it endeavors to grasp.[20] The question for Weber is thus: "Can the disruptive distortions of unconscious processes be simply recognized, theoretically, as an object, or must they not leave their imprint on the process of theoretical objectification itself? Must not psychoanalytical thinking itself partake of—repeat—the dislocations it seeks to describe?"[21]

Because this question serves to orient my own interrogation of Freud's texts, it is important to clarify what precisely is at stake in reading Freud in this way. As is apparent in the passage cited above, the accent in Weber often tends to fall on the prefix *dis-* (that is, on moments of disruption, distortion, and dislocation). This emphasis has in some cases led analysts like Coen to believe that the task for Weber consists merely in using "Freud against himself" in order to demonstrate how "any attempt to theorize about unconscious conflict must be subverted by the latter, which will always have the last laugh."[22] While Weber does tend to read Freud's writings as an "other scene" in which unconscious conflicts are not simply described but also symptomatically acted out, such enactments do more than simply subvert attempts to theorize about conflict. Indeed, rather than simply neutralizing or undermining the claims of theory, such subversions force us to reconsider what the process of psychoanalytic theorization actually entails.

It is significant in this regard that Coen describes the literary-critical return to Freud as a "move away from what Freud said and meant to how Freud said what he did and what we are to do with this" (483). What is lacking in this description is precisely the sense (so crucial to the literary reading) that it is necessary to study not only "how Freud said what he did" but moreover how his text does more than it says it is doing. In short, what Coen views as a subversion of psychoanalytic theory is treated by literary critics as the theory's irreducibly performative dimension.

Furthermore, as Coen himself suggests, what is at stake here is not simply a difference of perspective but a disagreement over the very status of perspective. "An exclusive emphasis on the role of unconscious conflict," he says, "refuses to leave anything alone, as possibly, even temporarily, outside of conflict": "This is not just a debate between French and Americans about ego psychology, metapsychology, and the unconscious; it is also a critical position from which it is impossible to maintain perspective, in which unconscious conflict *must* always subvert one's position. In less extreme form, such radical questioning of Freud's texts by Weber and Felman is fascinating and useful."[23]

Once again, it is the issue of subversion and, more particularly, the fate of an observer who is no longer able to distance himself from the conflicts he observes that form the crux of Coen's critique. It is therefore significant that what he perceives as a compromising loss of objectivity and "perspective" is viewed by Weber and Felman as a new and indeed "revolutionary" type of "scientific rigor" involving a radically different mode of scientific engage-

ment, participation, and necessary self-implication.[24] Troubled by
what he views as the radicality of Weber's and Felman's questioning of Freud's text (so much so that he tends to overstate their
claims), Coen fails to see what is potentially productive about the
subversions he describes. For if these authors do indeed argue that
unconscious conflict always has *at least the potential* to "subvert
one's position," the consequences of this are twofold: first, that
one may be *positioned by* such conflicts in a shifting field of forces;
second, that this *disposition* makes possible alternative modes of
critical and analytic intervention. Felman's comments on Lacan's
"Seminar on 'The Purloined Letter'" are particularly pertinent in
this regard:

> The intervention of Dupin, who restores the letter to the Queen,
> is . . . compared, in Lacan's interpretation, to the intervention of
> the analyst, who rids the patient of the symptom. *The analyst's ef-
> fectiveness, however, does not spring from his intellectual strength
> but . . . from his position in the (repetitive) structure.* By virtue of
> his occupying the third position—that is, the *locus* of the uncon-
> scious of the subject as a place of substitution of letter for letter (of
> signifier for signifier)—the analyst, through transference, allows at
> once for a repetition of the trauma, and for a symbolic substitution,
> and thus effects the drama's denouement. (Emphasis added)[25]

If Felman describes this "analysis through repetition" as an *"allegory of psychoanalysis,"* her description applies not only to the
analytic situation per se, as it is sketched above, but also to the
contemporary situation of analysis vis-à-vis the texts of Freud. For
while Lacan's "Seminar" deals explicitly with the theft and even-
tual restoration of a letter to its rightful owner, his literary-analytic
intervention is even more obviously—perhaps a little too obviously—an attempt to return *to the letter* of Freud's text. Needless
to say, such a return oriented by a reading of Poe aims less at restoring to Freud's texts a lost literal meaning or proper sense they
might once have had than at rediscovering the *literariness* of those
texts—that dimension of Freud's writing which is repeatedly over-
looked because, like the purloined letter, it is hidden out in the
open.[26] In the most basic sense, this return to the letter heightens
the focus upon Freud's language, style, figures, repetitions, allusions, terminological borrowings, narrative voices, modes of ad-

dress, and use of quotations. In short, it returns to those aspects of his text which are systematically disregarded and, I daresay, *repressed* when we try, as Coen says, merely "'to get' Freud's ideas" (513). If, as Coen observes, recent literary readings of Freud have taken a new approach "in which content is subordinated to process, style, and what transpires between author and reader," it should be stressed that this shift in focus has been motivated by a sense that the so-called content of Freud's work is more intimately and equivocally bound up with its mode of presentation—or to stay with Lacan's postal metaphor, its manner of *delivery*—than has hitherto been noticed.[27] In Chapter 2 I seek to develop such an approach through an examination of the functioning of the metaphor of censorship in *The Interpretation of Dreams*. The originality of Freud's work, I argue, consists as much in his novel approach to dreams and their censorship as in his implicit rethinking of the issue of metaphor in general.

While it is certainly true that analysts in particular have always paid close attention to the metaphors, images, and analogies used by Freud, they have nevertheless tended to treat these figures more or less as visual aids—as didactic illustrations of abstract and relatively unfamiliar ideas.[28] By contrast, critics inspired by the work of Derrida and Lacan have recently begun to focus on the ways in which Freud's figures *insinuate* themselves into the very texture of his writing, thereby enmeshing themselves in the fabric of relationships they are initially called upon simply to clarify and concretize.

No doubt this approach, which ascribes such importance to the figurative dimension of Freud's text, will strike many as an unwarranted attempt to read documents of inestimable scientific value merely as so many works of literature. Before drawing such conclusions, one would do well to recall Freud's own metalinguistic comments in *Beyond the Pleasure Principle,* in which he underscores the primary and enabling function of figurative language in the process of psychoanalytic observation:

> We need not feel greatly disturbed in judging our speculation upon the life and death drives by the fact that so many bewildering and obscure processes [*befremdende und unanschauliche Vorgänge*] occur in it—such as one drive being driven out by another, or a drive turning from the ego to an object and so on. This is merely due

to our being obliged to operate with the scientific terms, that is to say with the figurative language [*Bildersprache*] peculiar to psychology (or more precisely, to depth-psychology). We could not otherwise describe the processes in question at all, and *indeed we could not even have perceived them*. (*S.E.*18, 60; emphasis added)

Commenting on this passage, Samuel Weber astutely remarks that "far from translating observed data into the language of theory, what psychoanalysis actually does . . . is to transcribe a translation that itself is rendered perceptible, observable, cognizable only through the *Bildersprache* that repeats and replaces it."[29] In other words, the figurative language of psychoanalysis provides indirect, mediated, and necessarily *distorted* access to processes that are not otherwise available to analytic scrutiny; as such, this language functions as a kind of (mis)translation of a translation without original.

While it may thus be said that Freud's figurative language serves as a kind of Celanian "crookstick," a prosthetic supplement that enables him to depict in a necessarily roundabout way relationships that cannot be observed more directly or described in more straightforwardly literal terms, it is equally important to emphasize the necessity of finding ways around this *Bildersprache*.[30] For the very figures that serve to extend Freud's conceptual reach and that make unconscious processes observable in the first place also at times function like screen memories; that is, they often obfuscate and distort relationships by virtue of their very clarity.[31] In such cases, the similarities and homologies suggested by Freud's metaphorical language threaten to arrest the very movements of thought they otherwise make possible.[32] To break the spell of fascination exerted by these strikingly vivid images (in order to be able to arrive at other such compromise formations), it is therefore necessary to pay equal attention to the *dissimilarities* and *incongruities* engendered by Freud's metaphors; the overdetermination of his figures; and his peculiar use of a language of quantity which at times is employed not only to describe particular economic relationships but also to *avoid* a language of positive description, attribution, and qualification.

Because the *Bildersprache* of psychoanalytic discourse inevitably withholds as much as it delivers, conceals as much as it reveals,

Samuel Weber suggests that it be read with the same circumspection Freud applies to the "epistemophobic" language of dreams. This language, Weber observes, "is precisely *not* a theoretical discourse, in any traditional sense, for rather than seeking to disclose and discover, it [strives] to dissimulate and, moreover, . . . to dissimulate its own dissimulation."[33] In a well-known simile, Freud compares the dream language to a kind of *Bilderschrift* or hieroglyphic inscription:

> The dream-thoughts are immediately comprehensible, as soon as we have learnt them. The dream-content, on the other hand, is, as it were, given in a pictographic script [*Bilderschrift*], whose characters [*Zeichen*] must be transposed individually into the language of the dream-thought. If we attempted to read these characters according to their pictorial value instead of according to their semiotic relations [*Zeichenbeziehung*], we should clearly be led into error. . . . A dream is a picture-puzzle. (*S.E.*4, 277; trans. mod.)

Struck by the peculiarly Saussurean tone of these remarks, Weber notes that "Freud's conception of the dream-language seems structuralist *avant la lettre:* it is not the representational, thematic, 'pictorial' content of the dream-signs that determines their 'value,' but rather their relations to other signs."[34] As was noted above, Weber argues that this "semiotic" approach to the reading of the dream's *Bilderschrift* should be extended and applied to a study of the *Bildersprache* of Freud's texts in general. Such an approach, it should be stressed, involves more than an attempt to identify traces in Freud of a structuralism *avant la lettre*. On the contrary, Weber endeavors through a return to Freud's German—a return *à la lettre*—to unsettle and displace the very reading of his work which has emerged recently in the wake of structuralist efforts to articulate psychoanalysis with linguistic theory.

To appreciate the polemical thrust of Weber's argument, it is important to bear in mind that his critique is directed less at the "return to Freud" initiated by Lacan than at the fetishization of a certain "Lacan" by a new generation of disciples. It is significant in this regard that Weber's essay "The Meaning of the Thallus," ostensibly a critique of Lacan—thus the twist on the latter's title, "The Signification of the Phallus"—concludes by reminding the reader of Lacan's own injunction that the phrase *Le Nom du Père*

(The Name of the Father) must *also* be read as *le non-dupe erre* (the non-dupe errs). What Weber is thus criticizing in the name of "Lacan" is not simply the teaching of a particular individual but also and above all the reconstitution of a structure of discipleship and the new, albeit highly sophisticated, mode of "applied psychoanalysis" currently conducted in his name.[35]

It should be noted, however, that this transference onto "Lacan" alluded to by Weber is not merely to be traced back to the personality of a certain charismatic individual nor is it a matter that can be explained (away) in terms of psychoanalytic group dynamics. Even less can this transference be avoided simply by identifying it or calling it by *its* "proper name." It is therefore no accident that Weber's discussion of the punning Lacanian admonition *"le non-dupe err"* closes with the following qualification: "Yet if this error must be understood as constitutive of the very gesture of denomination itself, then this cannot be without consequences for every form of discourse that seeks to articulate truth by means of naming: be it that of Freud, of Lacan, or of this text itself."[36]

In this passage, which ironically concludes with a string of proper names, Weber seems to alert the reader to both the object and the strategy of his own polemics. As we have already had occasion to notice, these attacks are directed as much at those who would claim to *speak* the truth in the name of Lacan as at those who would *seek* that truth exclusively in the constative dimension of his (or for that matter of Freud's own) discourse.

The radical reduction of Lacan's notoriously difficult texts to a few mechanically repeated dictums, slogans, and instrumentalized "concepts" is no doubt a significant symptom of the prevailing tendency to read his writing as an essentially denominative and descriptive theoretical discourse. While such a reading is certainly useful, it nevertheless tends to lose touch with a sense of the diachronic movement of his thought. In other words, it risks losing touch with the displacements of a discourse whose own place is differentially and agonistically determined by virtue of what and whom it strategically sets itself off against. It is for this reason that Jean-Luc Nancy and Philippe Lacoue-Labarthe make emphatic use of a notion of *détournement* in their reading of Lacan's essay "The Agency of the Letter in the Unconscious." As the English translators of *The Title of the Letter* explain,

Détournement . . . is borrowed . . . from Lacan himself who used it in "Subversion of the Subject and the Dialectic of Desire" to designate his treatment of logic. The authors assign a special value to the term: the multiple borrowings, perversions, subversions, repetitions, and alterations of various theoretical fields with which Lacan's discourse institutes itself. . . . Détournement is . . . a distortion, but in the sense of a *deviation* or *change of course* of the distorted element. . . . The *distorted* element is *diverted* with the intent of making it enter into a new context. . . . [Lacoue-Labarthe and Nancy] are careful to contrast *détournement* with the *importation* of a concept: whereas an importation borrows a conceptual unity in order to appropriate it into a new system in a regulated way, *détournement* borrows a concept "without *working* it," that is, leaves room for a certain alterity or polysemy which resists containment and appropriation.[37]

It is precisely this sense of the strategic *détournements* with which, as the translators say, "Lacan's discourse institutes itself" that has often been lost in recent attempts to apply his "theories" to the study of literature (and film) in this country. Substituting more traditional notions of importation and appropriation for the Lacanian praxis of deviation, distortion, and diversion, critics have also tended to misconstrue the significance of structural linguistics for Lacan. Such a tendency is evident, for example, in the editors' introduction to a recent collection of essays, *The Ends of Rhetoric:* "At least in retrospect, Lacan's famous dictum that the unconscious is structured like a language seems to follow inevitably from the juxtaposition of Freud's treatises on dreams and jokes with Jakobson's specification of metaphor and metonymy as the basic mechanisms of discourse production, since these figures, as Jakobson notices, are the rhetorical equivalents of condensation and displacement—the fundamental processes of Freud's 'dream work.'"[38]

What tends to be passed over in such asertions is not only the relationship of these processes of the dream work to the dream censorship, but moreover the irreducibly agonistic nature of that relationship. Wrenched from this context of conflict and compromise, condensation and displacement are presented merely as neutralized psychical "equivalents" of the tropes of metaphor and metonymy. While the editors are not wrong to locate Lacan's dictum at the historical crossroads of a path suggested but not taken by Freud in his work on dreams and jokes and a structuralist theory of language eager to extend its claims about the "basic mechanisms of discourse production" to the realm of the unconscious, they fail to convey a sense of the specific twist that Lacan gives to each of these fields in the process of bringing them together. By contrast, Samuel Weber contends that "to properly understand the significance of structural linguistics for Lacan, one cannot overlook its internal contradictions. Saussure's writings are of interest to him, less as the site where a certain strain of modern linguistics sought to pose its foundations, than as a theater in which the structure of language and its relation to the subject are staged as questions."[39]

For Weber, then, it is not a matter of mechanisms but of contradictions and questions. Indeed, I would suggest that Lacan is less interested in pairing psychoanalytic terms with their "rhetorical equivalents" in the hope of assimilating one to the other than in exposing what remains *unassimilable* and internally contradictory in each as a way of opening it to a more fundamental interrogation. In contrast to the editors of *The Ends of Rhetoric,* who view Lacan's "famous dictum" as following "inevitably" from the juxtaposition of two foundations—the "basic mechanisms of discourse production" and the "fundamental processes of Freud's dreamwork"—I would further suggest that the function of Lacan's return to the writings of Freud, Jakobson, and Saussure is not so much to cite what has already been established as to renew contact with the conflicts, problems, and questions that dislocate and unconsciously impel those texts.

That the direction of this return is faithful to the spirit of Freud's own sense of his endeavor is implied by the following words he wrote to his future wife, Martha Bernays, in a letter of October 31, 1883: "A failure [in research work] makes one inventive, creates a free flow of associations, brings idea after idea, whereas once success is there a certain narrow-mindedness or thick-headedness sets in so that one always keeps coming back to what has been already established and can make no new combinations."[40] It is of course our luck that it is not always easy to tell the difference between Freud's moving failures and his arresting achievements. It is the tale of this fateful irony that the following chapters seek to tell.

2

Freud and the Scene
of Censorship

In a letter to his friend Wilhelm Fliess, announcing the completion of *The Interpretation of Dreams,* Freud compares his own style to that of the dreamer described in his pioneering work.

> The dream material itself is, I believe, unassailable. What I dislike about it is the style, which was quite incapable [*unfähig*] of noble, simple expression and lapsed into facetious [*witzelnde*] circumlocutions straining after metaphors. I know that, but the part of me that knows it and knows how to evaluate it is unfortunately the part that does not produce.
>
> It is certainly true that the dreamer is too witty, but it is neither my fault nor does it contain a reproach. All dreamers are equally insufferably witty, and they need to be because they are under pressure and the direct route is barred to them.[1]

The contrast here is clear enough. While the dreamer is obliged to be overly clever, the writer (who would one day be awarded the Goethe Prize for Literature) simply cannot help himself. While the former uses circumlocutions to get around obstacles, the latter merely "lapses" into them. While the creative, wish-constructing part of the dreamer works in tandem with its censorial counterpart, in the author the hand that evaluates "unfortunately" has nothing to do with the one that produces.

A little over a week later, Freud returns to the matter of style in another letter to Fliess.

> Somewhere inside me there is a feeling for form, an appreciation of beauty as a kind of perfection; and the tortuous sentences of my dream book [*Traumschrift*], with their parading of indirect phrases and squinting at ideas, deeply offended one of my ideals. Nor am I

far wrong in regarding this lack of form [*Formmangel*] as an indication of insufficient mastery of the material.[2]

Once again the self-deprecating tone and expression of an of-
fended aesthetic sensibility give voice to insecurities, as though
Freud were still wondering at this point just how finished his manuscript really was. Yet the insistent identification of his own style with
that of the dreamer—even as he excuses the latter while finding
fault with the former—suggests another way of understanding the
professed shortcomings of his text. In "straining after metaphors"
to describe the unconscious activity of dreaming, it is no accident
that Freud makes repeated use of *textual* metaphors throughout
The Interpretation of Dreams. As has often been observed, he compares dreams to pictograms, rebuses, and hieroglyphs and describes
the dream content as a kind of "transcript of the dream-thoughts
into another mode of expression" (*S.E.*4, 277). He even goes so far
at one point as to claim that "the phenomena of censorship and
of dream distortion correspond down to their smallest details"
(*S.E.*4, 143). Thus, while the tortuous sentences of his dream book
remind him of the indirect modes of expression proper to dreams,
a proper understanding of those dreams in turn requires that they
be treated as enigmatic, transcribed, and censored texts. Freud's
chiasmatic coupling of text and dream—of text-as-dream and
dream-as-text—effectively displaces the relative value of each of
the terms brought together here. While he complains to Fliess that
his dream book is "lacking in form," one begins to suspect that this
alleged deficiency is not merely an indication of "insufficient mastery," as Freud suggests, but instead the index of a *different kind of
relationship* of the psychical and the textual.

In his pathbreaking essay "Freud and the Scene of Writing,"
Derrida begins to outline just such a relationship. If his reading
is, as he says, guided by Freud's investment in the metaphor of
nonphonetic writing, his aim is less to determine how Freud uses
such metaphors for didactic ends than to ask how the insistence of
such terms "makes what we believe we know under the name of
writing enigmatic."[3] In other words, the question for him is not
whether

a writing apparatus—for example, the one described in the "Note
on the Mystic Writing Pad"—is a *good* metaphor for representing

the working of the psyche, but rather what apparatus we must create in order to represent psychical writing. [The question is] not *if* the psyche is indeed a kind of text, but: what is a text, and what must the psyche be if it can be represented by a text? For if there is neither machine nor text without psychical origin, there is no domain of the psyche without text. (199; emphasis added)

Derrida's decision to focus on the metaphor of writing is thus motivated by a desire to reinterpret and displace the traditional status both of metaphor and of writing—the point being that these issues are so bound up with each other that to address the one is always in a sense to talk about the other. Derrida argues that "scriptural images have regularly been used to *illustrate* the relationship between reason and experience, perception and memory" (199) from Plato and Aristotle on. What for him distinguishes "the gesture sketched out by Freud" is the way that metaphor and writing come to inhabit and constitute the very relationships they are usually called upon simply to illustrate.

While Derrida reads the tracing of this gesture in a wide range of texts, the professed aim of his essay is to follow "a strange progression" in Freud's work from the *Project* of 1895 to the "Note on the Mystic Writing-Pad" (1925). Charting the course of this progression, which along the way follows the "advance of the metaphors of path, trace, breach," etc., Derrida describes how

the structural model of writing, which Freud invokes immediately after the *Project,* will be persistently differentiated and refined in its originality. All the mechanical models will be tested and abandoned, until the discovery of the *Wunderblock,* a writing machine of marvelous complexity into which the whole of the psychical apparatus will be projected. The solution to all the previous difficulties will be presented in the *Wunderblock,* and the "Note," indicative of an admirable tenacity, will answer precisely the questions of the *Project.* (200)

If all roads thus seem to lead to the *Wunderblock,* it is not simply because this text provides the solution to a longstanding problem but rather because it restages in a more complex, dynamic, and rigorous way *an earlier question* already raised in the *Project* concerning the relationship of metaphor, writing, and spacing. Leaving aside for the moment the details of Derrida's discussion of Freud's "Note," to which I return in Chapter 5, I would instead like to call attention to the way the question of censorship emerges at this point in his essay.

"Writing," he says, "is unthinkable without repression. The condition for writing is that there be neither a permanent contact nor an absolute break between strata: the vigilance and failure of censorship" (226). While these remarks undoubtedly have a more general import, they refer specifically to Freud's *Wunderblock* and the two hands required to operate it. As Freud says, to appreciate fully the comparison of the writing-pad to the functioning of the psychical apparatus, we need to "imagine one hand writing upon the surface . . . while another periodically raises its covering sheet from the wax slab" (*S.E.*19, 232). As was noted in Chapter 1, Derrida reads this scene of two-handed writing described by Freud as gesturing toward a different kind of relationship between writing and repression, one that may no longer be understood simply in terms of the alternating logic of "on the one hand, on the other." To follow the movement of these hands is, in other words, to approach writing and repression as processes that are at once more intimately connected and more internally divided than has hitherto been imagined. It is for this reason that Derrida speaks of both "the vigilance *and* failure of censorship."

Yet why does Derrida find it necessary to wait until the "Note on the Mystic Writing-Pad" to begin to address the question of censorship in Freud? Certainly the most obvious place to broach the issue would be *The Interpretation of Dreams,* in which the notion of a dream censorship is assigned a pivotal role in Freud's understanding of the dream as a "(disguised) fulfillment of a (suppressed or repressed) wish."[4] If Derrida only seriously takes up the issue of censorship in his reading of Freud's "Note," this delay is at least in part related to the fact that he does not take the Freudian notion of dream censorship all that seriously. "At the beginning of the *Traumdeutung,"* he says, "Freud seems to make only a conventional, didactic reference to it" (226). As to the question of what Freud does with it elsewhere in the text, Derrida does not say.[5] What remains to be explained, then, is how one might move from this "conventional, didactic," and illustrative use of the "metaphor of censorship" to the more complex articulation of writing and repression discussed in the context of Freud's note on the *Wunderblock*.

Although Derrida's essay tends to pass lightly over the topic of dream censorship, "Freud and the Scene of Writing" nevertheless sets the stage for a reading of *The Interpretation of Dreams* and its own staging of another scene of censorship. In order to follow the complication and destabilization of a metaphor that, as Derrida observes, *is* used in a rather conventional way at the beginning of Freud's text, it is necessary to examine not only certain shifts in the use of the particular metaphor of censorship but also the general displacement of the very status of metaphor in this text. While Freud claims that "the kernel of [his] theory of dreams lies in [his] derivation of dream distortion from the censorship" (*S.E.*4, 308), a close examination of the strains, breakdowns, and dissimilarities engendered by his comparisons reveals a different mapping of the relationships among textual, psychical, and political spaces and a very different notion of censorship. Not only does this notion clearly diverge from the model of press censorship upon which it is initially based, but—in a twist comparable to the Lacanian strategy of *détournement*—it also and above all transforms and distorts that model in the process of translating it.

To begin to grasp some of the problems involved in understanding Freud's borrowing of the notion of dream censorship from the area of politics concerned with the deletions, blanks, and disguises of writing, it might be instructive to return to a well-known story recounted in the course of Freud's analysis of the seminal dream of Irma's injection.

> The whole plea—for the dream was nothing else—reminded one vividly of the defense put forward by the man who was charged by one of his neighbors with having given him back a borrowed kettle in a damaged condition. The defendant asserted first, that he had given it back undamaged; secondly, that the kettle had holes in it when he borrowed it; and thirdly, that he had never borrowed a kettle from his neighbor at all. So much the better; if only a single one of these three lines of defense were to be accepted as valid, the man would have to be acquitted. (*S.E.*4, 119–20)

Before commenting on this story and its connection to censorship, it should be noted that Freud rarely speaks of a dream *censor* (*Traumzensor*) in his work. Indeed, his lecture on "The Censorship of Dreams" explicitly warns against picturing this instance "as a severe little manikin or a spirit living in a closet in the brain and there discharging his office" (*S.E.*15, 140). In fact, if Freud almost exclusively uses the term "dream censorship" (*Traumzensur*), it is clearly in order to exploit its institutional connotations — its various levels of authority and delegated responsibility, and the censoring and policing of one level by another.[6]

Yet, the Freudian notion of censorship would be rather trivial were it modeled simply on an organizational flow chart. What gives the term its dynamism is the fact that in addition — and in opposition — to its bureaucratic aspects, it also involves processes comparable to the activity of *self*-censorship. As has already been observed, this latter form of censorship is itself internally conflicted and must be understood as a practice structured by the interplay of competing forces which, on the one hand, attempt to circumvent official sanctions and, on the other, cannot help but internalize them to varying degrees as forms of writer's block. What is thus gathered together and condensed under the rubric of the single covering term of dream censorship is a complex of incompatible pressures and opposing tendencies. Freud thus introduces a term that is not only lacking in conceptual integrity but that might also be brought up on charges of conflict of interest. One imagines a trial proceeding along the lines of the kettle story defense: the order to censor was received and duly executed; the order already had loopholes in it when it arrived; the order was never received in the first place. Obviously, none of these versions alone can account for the paradoxical functioning of censorship as it is elaborated in *The Interpretation of Dreams*. Yet, if one is prepared to consider these competing "pleas" together, it becomes possible to follow the dynamic interaction of the forces driving, structuring, and dislocating this internal border guard.

The Barred Path to Censorship

As Mikkel Borch-Jacobsen observes, at the beginning of Freud's text it would appear that if an unconscious wish is never clearly represented to consciousness, "no inherent opacity on the part of the wish is to blame. The wish is not clearly represented because access to consciousness is denied it by an 'agency' assigned the task of sorting out representations at the entrance to the preconscious-consciousness."[7] Thus, the wish must somehow be concealed and disguised if it is to get around this censorship. As Freud says:

> A similar difficulty confronts the political writer who has disagreeable truths to tell to those in authority. If he presents them undisguised, the authorities will suppress his words — after they have been spoken if his pronouncement was an oral one, but beforehand, if he had intended to make it in print. A writer must be aware of the censorship, and on its account he must soften and distort the expression of his opinion. According to the strength and sensitiveness of the censorship he finds himself compelled either merely to refrain from certain references or he must conceal his objectionable pronouncement beneath some apparently innocent disguise. . . . The stricter the censorship, the more far-reaching will be the disguise and the more ingenious too may be the means employed for putting the reader on the scent of the true meaning [*auf die Spur der eigentlichen Bedeutung*].
>
> The fact that the phenomena of censorship and of dream distortion correspond down to their smallest details justifies us in presuming that they are similarly determined. (*S.E.*4, 142–43)

In taking over the analogy of political censorship, Freud, at least at first, takes with it the accompanying hierarchies. Thus, as one might expect, he posits two separate and opposed forces or systems, one of which creatively "constructs the wish," while the other "forcibly brings about a distortion in the expression of [it]." To illustrate the effects of this distortion and its links to press censorship, Freud added a footnote in 1919 in which he adduced the so-called dream of the "love services." In this dream, the effects of the censorship may be discerned in the replacement of reprehensible statements by an incomprehensible mumble. Commenting on this dream in *The Introductory Lectures* (1916–17), Freud remarks:

> You will, I hope, think it plausible to suppose that it was precisely the objectionable nature of these passages that was the motive for their suppression. Where shall we find a parallel to such an event? You need not look far these days. Take up any political newspaper and you will find that here and there the text is absent and in its place nothing except the white paper is to be seen. This, as you know, is the work of the press censorship. In these empty places

there was something that displeased the higher censorship authorities and for that reason it was removed—a pity, you feel, since no doubt it was the most interesting thing in the paper—the "best bit" [*es war "die beste Stelle"*]. (*S.E.* 15, 138–39)

Freud's mention of *"die beste Stelle,"* an allusion to Heinrich Heine's famous poem *Germany: A Winter's Tale,* marks a shift in focus in his lecture. Whereas he had heretofore dealt only with the more blatant signs of censorship associated with the deletion of sensitive material, he now turns to the subtler ruses employed by the self-censoring author. That a passage from Heine serves to mark this transition is significant for a number of reasons: first, the passage referred to here—possibly the most famous "bit" of Heine's text—is one in which the censor's scissors do to the poet's body what they usually do to texts:

> The shears are clicking in his hand—
> He plunges like a possessed one
> Upon the body—hacks the flesh—
> Alas! that part was the best one.[8]

This allusion is but one indication of the way that Heine serves as a privileged point of reference for Freud in his thinking about censorship.[9] Moreover, in marking the transition in Freud's lecture from the blatant signs of external censorship to the subtler and more prevalent forms of dream distortion analogous to the politics of self-censorship, this passage literally places Heine and his own equivocal relationship to censorship somewhere between the two.[10]

At this point in his lecture, Freud describes the self-censoring author as one who "has contented himself with approximations and allusions to what would genuinely have come from his pen." According to Freud, this form of censorship is not only much more subtle and insidious but is also the form most often employed in the censorship of dreams. "The censorship," he says, "takes effect much more frequently according to the second method, by producing softenings, approximations and allusions instead of the genuine thing [*an Stelle des Eigentlichen*]" (*S.E.* 15, 139). This comparison of dream distortion to press censorship and the sense of propriety (*des Eigentlichen*) underwriting it is discussed by Borch-Jacobsen: "What these 'analogies' presuppose is obvious: the newspaper is legible before the censor's scissors make holes in it; the writer knows what he wants to say before he starts to play the game of conceal-ment. In other words, dream-thoughts are indeed thoughts, *cogita-tiones,* and they are perfectly intelligible ones. . . . Nothing sets them apart from conscious representations except the simple fact that repression keeps them inaccessible to consciousness."[11]

Borch-Jacobsen is undoubtedly correct in his assessment of the assumptions underlying one particular stratum of Freud's think-ing about censorship. Yet, in restricting his comments to this layer he fails to appreciate the significance of the general shift in Freud's brief lecture and more extensively in *The Interpretation of Dreams* toward the dynamics of self-censorship. For the more dream cen-sorship comes to resemble self-censorship, the harder it is to as-sign responsibility for the work of distortion and the more diffi-cult it is to say exactly whose interests are being served by it. While Borch-Jacobsen is not wrong in describing censorship as a one-sided "agency" whose function consists in denying representa-tions access to consciousness, Freud's texts also seem to suggest that censorship is a kind of double agent with multiple and di-vided allegiances. If these competing accounts are permitted to coexist side by side in Freud's texts, they are as much an indica-tion of the various thresholds and institutional levels of dream cen-sorship as a sign of the unconscious kettle logic structuring and unsettling this notion.

Freud may thus speak of "the presence of two psychical agen-cies and a censorship between them" (*S.E.*4, 235) while elsewhere warning against taking the term "in too 'localizing' a sense" and adding that "it is nothing more than a serviceable term for describ-ing a *dynamic relation*" (*S.E.*15, 140; emphasis added). If censor-ship thus tends to resist definition as a stable concept and seems to be difficult to locate simply as a particular psychical frontier, its instability is both an indication of the very dynamism of the rela-tions in which it is enmeshed and a sign of its close and equivocal connection to the Freudian notion of displacement. As is well known, Freud considered displacement to be the essential portion of the dreamwork. He describes it as "a psychical force . . . which on the one hand [*einerseits*] strips elements having a high psychical value of their intensity, and on the other hand [*andrerseits*], by means of overdetermination, creates new values from elements of low psychical value" (S.E.4, 307). Only these newly created values find their way into the dream content.

In contrast to the cruder forms of dream distortion in which the sides, battle lines, and traces of violence are all too clearly defined, displacement represents a two-handed process that redefines both the terms and the field of conflict. Whereas Freud earlier seemed to suggest that the diversions and detours imposed by censorship merely put greater physical distance between dream thoughts and their expression, decreasing their intensity through excisions, approximations, and circumlocutions, it now appears that the distortion of dreams can also involve the creation of new values. Rather than simply toning down and distancing highly charged material, displacement would thus effect a transvaluation of psychical values. Yet, how exactly it does this and on whose behalf it acts remain to be seen.

As to the question of whose interests are served by the mechanism of displacement, Freud's response is surprisingly unequivocal. An obvious consequence of displacement, he argues, is that the dream content no longer resembles the core of the dream thoughts and that the dream gives no more than a distorted version of the dream wish existing in the unconscious: "But we are already familiar with dream distortion. We traced it back to the censorship which is exercised by one psychical agency in the mind over another. Dream displacement is one of the chief methods by which that distortion is achieved. *Is fecit cui profuit.* We may assume, then, that dream displacement comes about through the influence of the same censorship—that is, the censorship of endopsychic defense [*jener Zensur, der endopsychischen Abwehr*]" (S.E.4, 308).

Thus, it seems that displacement and the distortions it brings about simply serve the interests of an endopsychic defense intent on censoring the expression of unconscious wishes. Yet, this conclusion is immediately called into question by a seemingly innocuous remark in the following paragraph, which closes the chapter on displacement. In the guise of summarizing his argument Freud surreptitiously reposes the problem: "We can state provisionally a second condition which must be satisfied by those elements of the dream thoughts which make their way into the dream [the first being that they must be overdetermined]: *they must escape the censorship imposed by resistance* [*daß sie der Zensur des Wider-*

standes entzogen seien]" (*S.E.*4, 308; emphasis in original).

Whereas a moment earlier Freud had claimed that displacement takes place under the influence of the endopsychic defense (*Is fecit cui profuit*), it now seems that this mechanism is also one of the means employed by elements of the dream thoughts *to escape* censorship. Is it in order to avoid this apparent contradiction that Freud introduces the terminological modification, "the censorship imposed by resistance"?[12] Here it seems that there is one form of censorship, a kind of precensorship, which enables dream thoughts to escape another form of censorship designated by the term "censorship of resistance." Or is it simply the case that, contrary to Freud's initial claims, displacement does not in fact occur in conjunction with or on behalf of the censorship imposed by the second agency on the first, but instead takes place prior to censorship, precisely in order to avoid it? If these questions are left unresolved in *The Interpretation of Dreams,* the space opened by Freud's equivocations, while perhaps indicating an "insufficient mastery of the material," also implicitly suggests a more complex interaction of displacement and censorship, a more layered, multiple staging of the latter, and finally even a dreamlike displacement of the very notion of censorship in Freud's text.

Such a displacement involves not only a rearticulation of psychical space but also a splitting of the very time frame in which censorship might be assumed to take place. For insofar as distortions that are produced in anticipation of censorship are already implicated in its dynamics — precisely to the extent that censorship must be taken into account as a real possibility — it becomes difficult to locate a stage clearly prior to (pre)censorship. Thus, not only will there have been a *censorship effect* before censorship ever actually occurs, but it is precisely this proleptic structure that effectively divides censorship from within and prevents it from ever simply being itself here and now. Similarly, in his *Introductory Lectures on Psychoanalysis* Freud identifies a related difficulty in locating the point where something like a (post)censorship will have ceased to function.

> The resistance to interpretation is only a putting into effect [*Objektivierung:* literally making objective — JS] of the dream censorship. It also proves to us that the force of the censorship is not exhausted

in bringing about the distortion of dreams and thereafter extinguished, but that the censorship persists as a permanent institution which has as its aim the maintenance of the distortion [*daß diese Zensur als dauernde Institution mit der Absicht, die Entstellung aufrecht zu halten, fortbesteht*]. (*S.E.*15, 141)

In short, there seems to be no getting around censorship — at least either as a moment simply before or after it — and if there is no ultimate detour around this instance, it is because censorship "itself" will have only taken place as pre- and/or postcensorship. Whereas the splitting of this instance undoubtedly reveals an extension and diffusion of its functioning not heretofore imagined, it also draws attention to censorship's inherent instability and untimeliness. To say that there is no proper time or place for it is above all to claim that censorship will have always taken place too early and/or too late. Indeed, it is precisely because censorship is always somewhat out of place that it can be so easily caught off guard. Yet, the question raised by the Freudian displacement of censorship is not so much why this instance is repeatedly taken unawares but rather what drives it to collaborate in its own undoing in the first place.

The Other Scene

Whereas censorship is initially described as an agent of repression situated at the entrance to the preconscious-consciousness system, Freud's displacement of it forces one to view it instead as a split and double agency with affiliations both to the repressing and to the repressed. The repeated undoing of censorship is thus merely an indication of the double bind that ties it to the mechanisms of the dreamwork in a relationship that can best be described as one of conflictual interdependence. What matters here is not so much *whether* an unconscious representation in fact gains access to a forbidden psychical realm but rather *what kind of link* is forged between the elements that do gain access and those that are kept out. Moreover, if what is in question here is precisely the status of a psychical frontier, one must further ask how such linkages may in effect constitute the very boundaries they cross and transgress.

Freud's description of the process of identification in dreams is particularly useful in helping one to grasp the compromises involved in the formation of these boundaries. In identification only one of the persons linked by a common element succeeds in being represented in the manifest content of the dream, while the second or remaining persons seem to be suppressed in it (*unterdrückt scheinen*). This single covering figure (*deckende Person*), Freud says, appears in all the relations and situations that apply either to him or to the figures that he covers. Freud further suggests that these covering persons not only come forth *into* the manifest content of a dream in the way characters in a play might appear on stage, but they may also come to the fore in it.

In an explicitly theatrical example of identification, Freud says that the scene of the dream (*die Szene des Traums*) is attributed to one of the persons concerned, while the other, usually more important person appears as an attendant figure without any other function. Insofar as little attention is paid to such figures, they tend to blend into the background and serve merely as backdrops for the action downstage. To put it in more dynamic terms, as one figure comes to the fore as a kind of "front" set up perhaps by those with a need to stay in the background, the other persons linked to it by a common element not only *seem* to be suppressed (*unterdrückt scheinen*), but in effect *are* absent insofar as no attention is paid to them. While the covering person thus takes his place on the scene of the dream as a stand-in for others, the link to those other concealed persons may never be discovered. This is precisely what Freud calls the objectification of censorship as resistance.

Because there are no set boundaries delimiting the front or back of the scene of the dream, the difference between an element coming to the fore *in* it and one coming forth *into* it, making it onto the stage at all, is one of quantity rather than quality. In other words, the borders of the scene are defined less by the criterion of actual existence than by that of effective appearance, less by the nature of the representations than by the intensity of their cathectic charge.[13] Only as figures fade, withdraw, or are driven into the background is the backdrop of the scene of the dream temporarily constituted. Whether attention is paid to such figures depends to a large degree upon the power of the actors downstage to monopolize the audience's attention.

Before asking who exactly the audience of a dream is and why the covering figures described by Freud should be worthy of special attention, it may be useful to read his discussion of identification in conjunction with his remarks about reversal added to the section on "The Means of Representation" in 1909:

> Reversal, or turning a thing into its opposite, is one of the means of representation most favored by the dreamwork and one which is capable of employment in the most diverse directions. It serves in the first place to give expression to the fulfillment of a wish in reference to some particular element of the dream thoughts. "If it had only been the other way round!" This is often the best way of expressing the ego's reaction to a disagreeable fragment of memory. Again, reversal is of quite special use as a help to the censorship, for it produces a mass of distortion in the material which is to be represented, and this has a positively paralysing effect, to begin with, on any attempt at understanding the dream. (*S.E.*4, 327)

Reversal thus involves nothing less than the transformation of a repressed wish into its opposite. The wish is "realized" in the double sense of being fulfilled and being represented as though it were actually happening. It thereby loses its subjective, subjunctive, and irreal character. As Freud says, "The dream represses [*verdrängt*] the optative and replaces it by a simple present" (*S.E.*5, 534). As the use of the term *repression* in this passage implies, the process of reversal also involves elements of conflict and compromise. Indeed, it is significant for our purposes that only a "particular element" (*ein bestimmtes Element*) of the dream thoughts is realized; that is, one particular element is singled out from a complex dream thought or from a complex of dream thoughts (the point being that the two are practically one and the same, since every dream thought insofar as it is overdetermined is complex).

Before proceeding, it is important to stress the shift in the status of the dream thoughts implied by this relationship. Whereas Freud's earlier descriptions of censorship led one to believe that distortions appear in dreams in place of something more genuine and self-identical (*das Eigentliche*), here it would seem that the dream thoughts subjected to distortion will have been less than authentic from the very beginning. Not only are these thoughts overdetermined in the sense of being polyvalent, they are also irreducibly plural because they are internally split by the *mutually contradictory* thoughts and desires that inhabit them. Such contradictions may thus coexist in the "same" thought complex or, what amounts to the same thing, each particular thought may serve as a substitute for another.[14]

Returning to the question of reversal, one recalls that it is from such a complex of dream thoughts that "a particular element" is singled out and allowed to come forth as a "realized" wish. Similarly, in the case of identification a covering figure is said to come forth in(to) the dream, upstaging a complex of related figures which are both represented and repressed by it.[15] In both cases, censorship seems to allow one particular element to come forth both as a way of keeping other associated elements in the background and as a means of avoiding a long and costly struggle.[16]

Yet like most halfway solutions, such compromises raise as many questions as they answer. For if a particular element of the dream thoughts comes forth into the dream as a realized wish, is it singled out and drawn forth as a "safety valve" or is it somehow pushed forward as a kind of front? Similarly, if the covering figures in Freud's discussion of identification serve both to represent and to repress a complex of related figures whom they stand in for, who exactly sets them up as "covers," and who is in turn set up by them into believing that they were more than mere fronts to begin with? If censorship itself is not merely deceived by material that gets past it, how exactly *does* it collaborate in its own subversion?

To begin to respond to these questions, it may be helpful to return to Freud's discussion of identification where, as it turns out, a certain *I* is said to be responsible for setting up covering figures.

> What the censorship objects to may lie precisely in certain ideas which, in the material of the dream thoughts, are attached to a particular person; *so I proceed to find a second person,* who is connected with the objectionable material, but only with part of it. The contact between the two persons upon this censorable point *now justifies me* in constructing a composite figure characterized by indifferent features derived from both. This figure, arrived at by identification or composition, is then admissible to the dream content without censorship, and thus, by making use of dream condensation, *I have satisfied* the claims of the dream censorship. (*S.E.*4, 321–22; emphasis added)

Whereas *The Interpretation of Dreams* often alternates between third- and first-person narration, here Freud impersonates the voice of the dreamer described within it. In thus identifying with the *I* of the dreaming subject, Freud seems to make a point of conflating the waking ego with that of the dreamer. Yet, while this conflation perhaps invites one to consider the *I* of the latter as a kind of alter ego modeled on the identity of the conscious self, it also leads one to ask how this *I* may in its turn alter the very sense of egoistic self-identity in the guise of simply repeating it.

> It is my experience, and one to which I have found no exception, that every dream deals with the dreamer himself. Dreams are completely egoistic. Whenever my own ego does not appear in the content of the dream, but only some extraneous person, I may safely assume that my own ego lies concealed, by identification, behind this other person; I may fill in my ego [*Ich darf mein Ich ergänzen*]. On other occasions, when my own ego *does* appear in the dream, the situation in which it occurs may teach me that some other person lies concealed, by identification, behind my ego. . . . Thus, my ego may be represented in a dream several times over, now directly and now through identification with extraneous persons. (*S.E.*4, 322–23)

Insofar as these remarks merely describe the various ways in which one's ego may be multiply represented in dreams while also serving to represent the identities of others, they never really put into question the identity of the dreaming subject as such. Yet, if such questions do arise in this passage, it is significant that they emerge only through the ambiguity of the German phrase *Ich darf mein Ich ergänzen*. In other words, they emerge not so much in the form of a competing, alternative account of the ego but rather in and as a moment of linguistic instability—as though the potential alterity of the dreaming *I* were of necessity related to the inherent otherness of linguistic equivocation. Commenting on the "notable ambiguity" of this passage, Samuel Weber explains that the phrase *Ich darf mein Ich ergänzen* "means both to complete my ego and to complete the scene by adding my ego to it, in the place of the non-ego that appears. But it would be more accurate to say, 'I may conceal and distort my ego,' for this is precisely what the subject does in the dream. And yet, precisely that is what 'filling in one's ego' amounts to: creating the illusion of fullness, of completeness, of the ego as a self-identical subjective instance."[17]

Here Weber subtly redefines the relation of the ego to the other in dreams and the play of substitution it involves in terms of an otherness *of* the ego and an incessant movement of supplementation (*Ergänzung*) in which it is caught. Instead of one particular ego filling in for another, an "illusion of fullness" fills in for the ego's "own" lack of identity. I would further suggest that it is precisely this uncompletable movement of supplementation which defines the ego *as process*. To put it in terms of Freud's description of identification, one might say that the pronoun *I* itself serves as a kind of covering figure that not only "fronts" for other egos but moreover acts as a "cover" for the dreaming subject's own multiple and divided identity.

While the notion of a covering figure initially led us to ask how such figures are set up and who could in fact be deceived by them, a certain reading of the phrase *Ich darf mein Ich ergänzen* suggests that these covers not only create a mirage of self-identity but moreover function as *self-deluding* illusions; that is, they do not merely delude the self but beguile with the very lure of identity. As is well known, the last section of the chapter on the dreamwork, which is devoted to the process of secondary revision, deals with just this kind of illusion. Here Freud explains how an audience might be driven to participate in its own deception.

> It is the nature of our waking thought to establish order in material . . . , to set up relations in it and to make it conform to our expectations of an intelligible whole. In fact, we go too far in that direction. An adept in sleight of hand can trick us by relying upon this intellectual habit of ours. In our effort at making an intelligible pattern of the sense impressions that are offered to us, we often fall into the strangest errors or even falsify the truth about the material before us. (*S.E.*4, 499)

To illustrate his point further, Freud draws on the everyday parapraxis of misreading. "In our reading," he says, "we pass over misprints which destroy the sense, and have the illusion that what we are reading is correct" (*S.E.*4, 499). In contrast to his earlier description of censorship as a process that either alone or in collaboration with the dreamwork produces "softenings, approximations and allusions instead of the genuine thing [*an Stelle des Eigentlichen*]," here the locus of distortion clearly shifts from the body of the text to the reading and interpretation of it. In other words, it is the reader who now supplies the text with the kind of smooth, homogeneous surface formerly constructed by the writer to outwit the censor and by the censor to cover his own tracks. It is also significant that the reader creates this surface not by actively constructing a façade but simply by overlooking apparent faults and discrepancies in the reading material. Here again the criterion of effective appearance seems to be as important as that of actual existence in determining the extent of textual distortion.

Similarly, in the case of secondary revision, gaps in the structure of dreams are filled both by positively adding extraneous material to it and by simply reading the ego's own expectations of intelligibility into it. While this fourth and final aspect of the dreamwork thus seems to be more closely allied to the interests of waking thought than to the processes of condensation, displacement, and considerations of representability, it also focuses more attention than the other three on the capacity of conscious thought to delude itself in its pursuit of coherent meaning.

If censorship in its turn is not always simply taken in by the deceptive appearance of fronts and covering figures but at times colludes in its own undoing, it does so precisely to the extent that it collaborates in the creation and perpetuation of illusions of intelligibility, wholeness, and subjective self-identity. Furthermore, because censorship is *set up* by a need "to establish order in material . . . , to set up relations in it and to make it conform to our expectations of an intelligible whole," this compromising activity must itself be supplemented by further acts of censorship.

While the process of secondary revision thus enables one to understand how censorship may be complicitous in its own subversion, it also raises more fundamental questions about the master whose interests it is supposed to serve. For insofar as *das Eigentliche* is no longer merely what is distorted by censorship but is itself the very means of distortion, what does this say about the alleged identity and integrity of the ego whose borders censorship is called upon to defend?

In *The Legend of Freud,* Samuel Weber follows an extension of the notion of secondary revision from *The Interpretation of*

Dreams, where, as he says, "its dissimulating function . . . is restricted to the dream-work" to *Totem and Taboo,* in which it is used "to characterize systematic thinking in general."[18] Describing the extended scope of this notion, Weber writes:

> Systematic thought organizes the world in the image of this organization [i.e., the libidinally cathected, narcissistic ego]. The intellectual construct we call a "system" reveals itself to be narcissistic, in its origin no less than in its structure: *speculative,* in the etymological sense, as a mirror-image of the ego, and "phobosophic" as well. If it is driven to fill in the "gaps and cracks" in the edifice of the universe, the fissures it fears are much closer to home. The "expectation of an intelligible whole" described by Freud, the expectation of a coherent meaning, appears thus to denote the reaction of an ego seeking to defend its conflict-ridden cohesion against equally endemic centripetal tendencies. The pursuit of meaning; the activity of construction, synthesis, unification; the incapacity to admit anything irreducibly alien, to leave any residue unexplained—all this indicates the struggle of the ego to establish and to maintain an identity that is all the more precarious and vulnerable to the extent that it depends on what it must exclude. In short, speculative, systematic thinking draws its force from the effort of the ego to appropriate an exteriority of which, as Freud will later put it, it is only the "organized part."[19]

While the notion of secondary revision will eventually come to be associated both with the animistic attempt to comprehend the external world in terms of unity and totality and with the efforts of the narcissistic ego to fill in the "gaps and cracks" in its own self-image, in *The Interpretation of Dreams* it is linked only to the notion of censorship.[20] Yet, what exactly does it mean at this point to speak of a connection to censorship? As I have tried to demonstrate, the term *censorship* does not so much denote a particular psychical frontier or stable psychoanalytic concept. Instead, it functions more like a covering figure whose single name serves to cloak an entire complex of incompatible pressures and opposing tendencies. At times, it is said to be as crude as the state censor who excises passages without covering his tracks; at other times, it seems simply to tone down reprehensible material or to replace it with circumlocutions; at still other times, it is said to distort the dream by filling in extraneous material and by creating a semblance of intelligibility. These competing accounts of censorship indeed seem difficult to reconcile. Moreover, it appears likely that any attempt to overlook the obvious differences between these versions, to privilege one version over another in order to view censorship as a localizable and stable instance modeled either simply on self- or on state censorship would be to distort it in exactly the same way that secondary revision is said to distort dream material.

In order to grasp the overdetermination of censorship, it is important to recall that for Freud, reading a dream involves not only its interpretation but its necessary *overinterpretation,* since "each of the elements of the dream's content turns out to have been 'overdetermined'—to have been represented in the dream thoughts many times over" (*S.E.*4, 283).[21]

Similarly, in attempting to read the notion of dream censorship, one must treat the different accounts of it presented in Freud's text as expressions of an overdetermined wish—or rather as the knotting together of a number of incompatible wishes. If one may thus speak of censorship in terms usually reserved for the unconscious material presumed to be censored by it, the ambivalent wishes of censorship express the efforts of this instance to accommodate the demands placed on it by the combined forces of repression and the unconscious repressed. Pulled in opposite directions, censorship thus finds itself doubly bound to the mechanisms of the dreamwork to which it is in principle opposed and with which it is nevertheless forced to conspire. Caught in and moreover *structured by* this double bind, censorship is fated not only to collaborate in its own undoing but also to put in question the very identity of the ego whose interests it is supposed to serve. Thus, as we have seen, it only defends its superior against the incursions of the repressed by betraying the "cracks and fissures" in the ego's own secondarily revised sense of identity. Such betrayals in turn adumbrate Freud's later extension of the notion of secondary revision, his redefinition of the relationship of the ego to the other, and his return to questions of censorship in his metapsychological papers on repression.[22]

What, then, is the effect of Freud's borrowing of the term censorship from the fields of politics and publishing? Are its political implications carried over in Freud's translation or are they simply neutralized and psychologized away? The intellectual historian Carl

Schorske tends toward the latter view when he describes *The Inter-pretation of Dreams* as "an epoch-making interpretation of human experience in which politics could be reduced to an epiphenomenal manifestation of psychic forces."[23] Commenting specifically on Freud's recourse to the metaphor of censorship, Schorske observes that the "selection of the analogy" bears witness to the way "the political realities of the nineties . . . had penetrated Freud's psychic life."[24] Yet, as the rest of his essay suggests, these realities find their way into Freud's inner world only to be depoliticized there. Thus, Schorske adds that the "social model [of censorship] provided an analogy for Freud to show us 'a quite definite view of the "essential nature" of consciousness.'" The analogy to press censorship would thus in effect only illustrate certain *intrapsychic* conflicts to the ex-tent that it essentializes the historical dimension of *political* conflict. Such an approach for Schorske is typical of Freud's more general reduction of "his own political past and present to an epi-phenomenal status in relation to the primal conflict between father and son."[25] In short, Freud would avoid the struggles of contempo-rary political life by devising a more global, primal, and personal theory of conflict.

Yet, how coherent is Freud's theory, and to what extent is a term as unstable as dream censorship assimilated and indeed assimil-able to it? Does not the volatility of the metaphor of censorship in Freud's text bear witness first and foremost to a theory *in conflict,* a theory that is distorted and dislocated by its own attempts to the-orize conflict? Indeed, it would seem that if there is a politics of censorship articulated in *The Interpretation of Dreams,* it is to be sought less in any secondarily revised theory of psychic conflict than in Freud's own writing praxis.

Thus, in contrast to Schorske, who reads the metaphor of cen-sorship merely in terms of its illustrative, didactive value—that is, in terms of what it "shows us"—I maintain that it is more impor-tant to ask how and why this analogy breaks down. For it is only by studying these breakdowns that one begins to appreciate the extent to which censorship in Freud itself only "works" as a neces-sarily dysfunctional and self-subversive operation. Moreover, it is this dysfunctional notion of censorship that in turn gives one a sense of the psychological, textual, and political problems faced by writers caught in the double binds of self-censorship. For while such writers are compelled, on the one hand, to develop strategies of dissimulation in an attempt to circumvent censorship, on the other hand, they cannot help but internalize it as various debilitating forms of writer's block. If there is indeed a politics of (self-)censorship articulated in *The Interpretation of Dreams,* it is perhaps to be read, as Derrida suggests, on the level of a certain gesture—namely, as the text's own dumb-show performance of a wringing of the two hands of writing and repression: "the vigilance and failure of censorship."

Heine and
the Dream Naval

Reframing the Question
of Censorship

Fluctuat nec mergitur
Motto of Paris cited in Freud's letter to Fliess of September 21, 1899

Our footman was called Prrschtzztwitsch.
To pronounce this name properly one must sneeze at the same time.
Heine, *From the Memoirs of Herr von Schnabelewopski*

What kind of position can a writer take in relation to censorship? How is one positioned and even prepositioned by it? The second section of Heine's book *The Romantic School* addresses these questions with characteristic irony:

> Writers suffering under conditions of censorship and intellectual constraints of all kinds who nevertheless cannot silence the promptings of their hearts are particularly dependent upon humorous and ironic modes of expression. These are the sole outlets still open to the honest man. In fact, it is through such humorous ironic dissimulations that honesty reveals itself in its most stirring manner. This reminds me again of the marvelous prince of Denmark. . . . Hamlet is honest through and through; only the most truthful person could say, "We are all arrant knaves" and while he pretends to be mad, he does not mean to deceive us; inwardly he knows [*ist sich innerlich bewußt*] that he is truly mad.[1]

As the irony of Heine's remarks suggests, writing under censorship involves devising strategies of dissimulation which, once set in motion, can develop an impetus of their own. As this momentum increases, it becomes harder to distinguish dissembling strategies from forms of self-deception. Thus, Heine describes the marvelous prince of Denmark as someone who feigns insanity, all the while "knowing" he is really mad. That Heine's comments are themselves progressively drawn into the vortex of "humorous ironic dissimulations," which they initially set out only to describe, suggests that self-censorship may be not only a particularly unwieldy political weapon but also an elusive object of investigation, one that may be difficult to grasp without in turn becoming caught in its grip.

As was noted earlier, Heine's struggles with censorship have been the subject of intense critical scrutiny.[2] Yet, within the framework of this scholarship relatively little attention has been paid to what might be described as the ironies of self-censorship. Indeed, until fairly recently the entire question of self-censorship was treated as a relatively marginal issue by Heine specialists and was considered only in the context of discussions of *Fremdzensur*. As Michael Werner observes in an article published in 1975, "A detailed investigation of self-censorship still needs to be undertaken. Yet for the time being we are obliged to take it into account only insofar as considerations of external censorship [*Fremdzensur*] make it necessary, i.e., insofar as one is unable to positively attribute the blunting and toning down of a text to a foreign instance."[3]

It is not difficult to understand why philologists concerned primarily with determining the extent to which outside influences may have been responsible for the distortion of Heine's texts should wish to treat the question of self-censorship as a special and relatively inconsequential case of external censorship. Yet, insofar as this scholarship is based on the assumption that the borders of a text are already defined and intact before being corrupted by outside forces, one wonders how such an approach could in fact accommodate the kinds of borderline issues raised by the practice of self-censorship. If in this kind of writing the outside forces are by definition already on the inside, how is it possible to differentiate authorial intention from foreign intervention?

The response of Heine scholars has been quite simply to split the question of self-censorship in two and to study how this practice, on the one hand, remains under the author's command and, on the other, takes on a life of its own (thereby manifesting its remote control by interiorized foreign powers). The most striking example of this kind of approach is to be found in Michael Werner's later essay "Der politische Schriftsteller und die (Selbst-)Zensur" (The political writer and (self-)censorship), published in 1987, which is divided into two main sections separated by the following remarks:

> If in a first moment we were concerned with describing self-censorship as a strategy of dissimulation dominated by the author to the point of mastery and finely tuned to particular conditions of publication and censorship, it now turns out that self-censorship can develop its own dynamic [*eine Eigendynamik*], detach itself from the external conditions out of which it initially arose and constitute itself as a general and autonomous condition of writing [*unabhängige, generelle Schreibbedingung*].[4]

In contrast to Heine, who describes a *dynamic* of self-censorship in which it becomes increasingly difficult to distinguish strategies of dissimulation from forms of self-deception, the *Eigendynamik* described by Werner refers only to the negative, debilitating side of this power play. Nevertheless, while Werner perhaps sidesteps some of the more equivocal issues raised by Heine's writing practices, his painstaking analysis of manuscript and published versions of the author's journalistic writings of the 1840s provides invaluable insight into processes Freud would later describe in a different but related context as movements of distortion (*Entstellung*) and secondary revision (*Sekundäre Bearbeitung*). Thus, in the first part of his article Werner describes the ways in which Heine attempted to slip sensitive material past the censors by disguising personal opinions as objectively reported statements of fact; shifting the speaker to have another give voice to his own views; feigning a tone of indifference; and using a parabolic style. As was noted above, the second half of Werner's essay is devoted to the more crippling aspects of self-censorship. There he documents Heine's tendency to avoid unambiguous formulations, his at times pathological fear of speaking his mind, and his related concerns about being misunderstood. Werner also discerns a kind of stuttering in the manuscripts where the author broaches a topic, interrupts himself, and starts over again repeatedly. As a kind of counterpart to this stammering he identifies a form of deferral whereby Heine promises his readers that clearer, more complete explanations will be forthcoming. Needless to say, these promises are rarely fulfilled. Certainly the most paralyzing form of self-censorship analyzed in Werner's article involves a total breakdown of the process of composition — the point where, as he says, the author "is condemned to silence": "This silence represents the obverse or underside [*Kehrseite*] of the artfully conceived practice of self-censorship, the price to be paid for the interiorization of the conditions of censorship by the politically engaged writer. [Here] the original goal of self-censorship has been transformed into its opposite [*in sein Gegenteil verkehrt*]."[5]

Werner's description of this silence as the *Kehrseite* of a productive strategy of dissimulation is telling, for it is symptomatic of a more general tendency among Heine scholars to treat self-censorship as a relatively static *two-sided* issue rather than as an unwieldy *double-edged* dynamic. While such a tendency undoubtedly bears witness to the investment of Heine criticism in traditional notions of authorial intention and the lengths to which it will go to preserve such notions, it also leads one to ask what it is about self-censorship that seems to lend itself to such interpretations. In other words, is it somehow inevitable that in speaking about this unstable practice one reverts to terms that tend to polarize and domesticate its very dynamism?

A Node of Resistance

In order to respond to this question, it may be helpful to return briefly to *The Interpretation of Dreams* and a lengthy footnote Freud felt compelled to add to it in 1925. In this note, Freud confronts the problems raised by analytic efforts to appropriate and apply his theory of dreams.

> I used at one time to find it extraordinarily difficult to accustom readers to the distinction between the manifest content of dreams and the latent dream-thoughts. . . . But now that analysts at least have become reconciled to replacing the manifest dream by the meaning revealed by its interpretation, many of them have become guilty of falling into another confusion which they cling to with equal obstinacy. They seek to find the essence of dreams in their latent content and in so doing they overlook the distinction between the latent dream-thoughts and the dreamwork. At bottom, dreams are nothing other than a particular *form* of thinking, made possible

by the conditions of the state of sleep. It is the *dreamwork* which creates that form, and it alone is the essence of dreaming — the explanation of its peculiar nature. (*S.E.*5, 506–7)

Freud's followers would thus misconstrue his theory insofar as they seek the essence of dreams in their latent content rather than in the conflictual interaction of the dreamwork with the dream censorship and the dynamic form of thinking this collaboration comprises. Yet, as the remarks cited above suggest, what is important here is not only the particular point these analysts fail to grasp but moreover the *way* in which they miss it. It is therefore significant that Freud's call for a return to the true "essence of dreaming" is made by evoking the history of a certain resistance within psychoanalytic thinking itself. Such *internal* resistances, he implies, do not simply manifest themselves as counterpositions but instead as attempts to meet his theory halfway. Indeed, it is precisely by agreeing with, appropriating, and *"obstinately clinging to"* the least threatening aspects of his approach that Freud's followers betray their unwitting intolerance of its repressed core. Conversely, it is only by measuring the strength and relative stability of these compromise formations — the misinterpretations to which his followers tenaciously cling — that Freud is able effectively to gauge what is most challenging, unassimilable, and perhaps most essential about his theory. Moreover, implicit in Freud's description of the tendentious misreading of his work by those in principle most favorably disposed to it is the suggestion that one may return to the true essence of dreaming only to discover that *The Interpretation of Dreams* will itself have been pregnant with a different approach to interpretation, an approach in which resistance would no longer be conceived of as a negative obstacle but instead as an equivocal *connection to the repressed* — which in a certain sense is what Freud had been saying all along.

As Samuel Weber and Shoshana Felman suggest in their respective readings of Freud, such an approach is already legible in the margins of *The Interpretation of Dreams* precisely in those places where the text itself seems to stand on the threshold both of the "unknown" and of another as yet unconscious way of acceding to it. This threshold, it is argued, is marked by the unusual figure of the dream navel first introduced by Freud in a footnote appended to his analysis of the dream of Irma's injection in the chapter "The Method of Interpreting Dreams." "There is," he says, "at least one spot in every dream at which it is unplumbable — *a navel,* as it were, that is its point of contact with the unknown" (*S.E.*4, 111, n. 1).

As both Felman and Weber suggest, the metaphor of the navel not only describes a certain threshold, it also and above all embodies one. For at the same time that the navel figures an interpretive impasse — the spot at which the dream is said to be "unplumbable" — it also serves as a kind of communicating link, "*a point of contact* with the unknown." Moreover, this figure not only marks the point at which the individual interpretation of any particular dream must break off but also the place where *The Interpretation of Dreams* in general seems to describe its own limitations — the place, that is, where it simultaneously makes contact with a different approach to interpretation.

If the usual method of interpreting dreams described by Freud involves an attempt to reverse the path traveled by the psyche in composing the dream, proceeding from the "manifest" content to the dream's hidden, "latent" meaning, the approach tacitly associated with the figure of the dream navel focuses instead on those heavily trafficked places where a reversible path becomes a choked and congested intersection. It is therefore no accident that when Freud returns to the figure of the navel in the seventh chapter of *The Interpretation of Dreams* he describes it as an overdetermined and inextricable *knot:*

> Even in the best interpreted dreams there is often a place that must be left in the dark, because in the process of interpreting one notices a tangle [*Knäuel*] of dream thoughts arising which resists unravelling but has also made no further contributions to the dream content. This, then, is the navel of the dream, the place where it straddles the unknown. The dream thoughts, to which interpretation leads one, are necessarily interminable and branch out on all sides into the netlike entanglement of our world of thought. Out of the denser places in this meshwork, the dream wish rises like a mushroom out of its mycelium. (*S.E.*5, 530; trans. mod.)

Insofar as the metaphor of the dream navel figures an impasse which is at the same time a kind of communicating link, Freud's description of "a tangle of dream thoughts . . . which resists unravelling" itself must be read as a node of resistance which also *ties* interpretation to the "unknown." In order to specify this unknown, it is important to bear in mind that the tangled figure of the dream navel is itself tied in a very specific way in Freud's text to the dream of Irma's injection, to its knot of resistant female figures, and to the pain in Irma's throat which literally "ties her up in knots [*es schnürt sie zusammen*]." In her intricate reading of these entanglements, Shoshana Felman demonstrates how the dream navel only connects with the unknown to the extent that it *unknowingly* articulates a very different mode of connection—one that is at once impeded and made possible by the knotting of resistance. Summarizing her reading of Freud's specimen dream, Felman writes:

> From the singularly silent and resistant navel of Freud's pregnant wife, to the singularly painful and resistant knot in Irma's throat, through the mediating notion of the navel of the dream, Freud discovers that resistance, far from being simply negative, is a positively pregnant concept; that resistance is a textual knot, a nodal point of unknown significance, the navel of an unknown text; and that the psychoanalytic dialogue is a new way of reading, and of working with, the pregnancy of this unknown and the fecundity of this resistance. This is what the Irma dream *makes contact with,* precisely, through the navel of its female knot ("a navel, as it were, that is its point of contact with the unknown"), but what the dreamer and the dream interpreter *do not yet know.*[6]

As the gnarled texture of Felman's own writing suggests, the dream navel is not just a figure in Freud's text—a metaphor used to describe the place where the dream "straddles the unknown." It is instead the very trope of intertextuality. In other words, it is a metaphor that unwittingly weaves textual, corporeal, and oneiric figures through one another, knotting them together in such a way that each reads as the signifier of the other. At once a painful knot in the throat, a choked and overdetermined nodal point in the dream, and the "navel of an unknown text," these figures simultaneously complicate and explicate one another.

Whereas nothing seems more familiar than a navel—that place where the body was last joined to its maternal origins—the irreducible metaphoricity of the navel of Freud's dream text suggests a different kind of filial relationship. For here each filament of the tangled umbilical knot is at once mother and child, bearer and born, vehicle and tenor of the other. It is perhaps for this reason that the initial mention of the navel with its all too obvious connotations of diachronic continuity, generation, and originality is later linked by Freud in the seventh chapter to the synchronic figure of the *mycelium*—a mass of interwoven filamentous hyphae which spreads by breaking down the tissue of the host body it inhabits.[7] Although Felman never puts it in exactly these terms, her reading strongly suggests that the navel functions as a trope of intertextuality insofar as this metaphor insinuates itself in the very texture of Freud's writing, enmeshing itself in the fabric of relationships it is initially called upon simply to illustrate.

Viewed in this way, the "intertextual" would be not merely a space between texts but a difference within them—or rather, a *movement of self-difference* in which the very notions of text, body, and dream become so entangled in one another that each takes its place only as the differential placeholder of the others. To be joined at the level of the navel, then, is to be ensnared in a differential knot. It is to be connected, paradoxically, in a relationship of self-difference, in a relationship, that is, in which each term is open to and opened by the difference of the others.

If Felman's analysis effectively alters the way one reads Freud, it does so by introducing what she describes as "a self-subversive (sexual) difference into Freud's own discourse."[8] Her strategic intervention thus works to dislodge an intertextual (and intersexual) space in which heretofore unrelated—or rather, tendentiously separated—issues are allowed to "make contact with" and proliferate through one another. The disseminating energy of her reading thus makes it possible to articulate the issue of feminine desire—"the question that psychoanalysis leaves answerless": "what does a woman want?"—with a "positively pregnant concept" of resistance, a different approach to dream interpretation, and another way of reading texts in general. As these connections proliferate, the figure of the navel, initially used by Freud simply to designate a particular spot in the dream, becomes increasingly identified with the more general texture of these "netlike entanglements." Accompanying this shift in the status of the navel is a similar dislocation of the very notion of desire. Whereas Freud at times describes unconscious wishes as though they were simply localized, "latent" meanings or repressed contents, Felman's reading of the irreducibly metaphorical fabric of Freud's text teases out an unstable and tangled movement of conflictual ambivalence.

The Texture of Self-Censorship

As Freud's 1925 footnote to *The Interpretation of Dreams* itself suggests, these different conceptions of unconscious desire—as a repressed content or as a movement of conflictual ambivalence—stand in a dynamic relation to one another. For if, as he says, analysts are mistaken in seeking the essence of dreams in their latent content, it is precisely this obstinate search for hidden meaning that makes it so difficult for them to understand how dreams *think through* the nodes of resistance described by Felman. The reductive appropriation of his theory would thus obscure a more dynamic understanding of the conflictual interaction of the dreamwork with the dream censorship and the tangled meshwork of desire this collaboration articulates. Similarly, insofar as Heine scholarship restricts its analysis of (self-)censorship to the question of reprehensible *contents* and the manner in which they are smuggled into the public sphere, it fails to understand how self-censored writing also and above all gives voice to a complex network of internalized power relations.

In order to examine the way these relations insinuate themselves in the very fabric of Heine's writing, I turn now to his narrative fragment, *From the Memoirs of Herr von Schnabelewopski*. This text has been described as one of Heine's oddest works and one of the most difficult to interpret.[9] Narrated in the first person by a young Pole who travels via Hamburg to the Dutch city of Leiden to study theology, the fragment ironically quilts together biblical citations, theological debates, theatrical productions, social commentary, art criticism, dream narration, and even reflections on the history and significance of dreaming. While the interaction of these heterogeneous elements in *Schnabelewopski* makes it difficult to summarize the text in terms of its plot, the very complexity of this interaction suggests that the brittle, uneven texture of the fragment may be of greater significance than its story line.

To refer to the text as a "fragment" is not only to acknowledge what Jeffrey Sammons has described as its "failure as a novel" but also and above all to take note of its *internal* rupturing—the way its individual pieces at once break off from and irrupt through one another. While Michael Werner has already documented a kind of stuttering in Heine's manuscripts and has suggested that writing which is repeatedly forced to break off and begin again bears witness to censorship's self-administration, in *Schnabelewopski* a self-interruptive, faltering style comes to define the text's very mode of narration.

Whereas traditional approaches to the question of censorship are based on the assumption that the borders of a text are already defined and intact before being corrupted by outside forces, *Schnabelewopski* challenges such assumptions by making fragmentation its positive, if highly equivocal (dis)organizing principle. Before turning to the internal disruptions of the narrative itself, it is worth noting a number of peculiarities concerning the composition of this text. Heine scholars have been unable to ascertain whether *Schnabelewopski* was originally conceived of and executed as a fragment or whether it merely stands as the ruin of a novel that was never completed. Unlike many other works by Heine, the manuscript versions of this text have either been lost or destroyed. And while Heine's correspondence usually enables one to chart the development of his work in progress, there are few direct references to *Schnabelewopski* in his letters of the period. As Sammons notes, "A remark to a friend in a letter of August 24, 1832, 'a novel has miscarried [*ist mir mißglückt*]' is usually referred to *Schnabelewopski*, but even that is not certain." Sammons nevertheless goes on to observe that

> it is easy to see that the novel "miscarried" quite early on. Heine at first made an abortive attempt to alter his customary narrative strategy. Instead of employing his own poetic persona, who simultaneously is and is not identical with his empirical self, he installed as narrator an initially completely fictive persona, the aristocratic, somewhat picaresque Polish student Schnabelewopski, born on April Fool's Day, who at the outset is a comic figure and the butt of what not uncharitably might be called Polish jokes. But Heine did not have the gift for this more conventional kind of narration, located in a self distinct from his own. When Schnabelewopski begins to speak of his father, we detect in the two or three sentences a portrait of Samson Heine, a fictionalized fragment of Heine's memoirs such

as we find in *The Book of Le Grand* and from that point on the Polish persona practically disappears, metamorphosed into the familiar narrative persona of the *Travel Pictures,* a sentimental student with a love of freedom and satire, standing largely outside of events and commenting on them.[10]

In rendering the German phrase *"ein Roman ist mir mißglückt"* as "a novel has miscarried," Sammons inflects the translation in such a way as to accentuate the connection between writing and child bearing. Extending the metaphor, he suggests that this "miscarriage" may be traced to "an abortive attempt" on Heine's part "to alter his customary narrative strategy." If the attempt fails and the pregnancy does not come to term, Sammons argues, it is because the literary offspring bears too close a resemblance to its author just as the portrait in the text of Schnabelewopski's parent is too closely identified with Heine's own father. In short, *Schnabelewopski* miscarries as a novel because it fails to have a navel; because the ties that bind the text to its author and the author to his own parent (via Schnabelewopski's depiction of his father) are never severed.

Yet, while *Schnabelewopski* perhaps miscarries as a novel, it nevertheless succeeds — as an ill-conceived fragment — in problematizing the very categories that inform Sammons's explanation of its failure. Whereas Sammons reads the literature in terms of the life, and the act of writing as a generative and intergenerational process, the fragment itself is concerned primarily with a certain suspension of life.

It is no accident, then, that the story of the Flying Dutchman forms the literal centerpiece of this text. In the central seventh section of a "fragment" consisting of fourteen chapters, the Dutchman is described as having to "endure the most unheard of tortures on the measureless waste of water; . . . his body is nothing but a coffin of flesh wherein his soul whiles away; . . . life casts him forth and death turns him away: like an empty cask tossed from one wave to another and contemptuously thrown back, the poor Dutchman is hurled back and forth between death and life, neither of which wanting to hold on to him" (132).[11]

Given the Dutchman's curse and his association in this text with the figure of the Wandering Jew, who, according to legend, is him-

self condemned to rove indefinitely between life and death, it is significant that Schnabelewopski's date of birth is given as April 1,
1795. Born on April Fool's Day, his origins would thus be as indefinite as the Dutchman's ends; his navel, far from simply being
absent, would be ambiguous—the trace of a fictive origin. As it
turns out, Schnabelewopski's origins are fictitious in a number of
unexpected ways. For his story begins not only in his mother's
womb but also in other literary works such as Plutarch's *Lives* from
which his mother reads to him during her pregnancy. He thus
comes to life literally engrossed in other texts. Yet in another
equally important sense, to be born on April first also means tracing one's beginnings to the mere fiction of an origin. In other
words, to come into the world on this date is at once to be born and
to have the illusion of being born. An inverted double of the Flying
Dutchman whose death is perpetually deferred, Schnabelewopski
comes to life repeatedly without ever quite *being* alive. Just as these
doubly undeliverable figures are condemned to repeat a crossing
without end, unable either to arrive or return, so too is it the
uncanny destiny of Heine's text itself to hover ambiguously between an incomplete, aborted novel and a realized fragment. Little
wonder, then, that Schnabelewopski, an ill-conceived character
who emerges in and as the very suspension of an origin as an April
Fool's joke, should carry the trace of this original suspension in the
form of a *verbal navel* (in German, *Nabel*) inscribed in the midst
of his own very funny name.

The *Nabel* inscribed in Sch(nabel)ewopski's midsection would
thus mark his limbolike existence—or rather, his perseverating insistence—at the very limits of life and death as well as his suspended relationship to other liminal figures such as the outcast
Dutchman. While the fates of these two characters are implicitly
linked throughout the text, their paths explicitly cross only at one
specific point—namely, at the dead center of the fragment, a site
whose significance is underscored by the sole mention of a navel in
the text. This overdetermined intersection is also marked by an all
too conspicuous act of self-censorship.

> But no—the whole story that I planned to narrate here, and for
> which the Flying Dutchman was only to have served as a frame, I
> am now going to suppress. Thereby will I revenge myself on the

prudes who devour such narratives with delight, and are enraptured with them to their heart of hearts, and even further [*bis an den Nabel, ja noch tiefer*], and then chide the narrator and turn up their noses at him in society and decry him as immoral. It is a good story, delicious as pineapple preserve or fresh caviar or truffles in Burgundy, and would be pleasant reading after prayers; but out of spite, and as punishment for old offenses I will suppress it. Here I make a long dash [*Gedankenstrich*] ——.

This stroke signifies a black sofa upon which took place the story which I am not going to tell [*die Geschichte, die ich nicht erzähle*]. (135)

In order to appreciate the significance of this scene, it may be useful to summarize the various plot lines that converge at this moment. The narrative interruption comes at a point where one story of seduction has been broken off in order to tell another. That is, the narrator begins by describing a theatrical adaptation of the legend of the Flying Dutchman only to interrupt that account in order to describe his own encounter with a fellow spectator referred to as "an exquisite Eve." It is this story "for which the Flying Dutchman was only to have served as a frame [*nur als Rahmen dienen sollte*]" that is now suppressed.

Before actually describing these interrupted and interirruptive scenes of seduction, the narrator sets the stage by recalling a legend he had once heard involving a cursed vessel said to have wandered the seas from time immemorial, never able to dock in any harbor. When the ship comes upon another vessel, some of its unearthly crew approach in a boat and beseech the others to take a packet of letters along with them. These letters, so the legend goes, must be nailed firmly to the mast. Otherwise, some misfortune will befall the ship, especially if there is no Bible on board or horseshoe on the foremast. The letters are always addressed to unknown persons or to people who have long since passed away. The ship itself is said to be nothing more than a "wooden spectre" that takes its name from its captain, a Dutchman, who once swore "by all devils that he would sail around a certain promontory . . . , in spite of the most violently raging storm even if he had to sail to Judgement Day." The devil took him at his word and condemned him to wander the seas until the end of time or until he was saved through the faithfulness of a woman.[12] He is thus allowed to land every seven years to search for his redeemer. Yet, as the narrator caustically observes, "the Dutchman is often happy enough to be saved from his saviors and to escape back to his ship."

This, then, is the setting for the dramatic adaptation of the legend seen by Schnabelewopski in a theater in Amsterdam. The play itself, which was later to serve as the basis for Richard Wagner's 1843 opera, begins with the Dutchman meeting a Scottish merchant. He sells the Scotsman diamonds for a ridiculously low price; in return, the merchant offers to introduce him to his beautiful daughter. In the next scene, the daughter is observed sitting at home anticipating the Dutchman's arrival. On the wall hangs a large, weathered portrait of a man dressed in Spanish-Dutch clothing in which the Dutchman is depicted as he was last seen one hundred years earlier in Scotland. Along with the painting, which has been handed down from generation to generation, comes the warning that women of the family should avoid the "original" at all costs. When the Dutchman enters, the girl is taken aback, and the guest himself grows visibly uneasy upon noticing the portrait on the wall. When someone explains whose picture it is,

> he laughs at the superstition and even describes the Flying Dutchman as the Wandering Jew of the Seas; but then passing involuntarily into a melancholy tone, he describes how Myn Heer has had to endure the most unheard-of suffering on the measureless waste of water; how his body is nothing but a coffin of flesh wherein his soul whiles away, and how life casts him forth and death turns him away; like an empty cask tossed from one wave to another and then contemptuously thrown back, the poor Dutchman is hurled back and forth between death and life, neither of which wanting to hold on to him; how his pain is as deep as the sea upon which he wanders, how his ship is without anchor and his heart without hope. (132–33)

The girl observes him carefully and after casting numerous sidelong glances at the portrait appears to grasp his secret. When he finally asks her to become his faithful wife, she lovingly replies, "faithful unto death [*bis in den Tod*]."

It is at this point that Schnabelewopski breaks off his account of the play in order to narrate his own brief encounter with a woman in the audience. After his description of this amorous interlude, to which we will return shortly, the narrator relates the final scene of the play. The Dutchman's wife is seen standing on a cliff overlooking the sea as her husband's ship is about to depart. At this moment the Dutchman confesses his true identity and she responds that having been faithful to him up to this point she knows of one sure way of remaining true to him unto death. She then casts herself into the sea, the curse is lifted, and the ghost ship sinks into the abyss.

Significantly, it is in the interval between the exchange of wedding vows and this fatal consummation of the relationship that Schnabelewopski inserts a censored description of his own seduction by "an exquisite Eve" sitting in the balcony. In telling contrast to her biblical counterpart, this modern seductress rejects the traditional gesture of "symbolically" handing Schnabelewopski half of her apple (*Apfel*), choosing instead "metaphorically" to throw orange (*Apfelsine*) peels at his head. Although the narrator initially threatens to suppress the juiciest parts of this encounter, the tale does somehow manage to be told. Yet, as might be expected, it is told in a very different manner, one that not only subverts the normal opposition between suppressive acts and attempts at self-expression but, in the process, also reconfigures the relationship of fruit and skin, diegetic content and narrative frame.

In order to follow these shifts in the text, it may be useful to begin by recalling Manfred Frank's observation that Heine not only links the saga of the Flying Dutchman to the story of the Wandering Jew at this point in the narrative but also couples the biblical story of Adam and Eve with the legend of Don Juan.[13] This latter-day Eve is first portrayed as

> a fair and gentle girl, a thoroughly soft and feminine figure, not languishing yet delicate as crystal [*kristallig zart*], a picture of domestic propriety and fascinating amiability. Only that there was something on the left upper lip which curved or twined like the tail of a slippery gliding lizard. It was a mysterious trait, something such as is not found in pure angels, and just as little in mere devils. This expression boded neither good nor evil, but signified only wicked thoughts — it is a smile which has been poisoned by tasting the apple of the tree of knowledge. (133–34)

Having stimulated the reader's desire to know more about carnal knowledge in general and more of the details of his own carnal relations with this "exquisite Eve" in particular, Schnabelewopski now breaks off his description. In its stead he places a long dash (*Gedankenstrich*) —— representing "a black sofa upon which transpired the story" he refuses to tell. From this point on, the frustrated reader is forced to squint between the lines and read the text against the grain (*gegen den Strich*) in order to find out what happened. To do so, Heine suggests, involves reading his text obliquely through the perspective offered by another legend. After Schnabelewopski confesses that he had never been so wildly kissed as by this Dutch blonde, he adds:

> Now I understand why an English poet has compared such women to frozen champagne. In the icy crust lies hidden [*lauert*] the most ardent [*heißeste*] extract. There is nothing more piquant than the contrast between external cold and the inner fire which, Bacchante-like, flames up and irresistibly intoxicates the happy carouser. Ay, far more than in brunettes does the fire of passion burn in many a sham-calm holy image with golden-glory hair, and blue angel's eyes, and pious lily hands. I knew a blonde of one of the best families in Holland who at times left her beautiful chateau on the Zuyder-Zee and went incognito to Amsterdam, and there in the theatre threw an orange peel on the head of anyone who pleased her, and who now and then gave herself up to the wildest debauchery in seamen's lodgings, a Dutch Messalina! (135)

The English poet alluded to is of course Lord Byron, who in the thirteenth canto of *Don Juan* compares the seeming indifference of Adeline Amundeville to snow above a smoldering volcano. Yet, finding this "a tired metaphor," the narrator comes up with "another figure in a trice":

> What say you to a bottle of champagne,
>   Frozen into a very vinous ice,
>   Which leaves few drops of that immortal rain.
>   Yet in the very centre, past all price,
>   About a liquid glassful will remain,
>   And this is stronger than the strongest grape
>   Could e'er express in its expanded shape.

Commenting on this passage, Ernest Lovell observes that the figure of frozen champagne evokes a sense of "restraint and self-discipline which is won at the price of bottling up and suppressing emotions beneath a layer of ice, thus doubly distilling them and ironically intensifying their explosive qualities, enabling them the more effectively to break down the cold and icy walls of polished restraint."[14] In taking over the figure from Byron, Heine would thus seem to use it merely to describe a particular Dutchwoman whose icy exterior serves to concentrate and strengthen the intoxicating spirits bubbling within. Yet more generally, and I think more interestingly, Heine also invokes the figure as a way of alluding to the pressures that accumulate and intensify throughout his text by means of his own narrative suppressions. As Byron's avoidance of the "tired metaphor" of a dormant volcano suggests, such pressures do not simply build to a point where they suddenly erupt at determinate places in the text like a violent return of the repressed. Indeed, rather than simply breaking through an otherwise homogeneous narrative surface—one that (to use Byron's metaphor) would be as uniform as fallen snow—in *Schnabelewopski* these pressures tend to displace the narrative at every turn, transforming it into a self-interruptive mode of articulation in which ruptures and disjunctions are no longer the exception but the rule.

In order to follow this faltering movement, it may be useful to return to the interrupted story of the Flying Dutchman, which, it will be recalled, "was only to have served as a frame" for this narrative interlude. Given the way in which this strategically suppressed story of the narrator's liaison with a blonde Dutchwoman reworks the very notion of suppression through its allusion to Byron, one begins to wonder what kind of frame the story of the Flying Dutchman could ever have provided for it. The question of framing, which in this particular case seems only to involve narrative frames, takes on greater significance when one recalls that the Dutchman himself is referred to as "an empty cask tossed from one wave to another," while the ship he repeatedly boards and unboards is described as an errant "wooden spectre." More significant still is the unusual status of picture frames in *Schnabelewopski*. Instead of simply being added on to finished works of art as external decorations, these frames actively open a kind of buffer zone or temporary disjunction between inside and outside, art and life, copy and original. It is just such a frame that the Dutchman seeks to impose when he is struck by the sight of a portrait hanging in the home of the merchant's daughter he has come to court.

> When he is informed whose likeness it is, he . . . knows how to keep himself beyond suspicion [*weiß er jeden Argwohn von sich fern zu halten*]; he laughs at the superstition and even describes the Flying Dutchman as the Wandering Jew of the Seas; but then passing involuntarily into a melancholy tone [*Ton*], he describes [*schildert*] how Myn Heer has had to endure the most unheard-of suffering [*Leiden*] on the measureless waste of water; how his body is nothing but a coffin of flesh wherein his soul whiles away, and how life casts him forth and death turns him away: like an empty cask [*Tonne*] tossed from one wave to another . . . (132)

Here the only thing separating the "original" from the likeness is the Dutchman's own weak attempt at sarcasm. It is therefore significant that at the very moment he depicts himself as a floating wooden frame—as an empty cask (*Tonne*) tossed about at sea—the tonal frame itself suddenly and "involuntarily" slips from a mocking into a melancholy mood. (This element of slippage is further emphasized by the resonance in German between *Ton* [tone] and *Tonne* [cask].) No longer distinguishable from the picture hanging on the wall, neither simply the portrait nor the one who depicts himself as though describing another, *it is the floating frame itself that now speaks*—or rather that suddenly and involuntarily *misspeaks* itself. That is, it speaks only to communicate a curse, only to *let slip* the Dutchman's *excommunication* both from this life and from the eternal Life after. As the allusion to the Wandering Jew, Ahasverus, suggests, this exile at the limits of life and death is but the endless prolongation of Christ's *Leidensweg*: the Way of the Cross, but also (in the context of a fragment whose final chapters are set in the Dutch city of Leiden) his life of suffering. We will have occasion to return to the legend of the Wandering Jew below and in particular to the way this story itself weaves through other biblical narratives referred to in *Schnabelewopski*.

For the moment, however, it is important to consider what it might actually mean to pass on, to communicate, the curse of excommunication. How does this particular mode of communication differ from more conventional ways of transmitting information? It is certainly no accident that the Dutchman's words begin to wander at the very point where he would like most to conceal his fate. In other words, it is precisely at the moment he would wish to disavow his own vagrancy and present himself as something other than a "floating frame" that the curse itself seems to communicate through a dislocation of the speaking subject. What is referred to here as a curse is at once that which performatively dislodges the rigidly imposed tonal frame of this passage as well as that which seems to speak or rather to slip through the cracks opened by this "involuntary" tonal shift.

The passage thus suggests that in speaking about the damnation of exile, speech itself is condemned to wander. Furthermore, it implies that this wandering of speech goes beyond mere depiction (*Schilderung*) in its *enactment* of a radically uprooting sense of excommunication and dislocation. No longer at home in the world, the Dutchman is also linguistically a stranger to the vagabond words he lets slip—words that, properly speaking, belong neither to him nor to another and that in fact describe him as another. The curse of exile is thus communicated *to* these words in addition to being transmitted by or through them. As a way of alerting the reader to the play of description and enactment in this scene and, moreover, to the ways in which its language functions as yet another scene in which the issue of dislocation is staged as a problem in the text, Heine frames it explicitly as a moment in a theatrical production described by the narrator. In other words, between the description of a performance and the performance of a movement of displacement which cannot simply be described, something "involuntarily" slips—something like the floating frame of the Flying Dutchman.

Narrative Frames

In light of the foregoing discussion, it seems fitting that the narrator should have wished to use the story of the Flying Dutchman as a frame for the story he decides not to tell. For ultimately the Dutchman seems to consist of nothing but empty and unstable frames. While in one sense these frames do describe the contours of an empty space in the text—the place where a self-censored story was supposed to have been inserted—they also reinscribe this suppression in the more general narrative economy of what in German is called a *Rahmenerzählung:* a story or group of stories composed of interlocking narratives that repeatedly interrupt and frame one another.

As a *Rahmenerzählung,* Heine's text has much in common with Plato's *Symposium,* Mary Shelley's *Frankenstein,* Italo Calvino's *If on a Winter's Night a Traveler,* and Scheherezade's *Tales of the Thousand and One Nights.*[15] In order to understand Heine's particular contribution to this tradition, it may be useful to compare *Schnabelewopski*'s "frame narrative" to that of *The Thousand and One Nights.* As is well known, in Scheherezade's tale of tales, the very act of storytelling is a matter of life and death. She tells stories in order to defer her imminent execution and, as it turns out, also in order to have her death sentence eventually commuted to a marriage vow. Thus, in *The Arabian Nights* it is the narrator's potentially fatal relationship to her audience that functions as the story that contains and impels all the others. By contrast, in *Schnabelewopski* it is the story of a marriage that is ironically *saved* by the wife's suicide that serves as its all too literal "frame."

If *Schnabelewopski* makes a point of taking the question of framing a little too literally, it is precisely this accentuation of the literal, the literary, and the letter that discloses a different kind of relationship between skin and fruit, vessel and cargo, envelope and message, narrative frame and framed narrative. Indeed, insofar as Heine's account of the Flying Dutchman narrates the displacement of a floating frame, this "frame narrative" should itself be read as a story ironically displaced and reframed by the very stories it was supposed to have enclosed. It might be recalled in this regard how the narrator's "suppressed" account of his meeting with "an exquisite Eve"—an account that was to have been framed by the story of the Dutchman—breaks off with a final description of this woman as a "Dutch Messalina." This allusion to the Roman emperor Claudius's third wife, whose debauchery led to her execution, is obviously intended as an ironic counterpoint to the self-sacrificing faithfulness of the Dutchman's wife. Not only does the juxtaposition of these scenes—separated by another *Gedankenstrich*—tacitly call into question the apparent resolution of the Dutchman's story, but it also foreshadows a return of "the Wandering Jew of the Seas" at another point in the text where once again it is a question of a spouse's alleged infidelity.

What I am suggesting is that the spectral frame of the Flying Dutchman continues to float through Heine's narrative long after it is presumed to have sunken into the abyss and disappeared from the text. As though driven from one form of exile to another, the Dutchman ceases to wander between life and death only to be cast adrift again in the dreams of other characters in the narrative. Moreover, when this displaced figure resurfaces in later chapters, he no longer appears as he once was but rather as "the Wandering Jew of the Seas" he will always already have been. In other words, the Dutchman's patently improper "proper name" will have been nothing more than a floating signifier, a differential placeholder, always already open to and opened by the difference of another.

In order to be able to follow the movement of these long-suffering figures as they themselves are pursued by a wandering curse, it may be useful to note the way Heine's description of dreaming in the twelfth chapter of *Schnabelewopski* echoes his account of the Dutchman's suspension at the limits of life and death in chapter 7.

> What is dreaming? What is death? Is it only an interruption of life or its full cessation? Yes, for people who only know the Past and the Future, and do not live an eternity in every moment of the Present, death must be terrible! When their two crutches, Space and Time, fall away, then they sink into the eternal Nothing.
>
> And dreams? Why are we not more afraid before going to sleep than to be buried? Is it not terrible that the body can be as if dead all night, while the spirit in us leads the most animated existence — a life full of all those terrors of that parting which we have established between body and mind! When in the future both shall be again united in our consciousness, then there will perhaps be no more dreams, or else only invalids, those whose harmony has been disturbed, will dream. The ancients dreamed only softly and seldom; a strong and powerfully impressive dream was for them an event, and it was recorded in their histories. Real dreaming began with the Jews, the people of the Mind [*Volk des Geistes*], and attained its highest development among the Christians, the ghostlike, spiritual people [*Geistervolk*]. Our descendants will shudder when they read what a ghastly life we led, how Humanity was cloven in us and only one half had a real life. Our time — and it begins with the crucifixion

of Christ [*sie beginnt am Kreuze Christi*]—will be regarded as the great period of illness of Humanity.

And yet, what beautiful sweet dreams we have been able to dream! (157–58)

These remarks suggest that if sleep is akin to death, dreaming is a form of suspended animation. In dreams, the "parting which we have established between body and mind [*Geist*]" manifests itself as a supplementary division of *Geist* into mind and spirit. Thus, during sleep one part of the mind remains dead to the world, while its spiritual counterpart "leads the most animated existence." Such reflections on dreaming are certainly rather banal in their own right. Yet, considered in the context of the narrative economy of *Schnabelewopski,* they mark an important inward displacement of the horizon between life and death. What was formerly described as a place of exile at the uttermost limits of life now reappears as an unstable, oneiric borderland within it.

This movement of displacement is alluded to, albeit in much more sanguine terms, in a passage directly following the one cited above: "All the splendors of the world disappeared from around us, and we found them again in our own souls; yes, there the perfume of the trampled roses, and the sweetest songs of the frightened nightingales took refuge" (158).

If Heine seems to recirculate some of the more hackneyed commonplaces of romantic poetry in this passage, he does so precisely in order to capitalize on their bankruptcy; that is, in using them *as clichés* he allows these well-worn images to efface themselves all the more, thereby transforming every alleged place of refuge, every sanctuary for "frightened nightingales" into a mere way station along a path of migration, dislocation, and exile. It is no accident, then, that the narrator's subsequent attempt "to escape into the Land of Dreams" results in his being awoken from a dream at a critical moment so that he might accompany his landlady to her husband's bedroom where the latter is found to be talking in his sleep. Catching her husband again cavorting with Old Testament women in his dreams, the landlady tears away the bedclothes and begins to beat him with a leather hernia belt (*Bruchband*).

Shattered Dreams

Because ruptures—in the sense of both herniated navels and narrative interruptions—are in a sense what *Schnabelewopski* is all about, the interpretation of any of the dreams recounted in the latter sections of the text requires that they be treated as textual fragments broken off from and irrupting through one another. In other words, each interrupted dream must be read as a link in a chain of interirruptive dreams. Not surprisingly, the first link in this sequence is itself a dream in which the narrator finds himself reunited with a certain Jadviga, a woman who had appeared earlier in the text as a feminine prefiguration of the Flying Dutchman. Consider, then, the following dream recounted by Schnabelewopski in chapter 2:

> But then I began to perceive a noise in measured time, like the beat of oars, and there came a boat driven along by the waves. In it sat four white forms, with sallow, corpse faces, wrapped in shrouds, rowing with energy. In the midst stood a pale but infinitely beautiful woman, infinitely lovely and delicate, as if made from lily-perfume, and she sprang ashore. The boat with its spectral oarsmen shot like an arrow back into the rising sea, and in my arms lay Panna Jadviga, who wept and laughed, "I pray to thee!" (99–100)

Despite the fact that Jadviga is now lying in the narrator's arms, it is unclear who exactly is addressed by these words. For in chapter 1, Schnabelewopski describes a praying figure lying prostrate before the sarcophagus of Saint Adalbert in a church in Poland: "The church is empty, only there lies before the silver shrine . . . a woman of wondrous beauty who casts a sidelong glance at me and then turns as suddenly again towards the saint, and murmurs with yearning, cunning lips, 'I pray to thee!' . . . Were these words addressed to me or to the silver Adalbert?" (97).

Here, as elsewhere in the text, face-to-face confrontations give way to strategically skewed encounters and equivocal sideshows. Like the "dead letters" later forwarded by the Dutchman's unearthly crew to other passing vessels, Jadviga's words here remain in some sense undeliverable. Not only are they, too, condemned to wander, but the effort to deliver them is doomed to repeat itself throughout the narrative. It is not by chance, then, that the setting for this floating scene of repetition gradually shifts from the nave of a church to a ghost ship in chapter 2 and then to the deck of another naval vessel in the narrator's dream in chapter 12. Here, in place of the sound of oars glancing the water "in measured time" described in the earlier dream, one hears only the rhythms of the poet's "rapturous love songs," which he declaims to his beloved. Schnabelewopski is thus comfortably adrift in the "dreamland" (*Land der Träume*) of romantic poetry at the moment when he is suddenly roused by the "grating voice" of his landlady and conducted into her husband's bedroom: "There lay the poor man with his nightcap pulled over his eyes, apparently dreaming intensely. His body often twitched visibly under the covers, his lips smiled as if with ineffable happiness and often pursed fitfully in the form of a kiss, while he rattled and stammered, 'Vashti! Queen Vashti! Fear not Ahasverus [*Fürchte keinen Ahasveros*]! Beloved Vashti!'" (160).

As was noted above, this is not the first time that the landlady hears of her husband's oneiric infidelities. Earlier in the story, the narrator tells of how his landlord would sit at the breakfast table and recount his nightly visits with biblical women. One morning the faithless husband spoke of Queen Esther,

> who begged him to help her in her toilet so that through the power of her charms she could win King Ahasverus over to her just cause. In vain did the poor man explain that Herr Mordecai himself had introduced him to his fair ward, that she was already half dressed, and that he had only combed out her long black hair—in vain! The enraged wife beat the poor man with his own trusses, poured hot coffee onto his face, and would certainly have finished him off if he had not sworn in the most solemn manner to renounce all association with Old Testament women and in the future to keep company only with patriarchs and male prophets.
>
> The results of this ill-treatment were that from now on Mynheer kept timidly silent about his nocturnal happiness. (156)

Like the narrator's own "suppressed" account of his meeting with an "exquisite Eve" in chapter 7, the landlord's anxiously stifled reports of his encounters with biblical women also find a stuttering form of expression. Thus, instead of continuing to tell his dreams at the breakfast table, the landlord begins to talk—or rather, "to rattle and stammer"—in his sleep: "Queen Vashti! Fear not Ahasverus! Beloved Vashti!" As was suggested earlier, this stuttering not only rehearses a kind of standoff between an urge to express oneself and a need to censor what is said, it also gives voice to a tangle of interirruptive relationships. In other words, the landlord's biblical dream speaks out of an inmixing of subjects — out of a place, that is, where the subject is (k)not.[16] As we will see, not only does this dream mark a particularly dense nodal point in the text, but its stuttered outbursts literally break through a rupture in the speaking subject. That is, they speak in a voice that is neither exactly that of the landlord nor of someone else. It is therefore only fitting that the split subject of these somniloquies should "himself" be interrupted in flagrante delicto by his wife and beaten with a hernia belt of his own devising.[17]

If this section of *Schnabelewopski* thus appears to narrate another kind of *Rahmenerzählung* in which each interrupted dream frames another, it is necessary to ask at this point what exactly is displaced along this interirruptive concatenation of dreams. What is being communicated that cannot be contained within any one particular frame? What is it that is breaching a path through these dreams, causing them to break through one another?[18] When faced with similar questions in the case of the Flying Dutchman, it was found that this movement of displacement was related both to the communication of a curse and to a strategic conflation of the Dutchman's story with other legends. In the present context, Heine again seems to structure the narrative in such a way as to allow an overdetermined knot of figures to speak — or, more exactly, to stutter — through one another. Indeed, the landlord's stammered outburst: "Queen Vashti! Fear not Ahasverus! Beloved Vashti!" draws attention not only to a split in the speaking subject but also to the nonidentity of the subjects spoken about. While the immediate context suggests that the name "Ahasverus" be read merely as a reference to the Persian king mentioned in the Book of Esther, the proximity of Jadviga, herself a kind of feminine Flying Dutchman, suggests that this name might also allude to the legendary Wandering Jew, whose "proper name" is also Ahasverus. As it turns out, the fates of these two figures are both textually and historically intertwined through yet another case of mistaken identity. Consider in this regard the following entry contained in the *Wahrig Deutsches Wörterbuch* under the name "Ahasverus": "Hebrew form of the name of the Persian king Xerxes (486–465 B.C.) who, according to the Book of Esther, saved the Jews from their enemies; in the course of plays and theatrical performances taking place during the feast of Purim in commemoration of this event, Gentile spectators in medieval Europe confused the actor playing Ahasverus (an itinerant Jewish actor) with the legendary Wandering Jew" (translation mine).

If the landlord's stammering of the name "Ahasverus" plays on this confusion, it does so in order to suggest that even when the perpetually displaced figure of the Wandering Jew is called by name in this text, it is always another who will answer in his stead. In other words, as the very figure of the Other and as the very movement of a self-differing signifier, Ahasverus is condemned to wander through Heine's text appearing only as other figures — as the masculine Flying Dutchman, as Jadviga, as the Persian king — but also as the concatenation of interirruptive dreams and as the dislocation of floating frames.

This perpetual displacement of the Wandering Jew in *Schnabelewopski* is itself linked to Heine's own unstable and ambivalent relation to Jewish tradition. In chapter 9 of this text, the narrator remarks:

> Jews are ever the most devoted Deists, especially those who, like little Samson, were born in the free city of Frankfurt. These Jews are capable of thinking in such a republican way in political questions, yes they can even roll so sansculottically in the mud; but as soon as religious ideas come into play they remain humble servants of their Jehovah, the old fetish, who, however, wants nothing more to do with their whole tribe and who has had himself rebaptized as a God-pure spirit [*Gott-reiner Geist*].
>
> I believe that this God-pure spirit, this parvenu of heaven, who is now so morally, cosmospolitically and universally cultivated [*gebildet*], harbors a secret ill-will towards the poor Jews, who knew him in his first rude form, and who remind him every day in their synagogues of his early and obscure national relations. Perhaps the old Lord would feign forget that he was of Palestinian origin and once the God of Abraham, Isaac, and Jacob, and was in those days called Jehovah. (145–46)

Just as the Flying Dutchman passes involuntarily from a mocking to a melancholy tone when depicting the fate of the "Wandering Jew of the Seas," so too does the mood of this passage shift from biting sarcasm to a more tentative and less distant sense of irony when the issue of baptism and conversion explicitly surfaces.[19] Whereas the passage at first seems to advocate a dialectical sublation of the Jewish *Geist*—a process that would cancel its more nationalistic and fetishistic aspects while raising it to a higher level as Enlightenment morality, cosmopolitanism, and universality—Heine goes on to describe this "God-pure spirit" as a philistine social climber, "a parvenu of heaven." His irony thus allows him to distance himself, not only from the "poor Jews" who persist in clinging to an apparently outmoded faith, but also from the nouveaux riches who attempt to wrap their recent material prosperity in the patina of *Bildung* (one thinks here of the figure of Gumpelino in *The Baths of Lucca*). His attack also seems aimed at people like Eduard Gans (formerly a member of a Jewish cultural organization in Berlin to which Heine at one time also belonged), who converted in order to obtain a professorship. Finally, and most significantly, if the tone of this passage appears to shift precisely at the point where the issue of baptism is explicitly brought to the fore, this "slip" suggests that Heine's irony may be directed not only at other Jews but also and perhaps above all at himself. That is, listened to in a certain way the ironic ambiguity of the passage seems to give voice to Heine's own ambivalent feelings about the conversion experience he himself went through on June 28, 1825.[20]

As Jeffrey Sammons has argued, Heine's decision to convert to Protestantism must be understood in the context of Prussian anti-Semitic policies promulgated in the 1820s. These measures had as their aim the systematic restoration of a pattern of discrimination against the Jews that had been relieved during the time of Napoleon and the Prussian reform.

> In September 1819 Christian children were prohibited from attending Jewish schools; in June 1822 Jews were excluded from the higher ranks of the army; in March 1823 it was announced that the Jewish religion was only "tolerated." Of special significance to Heine was the decision taken in August 1822 and announced in December that

Jews would henceforth be excluded from academic posts; the immediate motive of this action had been to deny a professorship to Gans.[21]

While Heine publicly referred to baptism as "the entrance ticket to European culture,"[22] privately he confided to a friend in a letter of January 1826: "I regret very much that I had myself baptized; I cannot at all see that things have gone better for me since then, on the contrary, I have since had nothing but misfortune."[23] Certainly the most telling index of Heine's ambivalence is the story told not in any one particular text but rather through the very process of textual revision. Consider in this regard an initial reference to his baptism in the original version of *The Harz Journey,* published in *Der Gesellschafter:* "No one," he says, "will hold it against me that I did this, with such significant reasons, and I have not regretted it to this hour"; four months later, when the work was published in book form, this sentence was revised to read, "No one will hold it against me that I did this in such a precarious position."[24]

Returning to *Schnabelewopski,* I would like suggest in conclusion that the ambivalence Heine felt in regard to his own baptism, an ambivalence that is perhaps most poignantly articulated in and through a movement of textual displacement, itself constitutes a knot of pain that is ambivalently tied up with the suffering of Ahasverus, the Wandering Jew. This suffering, *Schnabelewopski* seems to say, is not merely the positive torment of exile but also the wandering of a pain difficult to locate, one that knots together legendary figures of dislocation and only suffers to be read through those knots.

Halt!

Freud and the Repression
of Censorship

Truth is not always in a well. In fact, as regards the more important knowledge, I do believe that she is invariably superficial. . . . To look at a star by glances—to view it *in a sidelong way,* by turning toward it the exterior portions of the ret-
ina . . . is to have the best appreciation of its lustre—a lustre
which grows dim just in proportion as we turn our vision
fully upon it.

Poe, The Murders in the Rue Morgue

My reading of Freud's *Interpretation of Dreams* began by asking
how the metaphor of censorship functions in his work and whether
the term *dream censorship* is in fact just a metaphor. As we have
seen, the figurative language used in this text serves both as a kind
of visual aid which helps the reader become accustomed to the
obscurities of dream interpretation and as a kind of blind man's
stick which enables Freud to feel his way in the absence of a more
straightforwardly descriptive, properly psychoanalytic terminology. The necessity of this ambivalent dependence on metaphor is
addressed in *Beyond the Pleasure Principle* in a passage already
touched on in Chapter 1:

> We need not feel greatly disturbed in judging our speculation upon
> the life and death drives by the fact that so many bewildering and
> obscure processes [*befremdende und unanschauliche Vorgänge*] oc-
> cur in it—such as one drive being driven out by another, or a drive
> turning from the ego to an object and so on. This is merely due to
> our being obliged to operate with the scientific terms, that is to say
> with the figurative language [*Bildersprache*] peculiar to psychology

(or more precisely, to depth-psychology). *We could not otherwise describe the processes in question at all, and indeed we could not even have perceived them.* (S.E.18, 60; emphasis added)

As was noted earlier, the prosthesis of a *Bildersprache* not only serves to augment, enhance, or clarify material that has already been observed but enables Freud to see in the first place.[1] While he goes on to concede that the "deficiencies in our description would probably vanish if we were already in a position to replace psychological terms by physiological or chemical ones," he adds immediately that "they too are only part of a figurative language albeit one with which we have long been familiar and which is perhaps simpler as well" (S.E.18, 60). In this strikingly Nietzschean formulation, Freud not only suggests that all scientific language is at base metaphorical, but more importantly he implies that with time and use the artificial limbs of figurative language may become naturalized and incorporated as the organic body of a more straightforwardly descriptive and "simpler" scientific discourse.[2]

In examining Freud's recourse to the language of politics and publishing as he attempts to articulate a properly psychoanalytic notion of censorship, two points need to be stressed: first, such borrowings indicate the extent to which political concerns shape Freud's thinking about seemingly private matters such as dreams; second, and perhaps more importantly, they suggest that the question of censorship may itself remain beyond the grasp of any one particular field of study or critical jargon. In other words, if censorship practices inevitably raise questions about discursive boundaries and their transgression, in order to address such questions it is perhaps necessary to work at the limits of a number of disciplines, reading the language of one field of study through the filter of another.

My own aim in the preceding chapters has thus been to tease out the contradictions inherent in the Freudian notion of dream censorship through an examination of the problem of (self-)censorship in Heine. Such a reading of *The Interpretation of Dreams* — and its own distortions — I have argued, in turn teaches one to follow a general movement of textual fragmentation and dislocation when attempting to trace the effects of self-censorship in literary texts. In pursuing this dual approach, I have attempted to demonstrate how Freud's metaphor of dream censorship—like Heine's unwieldy irony—ultimately cuts two ways; how it simultaneously invites one to interpret dreams as distorted texts and to read (self-) censored literature as a particularly unstable kind of compromise formation. While Freud's borrowing of the term *censorship* may thus enable him to describe processes that would not even have been perceptible otherwise, this appropriation in turn effectively remetaphorizes the all-too-familiar notion of press censorship, making manifest certain contradictions at the heart of *its* dynamics. Like the kettle in *The Interpretation of Dreams,* the term "censorship," it would seem, already had holes in it when Freud borrowed it.

The Repression of Censorship

As was already intimated at the end of Chapter 2, the notion of censorship in Freud is closely related to that of repression. The two even seem to be used interchangeably at times. Thus, in order to pursue the vicissitudes of censorship in Freud's writings, I turn now to its relationship to repression. My approach will again focus on the problem of conflict and particularly on those conflicts that intensify to the point where opposing forces are difficult to distinguish from one another. As we have seen, the site of these interactions and collaborations can no longer be construed simply in terms of a particular place such as a front, threshold, or border between two realms.[3] Moreover, as conflicts become more intense and clearly defined borders begin to blur, Freud tends to speak increasingly in terms of quantitative rather than qualitative relationships. Thus, for example, in *The Interpretation of Dreams,* when describing an "other scene" of dreams in which the relationship of spectator and spectacle can no longer be conceived of in terms of a face-to-face encounter, he reframes the question of who is perceiving what in quantitative terms that take into account the strength and relative stability of what he calls a cathexis of attention (*Aufmerksamkeitsbesetzung*).

The emergence of these economic relations in Freud's writing is linked not only to the intensification of conflict but also to the issue of anxiety. While it is certainly necessary to examine the different and often conflicting accounts of anxiety offered by Freud at various stages in his thinking, it is nevertheless worth noting at this point that he describes anxiety in his essay "The Unconscious" as a kind of affective universal commodity. "It is possible," Freud says, "for the development of affect to proceed directly from the system *Ucs;*[4] in that case the affect always has the character of anxiety, for which all 'repressed' affects are exchanged [*gegen welche alle 'verdrängten' Affekte eingetauscht werden*]" (*S.E.*14, 179). While this essay describes anxiety as a quantum of qualitatively indeterminate affect and as something to be defended against, six years later in *Beyond the Pleasure Principle* it is associated with a form of psychic defense.[5] Functioning like an indefinite and diffuse sense of apprehension or foreboding, it is said to "protect its subject against fright and . . . fright-neuroses" (*S.E.*18, 13).

In this chapter and the next I interpret these changes in Freud's approach as the signs of an effort to come to terms with a potent ambiguity at the very heart of anxiety. In exploring why anxiety may be described by Freud both as a form of protection and as a threat to be protected against, I attempt to link it to questions of quantity and quality in his writings on repression and to the issue of intensified conflict. Once again, in order to tease out certain movements in Freud's thought, it is necessary to stage a kind of dialogue between texts. Thus, in this chapter I begin with his metapsychological writings on repression and the unconscious and move in Chapter 5 to *Beyond the Pleasure Principle* and "A Note on the Mystic Writing-Pad," which will be read through the filter of Benjamin's discussion of shock defense and a scene of writing in Baudelaire.

The Interregnum of Repression

Whereas Freud would eventually (though not necessarily progressively) revise and complicate his notion of repression in the course of his metapsychological reflections, the term is at least initially couched in the familiar metaphorics of thresholds and border guards. Thus, toward the middle of his "Repression" essay, he describes the difference between *banishing* a drive representation if it has already entered consciousness and *keeping it out* if it was about to cross the threshold, only to add that the "difference is not important": "It amounts to much the same thing as the difference between my ordering an undesirable guest out of my drawing room (or out of my front hall), and my refusing, after recognizing him, to let him cross my threshold at all" (*S.E.*14, 153). To this,

Freud appends the only substantive footnote of the essay: "This simile, which is thus applicable to the process of repression, may also be extended to a characteristic of it which has been mentioned earlier: I have merely to add that I must set a permanent guard over the door which I have forbidden this guest to enter, since he would otherwise burst it open" (*S.E.*14, 153).

Before commenting on the content of this comparison, it is again worth considering its status as a simile. As was noted earlier, figures that help one to imagine processes that might otherwise have escaped notice always run the risk of becoming something like a screen memory. As Freud elsewhere explains, the problem with such memories is that instead of being too vague and fuzzy, the images they present are a little too good. Insofar as their unusual vividness and arresting clarity effectively immobilize one's attention, they make it difficult to pursue other less obvious connections and chains of association concealed behind them.[6] Thus, for example, in one of his earliest attempts to deal with the process of repression and its relation to the forgetting of proper names, Freud describes his own inability to remember the name of the Italian painter Luca Signorelli, even though he was able to conjure up the pictures painted by Signorelli on the walls of the cathedral in Orvieto "with greater sensory vividness than is usual" with him. As he says, "I saw before my eyes with especial sharpness the artist's self-portrait—with a serious face and folded hands—. . . but the artist's name, ordinarily so familiar to me, remained obstinately in hiding" (*S.E.*3, 291). This emphasis on the unusual vividness of the memory and "the especial sharpness" of the artist's self-portrait in Freud's recollection suggest that these images do not merely arise in place of the painter's proper name, but, in doing so, actively serve to keep the name itself out of the picture.[7]

More generally, it might be said that the metaphors used by Freud to help one imagine the process of repression at times function like his unusually vivid sensory memories of the paintings in Orvieto insofar as the imagery of his *Bildersprache* serves to distort and conceal the very relationships it helps bring into view. Needless to say, these images do not so much falsify relationships that could otherwise be presented more clearly as provide indirect access—like Poe's sidelong glances—to processes that are themselves engaged in activities of indirection and distortion. In short, illustrative metaphors like that of the sentinel of repression employed above may possess the same power of fascination attributed by Freud to screen memories and the process of secondary revision. These processes, it might be recalled, deceive by producing a semblance of unity and intelligibility in place of more fragmentary and discordant relationships, which need to be studied as discontinuous movements of displacement.

Thus, just as Freud's figurative language functions as a kind of supplement depicting in a roundabout way relationships that may not be perceived directly, it may in turn be necessary to find ways around these metaphors themselves, which at times obfuscate relationships precisely by making things a little too visible. To get around these problems, it is important to pay attention to the drift of Freud's language, the dissimilarities engendered by his analogies, and his peculiar use of a language of quantity which at times replaces one of positive description, attribution, and qualification.

Returning now to the content of Freud's simile in which he compares the process of banishing or keeping out a drive representation to the dismissal of an undesirable guest from the drawing room or forbidding him entry into the apartment at all, it would appear that repression consists solely in the activity of turning away an unwanted representation or repressed idea.[8] Yet his footnote, which adds a sentinel to keep *constant* watch over the door, suggests that such processes of exclusion are not carried out once and for all but instead need to be maintained. Here one recalls Freud's lecture on dream censorship, in which he describes the resistance to interpretation as a kind of postcensorship. This resistance, he says, "is only an objectification [*Objektivierung*] of the dream censorship. It also proves to us that the force of the censorship is not exhausted in bringing about the distortion of dreams and thereafter extinguished, but that the censorship persists as a permanent institution which has as its aim the maintenance of the distortion" (*S.E.*15, 141).

If the process of repression, like that of censorship, must thus develop ways of maintaining the exclusions it effects, we should not be surprised to find that its efforts to stabilize conflict require the formation of certain compromises. As was the case with censorship, it seems that the only way to keep the repressed out is to let it in, albeit in a highly compromised and distorted manner. Such ambivalent processes of inclusion are already alluded to in the opening paragraph of Freud's "Repression" article: "If it were a question of the operation of an external stimulus, obviously flight would be the appropriate remedy [*Mittel*]; with an instinct, flight is of no avail, for the ego cannot escape from itself. Later on, rejection based on judgement (*condemnation*) will be found to be a good weapon [*Mittel*] against the impulse. Repression is a preliminary phase of condemnation, something between [*ein Mittelding zwischen*] flight and condemnation."[9]

Here it is less a question of repression turning away an unwelcome guest than of the ego's own futile attempts to vacate the premises. Moreover, if flight is impossible when the demands of the drives (*Triebe:* translated by both Baines and Strachey as "instincts") make themselves felt, it may be because the drives pose a peculiar kind of threat to the ego.[10] Indeed, if Freud claims that the ego cannot escape from itself, this may also be an indication that the drives are neither simply internal nor external to it. The problem of positioning the drives in relation to the ego is itself figured in Freud's shifting use of the term *Mittel* in the course of this short opening passage. The term is employed three times and is translated by Baines respectively as "remedy," "weapon," and "something between." Following the movement of this signifier, one also traces a shift in the nature of conflict. Beginning with terms like "remedy" and "weapon," which are usually used to designate means of combating something external in a struggle where it is still possible to take sides, the paragraph culminates in a definition of repression as *ein Mittelding*—"something between" flight and condemnation.

Thus, at least at first, repression is defined only negatively as a process caught or suspended between two impossible alternatives. Describing it as *ein Mittelding,* "a cross between" a "subjective" turning away from (flight) and an "objective" turning away of (condemnation), Freud also seems to suggest that repression may somehow be at cross-purposes with itself. By drawing attention to the potential heterogeneity of this "middle thing" at the very outset, he also seems to allude to the problems involved in handling it as a discrete, self-contained object of study. Indeed, he concludes the first paragraph by claiming that the "concept" of repression "could not have been formulated before the time of psychoanalytic research."[11]

What the insistence of the signifier *Mittel* further suggests is that such novel concepts can only be grasped by paying attention to the quirks and idiosyncrasies of their mode of formulation.

In a sense, the term *Mittel,* which is silently foregrounded in the opening lines of this essay, serves as a cryptic epigraph presiding over the fate of this concept and the vicissitudes of its formulations. It is characteristic of Freud's writings on repression that the emphasis repeatedly shifts from clearly defined, oppositional terms and terms of oppositional conflict such as "remedies" and "weapons" to "middle things" and questions of intensified conflict where the privileged field of battle is often the very language used to describe such struggles. In short, Freud's writings on repression are about conflict to the extent that conflict is internal to the writing.

It is also important to note the temporal terms in which this initial description of repression is couched. As if to imply that flight is *no longer* a possibility, Freud adds, *"later on,* rejection based on judgement will be found to be a good weapon against the drive impulse."* Thus, no longer the passivity of flight, not yet active condemnation, repression seems to take place in the meantime. Here one is reminded of the split temporality of censorship, the untimeliness of which we saw had less to do with censorship's being repeatedly caught off guard than with the displacement of a process which will have only taken place as pre- and/or postcensorship. To describe this untimeliness in positive temporal terms, it is necessary to employ the future perfect tense, which in this case does not so much anticipate the completion of an operation at some future moment as join past and future, pre- and postcensorship, without the mediation of the present. In other words, these temporal terms themselves circumvent the present tense and thereby serve to accentuate two important points: first, that there is no proper time or place for censorship; second, that its encounters will never have been simply face-to-face confrontations.[12] Similarly, Freud's initial gesture of describing repression exclusively in the negative temporal terms of no longer flight/not yet condemnation itself suggests a more differential and conflictual approach; that is, rather than attempting to pin down repression at some point on a continuum between two unfeasible alternatives, Freud seems to view it instead as an instance that—like censorship—may be radically and necessarily out of sync with itself.

If the untimeliness of repression is thus difficult to appreciate on its own terms, its specificity may perhaps be brought out through a comparison to the more familiar temporality of "rejection based on judgement," which, Freud says, "later on . . . will be found to be a good weapon against the drive impulse." According to Strachey, Freud first describes repression as an earlier form of a negative judgment in *Jokes and Their Relation to the Unconscious*. There Freud introduces this relationship with a tone of perplexed frustration at the fact that his claim, voiced in *The Interpretation of Dreams,* that there is no way of deciding at first glance whether any element that admits of a contrary is present in the dream thoughts as a positive or as a negative "has not up to now met with any recognition" (*S.E.*8, 175). He goes on to stress the importance of this characteristic of unconscious thinking in which "no" does not seem to exist and "in which in all probability no process that resembles 'judging' occurs. In the place of rejection by a judgement, what we find in the unconscious is 'repression.' Repression may, without doubt, be correctly described as the intermediate stage [*Zwischenstufe*] between a defensive reflex and a condemning judgement" (*S.E.*8, 175).

As the reader will have noticed, the language of this description clearly anticipates the formulation appearing ten years later in the "Repression" essay. Before returning to that text, it is important to take note of two important points: first, Freud's stress on the absence of an ability to judge the difference between "yes" and "no," positive and negative, in unconscious thinking suggests that the process of repression may be more tolerant of ambiguity and contradiction than the faculty of judgment; second, it implies that repression may itself be infected by the "timelessness" of unconscious thinking and may therefore be difficult to locate temporally as an "intermediate stage." As Derrida remarks in his essay "Freud and the Scene of Writing," the "timelessness of the unconscious is no doubt determined only in opposition to a common concept of time, a traditional concept, the metaphysical concept: the time of mechanics or the time of consciousness."[13] He adds, "It is not a question of a negation of time, of a cessation of time in a present or a simultaneity, but of a different structure, a different stratification of time."[14] As Freud's own remarks suggest, the difference of this structure and stratification of time is related to a different way of dealing with the problem of contradiction. Just as the kettle logic of dreams allows competing, mutually exclusive wishes and identifications to coexist without canceling each other out, the intermediate stage of repression seems to represent some contradictory combination of flight and condemnation rather than some developmental stage midway between the two.

Thus, it would seem that the best way to locate repression as a *Mittelding* and as an intermediate stage is to follow a movement of contradiction in Freud's own text. To trace this movement, it is necessary to examine the contradictions explicitly raised by him as well as those he manages to avoid. A case in point is his way of dealing with the relationship of pleasure and "pain" in the "Repression" essay. Freud begins by asking why it is that a drive impulse should suffer the fate of repression in the first place. "For this to happen, obviously a necessary condition must be that the attainment of its aim by the instinct [*Triebziel*] should produce 'pain' instead of [*an Stelle von*] pleasure. But we cannot well imagine such a contingency. There are no such instincts; satisfaction of an instinct is always pleasurable. We should have to assume certain peculiar circumstances, some sort of process which changes the pleasure [*Lust*] of satisfaction into 'pain' [*Unlust*]."[15]

Freud's way of dealing with the question of how the satisfaction of a drive can at once be pleasurable and "painful" is to assign each affect to a different location. Such satisfaction, he says, "causes pleasure [*Lust*] in one part of the mind, 'pain' [*Unlust*] in another."[16] Moreover, it should be noted that this spatial distribution of two seemingly incompatible moments or qualitatively opposed kinds of affect itself depends upon a clear separation of psychical systems. Thus, Freud adds, "Repression is not a defense mechanism present from the very beginning. . . . it cannot occur until a sharp distinction [*eine scharfe Sonderung*] has been established between what is conscious and what is unconscious: . . . *the essence of repression lies simply in the function of rejecting and keeping something out of consciousness*" (emphasis in original).[17]

Because the emergence of repression already presumes an exclusivity of conscious and unconscious activities, its primary function seems to consist more in the maintenance of those distinctions than in their establishment — more in the function of keeping something out of consciousness than of defining its parameters. Yet, as we will see, it is precisely the problem of maintaining these exclusions which not only troubles the borders of consciousness but repeatedly displaces them. It might even be argued that the notion of repression was introduced by Freud less as a successor to the concept of censorship than as an attempt to dwell on the issues already raised by the untimeliness of a process that will have already succeeded itself as postcensorship. That is, censorship "goes beyond itself" not only in the secondary revision and retelling of dreams but also as a resistance to interpretation whose aim, Freud says, is "to maintain [*aufrechtzuerhalten*] the distortions" effected earlier.

In order to get a better sense of the way problems of (post)censorship return in Freud's writings on repression, it may be helpful to examine the terms he uses to describe the process of "keeping something out of consciousness." While in the lecture on dream censorship he speaks of an *Aufrechterhaltung* of the distortion, in the passage cited above from the essay on repression it is a question of a *Fernhaltung vom Bewußten,* of holding something at a distance from consciousness, and in the third section of his essay "The Unconscious" he describes the operation of repression in terms of an *Abhaltung vom Bewußtsein,* a withholding from consciousness.[18] As we will see, the insistence of the signifier *halt* in these descriptions is less a sign of terminological consistency than a subtle way of foregrounding a problem latent within the concept of repression. This problem has to do precisely with the tenuousness of repression's hold on the repressed and more specifically with its ability to hold on to and maintain the exclusions that have been brought about.[19] These issues emerge more clearly in the fourth section of "The Unconscious."

> Let us take the case of repression proper ("after-expulsion") as it affects an idea which is preconscious or even has already entered consciousness. Repression can consist here only in the withdrawal from the idea of the (pre)conscious cathexis which belongs to the system Pcs. The idea then remains without cathexis, or receives [*erhält*] cathexis from the Ucs, or retains [*behält*] the unconscious cathexis it previously had. We have, therefore, withdrawal of the preconscious, retention [*Erhaltung*] of unconscious, or substitution of an unconscious for a preconscious cathexis.[20]

As if to mark the different ways of getting a hold on a representation (*Vorstellung:* translated as "idea" by both Baines and Strachey) stranded at the border between consciousness and the unconscious, Freud uses the term *Erhaltung* in the final sentence to refer to the "retention" of unconscious cathexis, whereas in the previous sentence he had used the verb form *erhält* to mean "receive" and had used the term *behält* to mean "retain." These stylistic twists not only linguistically enact the pull of different forces upon a repressed representation, they also call attention to a trouble spot; that is, they mark out an unstable borderland somewhere between two systems that were described in the "Repression" essay as being sharply differentiated. In other words, the repetitions and quirks of Freud's style place the signifier *halt* in a kind of bas-relief which in turn marks a psychical location that is literally a *Haltestelle*, an unstable point of transit between psychical systems. This is a place where, according to Freud's definition, repression is supposed to deny passage to certain representations and impulses or at least make them wait for another connection.

A brief survey of other points of transit in the Freudian corpus may help one to situate the transitional place of repression and to understand what kinds of connections it both denies and makes possible. Moreover, this survey may help one to appreciate the way certain *Haltestellen* mark moments of particularly strained transition in Freud's own thinking. For example, in the seventh chapter of *The Interpretation of Dreams* precisely at the point where he prepares to move from the concrete elucidation of particular dreams and specific aspects of the dreamwork to the murky realm of metapsychological speculation, Freud writes: "The psychological hypotheses drawn from our analysis of dream processes will have to wait at the station until the transfer comes along [*an einer Haltestelle warten müssen, bis sie den Anschluß . . . gefunden haben*], linking them with the results of other investigations that seek to penetrate the nucleus of the same problem by other points of attack" (*S.E.*5, 511).[21]

Similarly, in *Jokes and Their Relation to the Unconscious*, the transition from what he describes as the "long detour" of the "analytical" first half, with its abundance of examples, to the tersely theoretical "short synthetic path" of the second half is marked by another *Haltestelle*. Although Freud does not use the term here, he does place a joke whose setting is a railway carriage sitting at a station in Galicia at this point in the text. "'Where are you going,' asks one Jew. 'To Cracow,' the other responds. 'What a liar you are! If you say you're going to Cracow, you want me to believe you're going to Lemberg. But I know that in fact you're going to Cracow. So why are you lying to me?'" (*S.E.*8, 115). Here the transition from the detours of the first half to the short, synthetic paths of the second is itself marked by a joke about routes and destinations in which the shortest, most direct statement made by one man is construed by the other to be but another misleading detour.

A third example returns us to Freud's discussion of repression in "The Unconscious," where it is once again a question of a transition from the system Ucs to the system Cs: "It is possible for affective development to proceed [*ausgeht*] directly from the system Ucs; in this case it always has the character of anxiety, the substitute for all 'repressed' affects. Often, however, the instinctual impulse has to wait [*muß . . . warten*] until it has found a substitute idea in the system Cs."[22]

Here the place where we find the drive (or "instinctual") impulse waiting for a connection is no longer simply another point of transit, but instead a place Freud will later call an *Ausgangsstelle*. In what follows I examine why at this point the metaphor of the *Haltestelle* itself seems to make way for another term. To appreciate this shift, it is also necessary to study the ways in which a language of *Abhaltung* and *Fernhaltung,* used to describe the ways in which repression holds representations at a safe distance from consciousness, itself proves inadequate to describe a more unstable and dynamic process.

Die Ausgangsstelle

While Freud describes repression as something between flight and condemnation in the very first paragraph of his essay on the subject, it is only in "The Unconscious" that he really specifies just how this process works. It is perhaps not by chance that his most detailed and stylistically most dazzling account of this *Mittelding* occurs in the middle of the central fourth chapter of an essay consisting of seven sections. The passage's pivotal position is further emphasized by the fact that it immediately follows his introduction of the notion of a "metapsychological mode of presentation," a title to be reserved for descriptions that succeed in portraying "a mental process in all its aspects, dynamic, topographic and economic."[23] The renewed attempt to describe the process of repression which follows thus promises to be Freud's most ambitious and synthetic effort yet.

While Freud deals specifically with the role of repression in the genesis of anxiety hysteria, the analysis has much more far-reaching implications. During a preliminary phase of this illness, Freud says, anxiety appears without the subject knowing what he is afraid of: "We must suppose that there was present in the Unc some love-impulse which demanded to be translated into the system Pcs; the preconscious cathexis, however, recoiled from it in the manner of an attempt at flight, and the unconscious libidinal cathexis of the rejected idea was discharged in the form of anxiety."[24]

In order to follow this process, it is important to notice how a language of quantity works here. Whereas one usually assumes that the term "cathexis" represents a particular quantum or investment of psychical energy, in this case it also seems to have the capacity of evaluating the threat posed by the unconscious love impulse, since somehow a decision is made to withdraw from it. It almost seems as though Freud were using the term as an abbreviation for "cathexis of attention" (*Aufmerksamkeitsbesetzung*), which he employs in *The Interpretation of Dreams* to describe an unusually complicated relationship between subject and object, spectator and spectacle.

Indeed, in the present case, what appears at first to be merely a one-sided process of retreat and withdrawal is in fact a double movement of aversion in which a mere turning away of the Pcs cathexis in the manner of an attempt at flight is sufficient to turn away an unconscious representation. In other words, at this point repression does seem to function as something between flight and condemnation — at least insofar as the flight of the Pcs cathexis effectively rejects an undesirable representation. Yet this process, which deals so effectively with the *representation* associated with an unconscious libidinal impulse, has no way of coping with the release of anxiety which occurs when the libido previously attached to the rejected representation now becomes unbound. Freud suggests thatthese doubly averting maneuvers will go on repeatedly until further steps are taken to master this unwelcome release of anxiety. He therefore proceeds to the next step: "The fugitive cathexis attached itself to a substitutive idea which, on the one hand [*einerseits*], was connected by association with the rejected idea, and, on the other [*anderseits*], escaped repression by reason of its remoteness from that idea (displacement-substitute), and which permitted of a rationalization of the still uncontrollable out-break of anxiety."[25]

The tenuous compromise thus arrived at is itself figured in the rhetoric of *einerseits, anderseits*. What gives the displacement-sub-stitute its stability is the fact that it is cathected both from the side of the unconscious libido and from that of the preconscious ca-thexis. Furthermore, the potentially interminable double move-ment of aversion described in the first stage is replaced and to some degree stabilized by a process of substitution. As Samuel Weber remarks, "If a representation can be shunted aside, excluded from consciousness, this can occur only by means of another representa-tion *taking its place*."[26] While one representation is thus repressed insofar as it is replaced by another, this process, which deals so ef-fectively with the repressed representation, manages only to de-flect and displace the now unbound affect originally linked to it. Thus, Freud continues: "The substitutive idea now plays the part of an anti-cathexis [*Gegenbesetzung*] for the system Cs(Pcs) by securing that system against [*gegen*] the emergence into conscious-ness of the repressed idea; on the other hand, it is, or acts as if it were, the point [*Ausgangsstelle*] at which the anxiety-affect, which is now all the more uncontrollable, may break out and be dis-charged."[27]

Here Freud again employs the rhetoric of "on the one hand, on the other" to describe a substitute representation that bears all the marks of a liminal compromise formation. It is at first described in the theatrical language of "playing a part" and then later in terms of "being or acting as if it were," thus apparently wavering between mere appearance and actual existence. In terms of its location, the substitute seems to straddle (and thereby to mark) the limit be-tween the repressing and the repressed. On the one hand, it serves the interests of the system Cs(Pcs) by playing the role of a counter-cathexis that secures the system against the emergence of the re-pressed representation by absorbing some of the energy hitherto attached to that representation. On the other hand, it is, or acts as if it were, an *Ausgangsstelle,* which Baines translates as "the point at which the anxiety-affect, which is now all the more uncontrollable, may break out and be discharged."[28] Yet, here again the formation of a compromise seems in the end only to displace the problem of anxiety—especially if its release is now said to be "all the more uncontrollable."

Before continuing to map this movement of displacement, Freud translates his psychoanalytic jargon into more everyday terms, explaining that a child suffering from an animal phobia may experience anxiety under two kinds of conditions. In the first, when a repressed love impulse becomes intensified from within; in the second, when the child perceives the animal it is afraid of. Thus, in the one case, repressed love impulses originally directed toward the father are rechanneled through the animal substitute. In the other, the animal itself becomes an independent source for the release of anxiety. It is worth noting in this regard the appropriateness of Freud's choice of the term *Ausgangsstelle* to describe the double role of the substitute representation, which functions both as a conduit (*Überleitung*) for and as an independent source (*Quelle*) of anxiety, for the term *Ausgang* can itself mean both an exit or egress and a starting point. Moreover, Freud's term not only describes the double role of a substitute representation, it itself functions as one; that is, its ambiguity allows it, on the one hand, to be translated as *"the point* at which the anxiety-affect . . . may *break out* and be discharged" and, on the other, to be understood as a synonym for an *Ausgangspunkt,* or starting point, in keeping with its function as an independent source of anxiety.

One thus begins to appreciate the difference between an *Ausgangsstelle* and a *Haltestelle.* While the latter functions merely as the point of transit where a drive impulse often has to halt and wait until it has found a substitute representation in the system Cs, an *Ausgangsstelle* functions as just such a representation; that is, it both transgresses and enforces the limit it straddles. It embodies an unstable compromise in which the difference between its two functions of conduit and source may be only a matter of a "dynamic" difference of accent rather than a "topological" distinction in kind or location.[29] Furthermore, the term *Ausgangsstelle* not only functions as an unusually equivocal substitute representation straddling the limit between a breakthrough point and a point of origin, it also plays out an ambiguity at the very heart of repression. Like censorship, repression is not merely opposed to representation (*Darstellung*) but rather functions as a compromised form of it. That is, the substitutions it effects serve both to represent and to repress the *Vorstellungen* whose place they take. It is this fundamental duplicity of the process of substitution which makes it impossible for repression ever to *take place* once and for all. As Lacan often writes, the signifier takes place "in [the] place of the Other [*au lieu de l'Autre*]": both "in the place of the Other" and "instead of another."[30]

While the equivocality of the signifier *Ausgangsstelle* and the rhetoric of "on the one hand, on the other" which accompanies it suggest the formation of a compromise, they also indicate the tenuousness of the solution offered. For, as we have already seen, the countercathexis of a substitute representation does not so much inhibit the release of anxiety as defer and deflect it. In continuing to follow the ways in which anxiety and the problems raised by it are displaced in Freud's account, it is also important to notice how the focus begins to shift from the problem of how to exclude a particular representation to ways of dealing with the displacements of unbound affect. As we will see, the notion of anxiety itself undergoes a kind of transvaluation in the course of these displacements. Whereas it at first signifies a qualitatively indeterminate quantum of energy—a universal "substitute for all 'repressed' affect"—and therefore something to be defended against, anxiety gradually becomes a "signal" (which is not to be confused with a representation) and something associated with mechanisms of defense. In order to follow this process of transvaluation, it will be important to understand how these displacements do not simply move from one conception of anxiety to another, but rather how they serve to tease out an instability at the heart of its functioning.

Freud begins by following a shift in which the *Angst* associated with a kind of quantitative pressure from within is exchanged for focused fear (*Angst vor*), which might be characterized as qualitatively defined oppression from without. As he says, "The extending control [*Herrschaft*] on the part of the system Cs usually manifests itself by a tendency for the substitutive idea to be aroused more easily as time goes on in the second rather than the first way [*die erste . . . gegen die zweite immer mehr zurücktritt*]. Perhaps the child ends by behaving as though he had no liking at all for his father but had become quite free from him, and as though the fear of [*Angst vor*] the animal were the real fear."[31]

Ironically, what is described above as an "extension of *Herrschaft* on the part of the system Cs" actually has less to do with its mastery of anxiety than with its subjection to another kind of pressure. Having managed to repress the originally threatening representation by replacing it with a substitute, repression must in turn find ways of averting the substitute itself, which in its turn can serve as an independent source of anxiety. Yet, whereas one might expect repression to fix on yet another displacement substitute, this time it is said to act in the following manner:

> all the associations in the neighborhood of the substitutive idea become endowed with a peculiar intensity of cathexis so that they may display a high degree of sensibility to excitation. Excitation at any point of this protective structure [*Vorbau*] must, on account of its connection with the substitutive idea, *give rise to a slight degree of development of anxiety, which is then used as a signal to inhibit, by means of a fresh attempt at flight on the part of the [precon-scious] cathexis, any further development of anxiety*. The further the sensitive and vigilant anti-cathexis becomes extended round the substitute which is feared, the more exactly can the mechanism function which is designed to isolate the substitutive idea and to protect it from fresh excitation.[32] (Emphasis added)

Whereas Freud earlier used the simile of a doorway to describe the location of a threat posed by a particular representation, in this context, where quantitative relations and signals take precedence over qualitative determinations and *Vorstellungen,* he speaks in terms of a more diffuse protective structure, or *Vorbau*. In other words, the *Ausgangsstelle* for the release of anxiety may no longer be located at a particular point or passageway but instead has to be understood more generally in terms of an entire associative network surrounding the substitutive representation. Moreover, as the threat posed by the substitute thus becomes more diffuse, it is in turn measured in quantitative terms—that is, in degrees of anxiety—rather than in positive, qualitative terms. In this case, what a particular association means and how it is related to the substitute is ultimately less important than the simple fact that it *is* associated. The ease with which these associative connections are made suggests a mode of thinking identified more with the primary than with the secondary process. And yet, this exchange of a diffuse protective structure for a localized point of effraction (*Einbruchspforte*) represents just such a blurring of boundaries between unconscious and conscious activities.[33] As Freud says, "the whole protective structure of the phobia corresponds to an enclave of unconscious influence" (trans. mod.).[34] In other words, the very defenses designed to ward off the unconscious repressed bear witness at the same time to the extent of its intrusion. Similarly, the very thing that was supposed to be protected against, anxiety, is here enlisted in the service of psychic defense. One begins to get a sense of the shift adumbrated in the opening paragraph of the "Repression" essay from clearly defined, oppositional terms and terms of oppositional conflict to "middle things" and questions of intensified conflict.

This blurring of boundaries between inside and outside, menace and defense, also enables the ego to behave in the following manner: "[It acts] as if the danger of an outbreak of anxiety threatened it not from the direction of an instinct, but instead from the direction of perception: this enables the ego to react against this external danger with the attempts at flight consisting of the avoidances characteristic of a phobia."[35] Yet, even these attempts at flight are in general useless, Freud says, since what they achieve in terms of a "damming up" of anxiety is insufficient compensation for the "heavy sacrifice of personal freedom" which is the cost of maintaining the avoidances characteristic of a phobia.

The futile necessity of these displacements thus ultimately outlines a series of unsatisfactory ways of coping with anxiety. In the process of tracing this movement, however, Freud also allows an important aspect of repression gradually to come to the fore: namely, that repression never takes place once and for all because the substitutions effected by it never entirely take the place of a repressed that is both kept out and carried over by them. Thus, no satisfactory response to the question of how repression stabilizes and maintains the exclusions it effects is forthcoming. Yet insofar as this question remains unanswered—and perhaps unanswerable, at least within the parameters set by Freud—it continues to act as a driving force of his thinking.[36] It compels him to redefine what appear to be thresholds and "sharp distinctions" between systems in terms of processes of substitution and as displacements of unresolved conflict. Thus, when he speaks in the sixth section of "The Unconscious" of the need to "assume that to every transition from one system to that immediately above it (that is, every advance to a higher stage of mental organization) there corresponds a new censorship,"[37] one might add that "to every advance" there corresponds not a *"new censorship"* but rather a displacement of *the problem* of censorship.

More importantly, to trace the displacements of (post)censorship and repression in this essay is also to follow a shift in the status of anxiety. Whereas it is described earlier as a qualitatively indeterminate quantum of affect which must be protected against, later on it is said to function as a signal of approaching danger. That anxiety may somehow be both at the same time — at once a defense mechanism and something to be defended against and moreover an internally conflicted form of defense — is a possibility that is not explicitly explored in this text, even though the outlines of the problem can begin to be discerned. Six years later, this problem would reemerge in *Beyond the Pleasure Principle* in the context of what Freud calls *Angstbereitschaft,* a term that is difficult to translate either simply as a preparation for anxiety or as anxiety preparedness. To tease out the ambiguity at the heart of this term and the equivocal kind of defense which *Angstbereitschaft* may provide, it is necessary to read Freud through the filter of Walter Benjamin, whose notion of shock defense is itself articulated by drawing out certain tensions in Freud. I therefore turn now to Benjamin's essay "On Some Motifs in Baudelaire."

En Garde!

Benjamin's Baudelaire and the
Training of Shock Defense

Er läßt sich nicht lesen
Poe, *The Man of the Crowd*

Freud's *Beyond the Pleasure Principle* and Benjamin's essay "On Some Motifs in Baudelaire" are both concerned with the issue of traumatic shock. Yet whereas the former tends to focus on the belatedness of traumatic experience and the ways in which the dreams of patients suffering from traumatic neuroses endeavor to master an overwhelming stimulus *retrospectively,* the latter's orientation is more prospective and anticipatory; that is, Benjamin's text tends to be more concerned with ways of preparing for and guarding against the threat of shock than it is with the deferred action of trauma. The distinction, however, is not as clear-cut as at first it might appear—not, at least, as regards the temporal structure of the two approaches. For while trauma involves an event that is not assimilated or fully experienced at the time, but only belatedly, in its repeated possession of the one who experiences it, Benjamin's discussion of shock defense deals with the prevention of an event that is experienced *only before the fact* as an anxious sense of anticipation and as a mode of defense which must itself be repeatedly defended against.[1]

Whereas Cathy Caruth persuasively argues that "the historical power of the trauma is not just that the experience is repeated after its forgetting, but that it is only in and through its *inherent* forgetting that it is experienced at all," Benjamin's notion of shock defense involves a future-oriented mode of repetition in which the rehearsal *for* conflict will have itself become an enactment of it. In short, what is at issue in both cases is a split inherent in the very stage of conflict. What was to have taken place as the rendezvous of a direct confrontation or head-on collision instead will have been experienced only as a curiously missed encounter. For Benjamin, this dislocation of experience ultimately has less to do with what actually comes to pass than with what comes, as it were, only en passant.[2]

Before turning to Benjamin's essay, it may be helpful to begin by recalling a distinction that Freud draws in "Drives and Their Vicissitudes" between the "momentary impact" of an external stimulus and the "constant force [*konstante Kraft*]" or "incessant urgency [*konstant drängende*]" of the drive. As he says, "The stimuli of the drives oblige the nervous system to renounce its ideal intention of warding off stimuli, for they maintain an incessant and unavoidable afflux of stimulation" (*S.E.*14, 120). Thus, the constant pressure exerted by drives cannot be conceived of as a particular stimulus requiring a particular response. Instead, their *incessant* stimulation suggests an equally vigilant mode of defense or—as I have argued throughout—a more intensely compromised and collaborative relationship between the drives and the defenses.[3] Whereas Freud claims that the "characteristic of urgency [*des Drängenden*] is common to all drives" and is in fact "the very essence of them," I would suggest that a similar sense of spatial, temporal, and emotional pressure (*Drang*) informs Benjamin's thinking about the urban throng (*Gedränge*) and the closely related issues of shock and shock defense. Although he usually employs the German terms *Menge* and *Masse* in his discussion of crowds in "On Some Motifs in Baudelaire," he does cite at length a passage from Engels's *The Condition of the Working Class in England* (first published in German as *Die Lage der arbeitenden Klasse in England*) in which the author's heavy-handed plays on the term *Gedränge* effectively disperse this isolated term in a crowd of associations.[4]

> Hundreds of thousands of people of all classes and ranks of society jostle past one another [*an einander vorbeidrängen*]. . . . Their only agreement is a tacit one: that everyone should keep to the right of the pavement, so as not to impede the stream of the crowd [*des Gedränges*] moving in the opposite direction. . . . The greater the number of people that are packed [*zusammengedrängt*] into a tiny

space, the more repulsive and offensive becomes the brutal indifference . . . of each person. (166–67)[5]

There are two reasons for dwelling on the specific wording of this passage. First, Engels's repeated use of the root *drängen* in various forms increasingly draws attention to the signifying surface of his text, thereby tacitly linking the social, economic, and political issue of urban crowding to questions of language. Second and more importantly, Benjamin himself speaks of a "phantom crowd of words [*Geistermenge der Worte*]" (165) at a pivotal moment in his essay. As we will see, it is at this point in the text that the language used to describe urban conflict itself becomes another scene of struggle; that is, in Benjamin's reading of Baudelaire a phantom crowd of words becomes both a field of battle and a spectral protagonist in the fray.

Whereas Benjamin speaks of the "close connection in Baudelaire between the figure of shock and contact with the metropolitan masses" (165), the proximity of the two is above all reflected in the critic's own style of presentation. For while the notion of shock defense receives no sustained, systematic exposition in this essay, it is no exaggeration to say that it is instead held in place and carried along by the movement of a crowd through the text. The reader encounters it only fleetingly as it surfaces from time to time in the midst of Benjamin's discussion of urban life in general and the Baudelairean throng in particular. In other words, one encounters it in much the same manner that the poet in Baudelaire's sonnet *A une passante* meets — or rather, passes by — an unknown woman borne along by the crowd on a deafeningly noisy street. Benjamin describes this missed encounter as the distinctly urban experience of "love at last sight" (169).

> La rue assourdissante autour de moi hurlait.
> Longue, mince, en grand deuil, douleur majestueuse,
> Une femme passa, d'une main fastueuse
> Soulevant, balançant le feston et l'ourlet;
>
> Agile et noble, avec sa jambe de statue.
> Moi, je buvais, crispé comme un extravagant,
> Dans son oeil, ciel livide où germe l'ouragan,
> La douceur qui fascine et le plaisir qui tue.

Un éclair . . . puis la nuit!—Fugitive beauté
Dont le regard m'a fait soundainement renaître,
Ne te verrai-je plus que dans l'éternité?[6]

What gives this poem its charm is the privilege it accords to what could have been rather than to what actually happens. Thus, the sonnet concludes:

Ailleurs, bien loin d'ici! Trop tard! Jamais peut-être!
Car j'ignore où tu fuis, tu ne sais où je vais,
O toi que j'eusse aimée, ô toi qui le savais![7]

Like the furtive glances exchanged in the poem, the sonnet as a whole presents itself as a negative image of glimpsed possibilities that need not and in fact should not be realized.[8] Like the ever-so-fleeting eye contact of the passers-by, the sonnet's positive content touches a realm of possibility, which it both conjures and staves off, as a tangent touches a circle lightly at one infinitely small point.[9]

Both here and in general, Benjamin seems less interested in the positive points of contact between different spheres than in the way a particular image veers away from what cannot be represented. This is precisely the approach he takes in the first section of the essay, in which he deals with Henri Bergson's alleged rejection of "any historical determination of memory." Benjamin claims that Bergson "manages above all to stay clear of that experience from which his own philosophy evolved, or, rather, in reaction to which it arose. It was the inhospitable, blinding age of big-scale industrialism" (157). According to Benjamin, Bergson is blind to that which he is blinded by—not something hidden away, but the very medium of vision. He continues, "In shutting out this experience the eye perceives an experience of a complementary nature in the form of its spontaneous after-image, as it were" (157). Here Benjamin uses the term *Nachbild* to describe a visual image that persists after the stimulus that had caused it is no longer operative.[10] This is the common experience one has of closing one's eyes after staring at a light source only to see the after-image of that which one had attempted to shut out.[11]

There are a number of reasons for paying close attention to this image (or is it an after-image?) used by Benjamin to help the reader imagine the experience in reaction to which Bergson's philosophy allegedly arose. The first has to do with Benjamin's claim that this philosophy "represents an attempt to give the details of this after-image and to fix it as a permanent record" (157). The second involves his contention that Bergson's philosophy "indirectly furnishes a clue to the experience which presented itself to Baudelaire's eyes in its undistorted version in the figure of his reader" (157). Thus, one might be led to expect that what Bergson could see only in a mediated form, only as a kind of after-image, Baudelaire was already able to observe directly in its undistorted version in the figure of his audience. Furthermore, whereas Benjamin himself employs the metaphor of the after-image in his remarks about Bergson to help the reader to see what he or she might otherwise have been blind to or perhaps even have been blinded by, we might now expect a more direct (less self-consciously metaphorical) mode of presentation from Benjamin as he turns to consider the experience that presented itself directly to Baudelaire's eyes.

What, then, is this experience presented to Baudelaire in the shape of his reader? If, as Benjamin suggests, Bergson's philosophy furnishes a clue to this experience, then let us recall that this philosophy not only excludes what it cannot contain—shutting out what blinds it—but, moreover, that its positive contents are nothing other than the trace or after-image of what is excluded. Were one to speak in Freudian terms, one might describe this philosophy as a kind of reaction formation, whose positive, manifest content becomes a negative image of that in reaction to which it arose. By contrast, the experience presented to Baudelaire's eyes in the form of his reader is less one of exclusion and repression than one of ambiguous identification and uncanny doubling. For, as Benjamin points out in his opening paragraph, Baudelaire opens *Les Fleurs du mal* with a poem addressed to the reader which ends with the apostrophe *"Hypocrite lecteur,—mon semblable,—mon frère!"*

Before hastening to assume that the poet and reader are linked in a dual and symmetrical identification, one should recall that in the poem *Au lecteur* this relationship is itself mediated by a third person or rather by the personification of a kind of middle voice. What is personified as *Ennui* in the poem's last stanza is a figure that is neither simply active nor passive, but instead is dreadfully active in its passivity.

Il en est un plus laid, plus méchant, plus immonde!
Quoiqu'il ne pousse ni grands gestes ni grands cris,
Il ferait volontiers de la terre un débris
Et dans un bâillement avalerait le monde;

C'est l'Ennui — l'oeil chargé d'un pleur involontaire,
Il rêve d'échafauds en fumant son houka.
Tu le connais, lecteur, ce monstre délicat,
— Hypocrite lecteur, — mon semblable, — mon frère![12]

Thus, in contrast to the blinding experience that Bergson's philosophy shuts out, Baudelaire's poem depicts an eye that is open yet doubly clouded. Lost in a waking reverie, this eye looks through the cataract of an involuntary tear welling up within it as well as through the smoke rising from a hookah. This doubly clouded vision of Boredom (*Ennui*) not only makes it twice as difficult to see clearly, but moreover, makes it unclear who exactly is seeing and whom or what is being seen. Thus, in place of the stable oppositions of activity and passivity, the apostrophized reader is read into a text that incorporates him like a yawn that swallows the world.

Yet, it is equally possible that this yawn belongs not to the text but rather to a bored audience that presumably has little stomach for the poet's demanding verse. Indeed, Benjamin begins his essay (and thus his own address to the reader) by stressing that "will power and the ability to concentrate are not the strong points" of the reader addressed by Baudelaire. These readers, he says, are "familiar with the 'spleen' which deals a fatal blow to interest and receptiveness [*Aufnahmefähigkeit*]" (155). Given this inhospitable climate, Benjamin must attempt to explain the extraordinarily favorable reception of *Les Fleurs du mal* over the years. Indeed, as he says, "there has been no success on a mass scale in lyric poetry since Baudelaire." His essay thus attempts to account for this unparalleled popularity. Yet more importantly, in doing so, it also develops a different way of approaching questions of reception — be it of texts, stimuli, impressions, or even of blows. As we will see, Benjamin's essay subtly reposes questions of reception in terms of what he calls parrying (*Parieren*) and interception (*Abfangen*).

Before exploring Benjamin's use of these terms, it should be pointed out that the term "boredom" (*Langeweile*) itself has unusual resonances in his work. In addition to having the sense of taedium vitae or world-weariness, it also signifies a certain relationship to time.[13] While the notion of ennui certainly implies a sense of stagnation and monotony, which is captured in the English phrase "killing time" or the German *die Zeit vertreiben,* Benjamin also describes it in *The Arcades Project* (*Das Passagen-Werk*) as "what we have when we do not know what we are waiting for. . . . It is the threshold to great deeds."[14] Indeed, not only does boredom have the status of a temporal threshold, but it signifies an ambiguous, borderline state in Benjamin's way of thinking.

Insofar as boredom is what we have when we do not know what we are waiting for, its lack of focus brings it closer to an anxious and indefinite sense of apprehension than to a definite and focused sense of fear or foreknowledge. This dim sense of expectancy is closely related to what Benjamin, following Freud, describes as *Angstbereitschaft.* Whereas Strachey and Benjamin's translator, Harry Zohn, both translate this term as "preparation for anxiety," the contexts in which it appears suggest that *Angstbereitschaft* would be better rendered as "anxiety preparedness."[15] Thus, for example, Freud writes in chapter 4 of *Beyond the Pleasure Principle:* "It will be seen, then, that anxiety preparedness [*Angstbereitschaft*] and the hypercathexis of the receptive systems constitute the last line of defense of the shield against stimuli. In the case of quite a number of traumas, the difference between systems that are unprepared and systems that are well prepared through being hypercathected may be a decisive factor in determining the outcome" (*S.E.*18, 31–32; trans. mod.).

Needless to say, Strachey and Zohn's term is not simply incorrect. Rather, as I suggested at the end of Chapter 4, these divergent translations make manifest an important equivocation at the heart of *Angstbereitschaft.* Before considering the essential ambiguity of this term, it may be helpful to begin by noting the distinction that Freud draws in Chapter 2 of *Beyond the Pleasure Principle* between fright, fear, and anxiety in terms of their relation to danger: "'Anxiety' describes a particular state of expecting danger or preparing for it, even though it may be an unknown one. 'Fear' requires a definite object of which to be afraid [*vor dem man sich fürchtet*].

'Fright,' however, is the name we give to the state a person gets into when he has run into danger without being prepared for it; it emphasizes the factor of surprise" (*S.E.*18, 12).

In contrast to "The Unconscious," where Freud (at least at first) describes anxiety as a danger to be prepared for or protected against, here it appears to be associated with an indefinite sense of expectancy which is prophylactic in nature.[16] As though to emphasize this point (and indeed, if it needs to be stressed it is because this sense of anxiety risks being misunderstood or mistranslated), Freud adds, "I do not believe anxiety can produce a traumatic neurosis. There is something about anxiety that protects . . . against fright" (*S.E.*18, 12–13).

What, then, is the connection between this notion of *Angstbereitschaft* (which, like Benjaminian boredom, seems to be what we have when we do not know what we are waiting for) and the notion of shock defense? In section 3 of his essay on Baudelaire, Benjamin explicitly refers to *Beyond the Pleasure Principle*. Yet, in "going back to Freud," as he puts it, Benjamin does not so much mine Freud's essay in search of a stable psychoanalytic foundation for his own notion of shock defense as pinpoint a problem central to Freud's writing in general.[17] Indeed, it is no exaggeration to say that the difficulty identified but not really developed by Benjamin is only fully elaborated close to fifty years later by Derrida in "Freud and the Scene of Writing."

The problem has to do with the liminal status of the system Freud calls Pcpt-Cs. He describes this system as a kind of shell or cortical layer which "lies on the borderline between inside and outside" (*S.E.*18, 24). "It yields perceptions both of excitations coming from the external world and of feelings of pleasure and unpleasure which . . . arise from within the mental apparatus" (*S.E.*18, 24). In contrast to other psychical systems in which excitatory processes are said to leave behind permanent traces, Freud says that it is hard to believe "that permanent traces of excitation . . . are also left in the system Pcpt-Cs" (*S.E.*18, 25). In short, the problem for Freud is the following: "If such traces remained constantly conscious, they would very soon set limits to the system's aptitude for receiving fresh excitations" (*S.E.*18, 25). In other words, "becoming conscious and leaving behind a memory trace are processes incompatible with each other within one and the same system" (*S.E.*18, 25).

Confronted by the incompatibility of these processes, Freud's tendency is to partition them; that is, what would be a contradictory function for one and the same system is divided up and assigned to two separate systems or adjacent strata of the psyche. Thus, according to Freud, the archive of permanent traces is kept on one level, while the reception of fresh excitations occurs on another, namely in the system Pcpt-Cs. Benjamin adds another wrinkle to the problem, for he recalls that "according to Freud, consciousness . . . has another important function, namely the protection against stimuli" (161). In other words, in addition to the fact that consciousness cannot receive any permanent memory traces, it cannot receive any fresh excitations either—at least, not without somehow being protected against them.

Here one begins to appreciate the contradictory pressures that make consciousness a truly liminal, heterogeneous instance and not just a stable borderline (or cortical layer) situated on the frontier between inside and outside. While Freud at first attempts to accommodate two incompatible processes by dividing them and assigning each to a separate system, this time his strategy of divide and conquer will not work.[18] Instead, one is forced to consider how consciousness must at once receive stimuli and somehow protect against them. It is at this point in Benjamin's reading that the language of reception, with which both he and Freud begin, becomes sufficiently problematic to necessitate a change in terminology. Hence, he introduces the notion of interception. In intercepting shocks, consciousness now neither simply receives them nor completely wards them off. Instead, as Benjamin says, it parries them.

As one might expect, the introduction of the notion of interception, which represents Benjamin's attempt to think together two seemingly incompatible processes, has important repercussions for an understanding of the role of memory. His citation of a remark by Valéry at this point in his essay is therefore extremely telling. According to Valéry, "Recollection is an elemental phenomenon which aims at *giving us time* for organizing the reception of stimuli which we initially lacked" (161–62; emphasis added). As we will see, this form of recollection has less to do with internal memory or "memory proper" (if such a thing exists) than with memory supplements and scenes of writing. In this regard, it is significant that

Benjamin develops his notion of interception through a discussion of a scene of dueling and "phantastic combat" in Baudelaire, which is also and above all a scene of writing.

To appreciate the full significance of Benjamin's treatment of parrying in Baudelaire, we should first return to the texts of Freud. While *Beyond the Pleasure Principle* considers becoming conscious and leaving behind a memory-trace to be processes incompatible with each other within one and the same system, Freud's brief "Note on the Mystic Writing-Pad," published five years later, attempts to reimagine the possible cohabitation of these processes. In fact, this move beyond the earlier essay is in a certain sense already legible within *Beyond the Pleasure Principle* at a moment when Freud, by his own admission, has reached the limits of his "often far-fetched speculation" (*S.E.*18, 24). Interestingly enough, it is a moment in which the spatial layering of the psychical strata is disrupted by what is described as a temporal moment involving a pulsating process of sampling. These periodic samplings, Freud says, "may perhaps be compared with feelers which are repeatedly making tentative advances towards the external world and then drawing back from it" (*S.E.*18, 28). Freud even dares to risk the suggestion that "our abstract idea of time seems to be wholly derived from [these pulsations and appears] to correspond to [an internal] perception of that method of working" (*S.E.*18, 28). He also adds significantly that "this mode of functioning may perhaps constitute another way of providing a shield against stimuli" (*S.E.*18, 28).

Although Benjamin never explicitly refers to this passage— indeed, his commentary breaks off shortly before coming to it— the power of Freud's suggestion is in no way lost on him. It seems to inform his description of the way that an individual moving through big-city traffic is involved "in a series of shocks and collisions" (175). These shocks have more to do with an assault on the senses and a related need for more frequent "samplings" of one's environment than with an actual physical collision between two bodies. To speak in terms of Freud's essay "The Unconscious," the faster the pace of modern urban life, the greater the shift from the physical contours of the body and the threat of a localized point of effraction (*Einbruchspforte*) to a diffuse protective structure (*Vorbau*) or "forebody" whose buffer zone of anxiety preparedness not only extends but also diffuses the borders of the self.[19] Thus, Benjamin writes,

> At dangerous intersections, nervous impulses flow through [an individual] in rapid succession, like the energy from a battery. Baudelaire speaks of a man who plunges into the crowd as into a reservoir of electric energy. Circumscribing the experience of shock, he calls this man "a *kaleidoscope* equipped with consciousness." Whereas Poe's passers-by [in "The Man of the Crowd"] cast glances in all directions which still appeared to be aimless, today's pedestrians are obliged to do so in order to keep abreast of traffic. (175)

As was suggested earlier, these nervous impulses are akin to the periodic samplings of which Freud speaks. In pursuing this connection, one should recall that for Freud the hypothesized periodicity of these samples is accompanied by the corollary assumption that consciousness is not simply "on" all the time. Rather, as Derrida remarks, Freud's "hypothesis posits a discontinuous distribution—through rapid periodic impulses—of 'cathectic innervations' [*Besetzungsinnervationen*] from within toward the outside, toward the permeability of the system Pcpt-Cs. These movements are then 'withdrawn' or 'removed.' *Consciousness fades each time the cathexis is withdrawn in this way*."[20] The rule seems to be: the greater the potential danger in a given situation, the more frequent the sampling, the greater the dominance of consciousness, the keener one's perception of time, the more consciousness itself is perceived as persisting uninterruptedly over time. Or, as Benjamin puts it:

> The greater the share of the shock factor in particular impressions, the more constantly consciousness has to be alert as a screen against stimuli; the more efficiently it does so, the less do these impressions enter experience [*Erfahrung*], tending to remain in the sphere of a certain hour in one's life [*Erlebnis*]. Perhaps the special achievement of shock defense may be seen in its function of assigning an incident a precise point in time in consciousness at the cost of the integrity of its contents. This would be a peak achievement of the intellect; it would turn the incident into a moment that has been lived [*Erlebnis*]. (163)

It is unclear, however, why assigning an incident a precise point in time in consciousness should represent shock defense's "special achievement [*eigentümliche Leistung*]" or why it should be described as a "peak achievement of the intellect [*Spitzenleistung der Reflexion*]." To understand the significance of this achievement and the weight Benjamin places on it, it may be necessary to translate this temporal sense of punctuality into Freudian terms and conceive of it literally as a kind of puncture wound.[21] In other words, assigning an incident a precise point in time in consciousness may have an effect similar to that produced by a wound or injury to the body during a traumatic occurrence. One recalls that, according to Freud, it is precisely the infliction of a wound that may in some cases work *against* the development of a traumatic neurosis. As Freud says, "On the one hand, the mechanical violence of the trauma would liberate a quantity of sexual excitation which, owing to the lack of *Angstbereitschaft* would have a traumatic effect; but, on the other hand, the simultaneous physical injury, by calling for a narcissistic hypercathexis of the injured organ, would bind the excess of excitation" (*S.E.*18, 33).

In other words, a share of the shock factor contained in frightening impressions is bound, focused, and localized through the simultaneous "puncturing" of one's sense of time.[22] Furthermore, this wounding of time—in the double sense of the wounds inflicted on and by it—is what makes one increasingly aware of its passage.[23] These wounds may be inflicted not only at the time of a trauma but also in advance, precisely as a way of preparing for that which one cannot expect. One thereby marks time not only when bored but, moreover, when boredom itself becomes associated with an anxious sense of anticipation.

Like so many forms of hypochondria, this heightened awareness of time, which seems to protect against the effects of traumatic neurosis, itself has to be guarded against. Thus, Benjamin can claim, on the one hand, that the ability to assign an incident a precise point in time in consciousness represents "the special achievement of shock defense," while, on the other, he notes later in the essay that "in [Baudelairean] spleen the perception of time is supernaturally keen; every second finds consciousness *ready to intercept its shocks*" (184; emphasis added). Here one begins to get a sense of the way that Benjamin's notion of interception is itself split in its relation to time. Like the Freudian notion of *Angstbereitschaft*, this hyperdeveloped sense of time is described both as part of the defense against shocks and as a source of shocks to be protected against.

In order to get a better idea of this split, which structures Benjamin's notion of interception, its connection to the figure of the parrying poet in Baudelaire, and its relation to Freud's speculations on time and sampling, let us turn briefly to Freud's "Note on the Mystic Writing-Pad." What delights Freud about this "small contrivance" is that its construction shows a remarkable agreement with his hypotheses concerning the structure of our perceptual apparatus; that is, "it can in fact provide both an ever-ready receptive surface and retain permanent traces of the notes that have been made upon it" (*S.E.* 19, 228). While Freud thus seems to have found a mechanism that could accommodate these seemingly incompatible processes, a closer examination of his actual description of the writing-pad reveals that all it does is repeat the now familiar strategy of dividing up and separating out. As he says, the writing-pad "solves the problem of combining the two functions by dividing them between two separate but interrelated component parts or systems" (*S.E.* 19, 230).

The situation thus remains more or less as it was until Freud reintroduces his speculations on time and sampling. This pulsating process of sampling represents an important modification of his initial view, for it suggests not only a discontinuous method of functioning of the system Pcpt-Cs but also a situation in which there can be neither permanent contact nor an absolute break between psychical strata. Thus, in order to accommodate these periodic samplings into his comparison, Freud is obliged to add one final note to his essay, which concludes: "If we imagine one hand writing upon the surface of the Mystic Writing-Pad while another periodically raises its covering sheet from the wax slab, we shall have a concrete representation of the way in which I tried to picture the functioning of the perceptual apparatus of the mind" (*S.E.* 19, 232).

Thus, in order to accommodate the incompatible functions of the system Pcpt-Cs, one literally needs two hands. One hand writes while the other erases. One hand engraves impressions with an inkless stylus while the other parries its styling thrusts. Ultimately, however, Freud's "Note" describes—or least makes certain gestures toward—a situation that exceeds the rhetoric and logic of "on the one hand, on the other"—on the one hand writing, on the other erasure; for here it is no longer a matter simply of what is written versus what is censored. Instead, what is enacted is a scene of writing—or, to be more precise, a scene of two-handed writing. Obviously, this is not the daily drama of the two-handed typist but instead an enactment of the cross-coupled rhetoric of a process of inscription fundamentally at odds with itself;[24] that is, it is at odds both with itself and with another that is supposed to guard against the registration of impressions but that in fact forms a "permeable" protective shield which is at once vigilant and distracted. Like self-censorship, this hand that erases as the other writes not only inhibits writing but also collaborates in its production.

Derrida links the two hands that it takes to maintain this apparatus to a primacy of conflictual relationships more original than the "ideal virginity of the present [*maintenant*]."

> Traces thus produce the space of their inscription only by acceding to the period of their erasure. From the beginning, in the "present" [*maintenant*] of their first impression, they are constituted by the double force of repetition and erasure, legibility and illegibility. A two-handed machine, a multiplicity of agencies or origins—is this not the original relation to the other and the original temporality of writing, its "primary" complication: an originary spacing, deferring, and erasure of the simple origin, and polemics on the very threshold of what we persist in calling perception? . . . If there were only perception, pure permeability to breaching, there would be no breaches. We would be written, but nothing would be recorded; no writing would be produced, retained, repeated as legibility. But pure perception does not exist: we are written only as we write, by the agency within us which always already keeps watch over perception, be it internal or external. . . . The subject of writing is a *system* of relations between strata: the Mystic Pad, the psyche, society, the world.[25]

Bearing in mind this equivocal scene, which rehearses the incompatible moments of writing at the end of Freud's "Note," let us now turn to the figure of the parrying poet in Baudelaire. According to Benjamin, Baudelaire "speaks of a duel in which the artist, just before being beaten, screams in fright. This duel is the creative process itself. Thus, Baudelaire placed the shock experience at the very center of his artistic production" (163). Yet, while the experience of shock may, according to Benjamin, be at the very heart of Baudelaire's work, it is precisely this centrality that makes it so difficult to locate anywhere in particular. Indeed, it is no exaggeration to say that the figure of shock literally loses itself in the crowd in Baudelaire. Because one can never encounter it in isolation, Benjamin is obliged to approach it indirectly—to intercept it, as it were—both in and as a crowd. He says as much when he draws the reader's attention to "the close connection in Baudelaire between the figure of shock and contact with the metropolitan masses" (165).

Yet, there is once again a certain irony in these remarks, for, as it turns out, these masses themselves cannot be encountered as such. According to Benjamin, they too "had become so much a part of Baudelaire that it is rare to find a description of them in his work" (167). As he says, Baudelaire's "most important subjects are hardly ever encountered in descriptive form" (167). As though to emphasize the extent of the problem, Benjamin repeats this contention elsewhere in the essay when he states, "This crowd whose existence Baudelaire never forgets has not served as the model for any of his works. It is, however, imprinted on his creativity [*seinem Schaffen*] as a hidden figure" (165). Thus, the crowd—like the figure of shock—cannot be located either within Baudelaire's work as a particular content described by him or outside that work as a model that he copied or reproduced.[26] Neither inside nor outside his writings, the crowd and the closely related figure of shock are instead imprinted on the writing process. It is for this reason that the figure of dueling is so important to Benjamin. "This duel," he says, "is the creative process itself. Thus Baudelaire placed the shock experience at the very center of his artistic production" (163).

Yet if, as we have seen, the center is repeatedly displaced to the periphery as the borders between inside and outside become increasingly embattled, we should not be surprised to learn that Benjamin's characterization of the creative process as a duel has the effect of transforming the experience of shock into a reflexive operation. In other words, in addition to being exposed to shocks, the figure of the poet is also shocking. Or, as Benjamin says, "since [Baudelaire] himself is exposed to fright, it is not unusual for him to occasion fright" (163). The remark obviously has more than anecdotal value—even though Benjamin goes on to cite reports of

Baudelaire's eccentric grimaces, alarming appearance, jerky gait, and the "italicizing" he indulged in when reciting poetry.

What gives particular value to these anecdotes is not only their content but their derivation. It is therefore significant that these reports do not come directly from Baudelaire but are furnished instead by other witnesses. It is as though the experience of shock *could only be described from the outside,* just as Baudelaire himself only seems able to talk about it when he is describing someone else.

It is not by chance, then, that Benjamin juxtaposes this testimony about Baudelaire with the poet's own description of his friend Constantin Guys, about whom he remarks

> how he stands there, bent over his table, scrutinizing the sheet of paper just as intently as he does the objects around him by day; how he *stabs away* [*ficht*] with his pencil, his pen, his brush; how he spurts water from his glass to the ceiling and tries his pen on his shirt; how he pursues his work intensely, as though he were afraid that his images might escape him; thus he is combative, even when alone, and parries his own blows. (163–64; emphasis in original)[27]

Here Baudelaire not only describes himself as though portraying another, but the other whose portrait he paints is himself a combative painter who wields his pencil, pen, and brush like a sword as he fences with himself. He parries his own blows as though dueling with another. Thus, the experience of shock, it turns out, involves an operation that is not so much self-reflexive as heteroreflexive; its parrying involves not only fending off blows dealt by another but also dealing them, yet dealing them to oneself as though fending off another, and dealing them to another as though parrying one's own blows. This heteroreflexive relationship, I would suggest, may be understood as the double bind of "the original relation to the other" described by Derrida—the relation to the other through whom, with whom, and for whom the subject experiences in a necessarily secondhand manner an event that will only have taken place in its prevention (literally in its coming before itself).

As though to remind the reader that this "phantastic combat" (*phantastisches Gefecht,* as Benjamin calls it) is also and above all a scene of writing, he goes on to cite the opening stanza of the poem *Le Soleil*. Of it he says, "Baudelaire has pictured himself engaged in just this kind of phantastic combat; this is probably the only place in *Les Fleurs du mal* that shows the poet at work" (164).

Le long du vieux faubourg, où pendent aux masures
Les persiennes, abri des secrètes luxures,
Quand le soleil cruel frappe à traits redoublés
Sur la ville et les champs, sur les toits et les blés,
Je vais m'exercer seul à ma fantasque escrime,
Flairant dans tous les coins les hasards de la rime,
Trébuchant sur les mots comme sur les pavés,
Heurtant parfois des vers depuis longtemps rêvés.[28]

Commenting on this passage, Benjamin unites the experience of shock with the image of the fencer and the hidden figure of the crowd. He says that the blows dealt by the poet are designed to open a path (*den Weg zu bahnen*) through the crowd for him.[29] Yet, where exactly is the crowd in this passage? As Benjamin himself points out, "The faubourgs through which the poet of *Le Soleil* beats a path [*hindurchschlägt*] are deserted." It appears that just as the figure of shock loses itself in Baudelaire's crowd, so too does that crowd seem to get lost in the deserted streets. In Benjamin's reading of this poem, however, the lost crowd reappears—or rather, appears to reappear—as "a phantom crowd of words [*Geistermenge der Worte*]." According to Benjamin, "It is the phantom crowd of words, the fragments, the beginnings of lines from which the poet, in the deserted streets, wrests [*ausficht*] the poetic booty" (165). In other words, Baudelaire does not merely use language to depict or even to fend off the shocks and crowds he sees. Rather, his language becomes a field of combat in which words are treated as things. Thus, the poet engages in verbal combat as though he were battling a crowd.

Yet if, as Benjamin claims, "the masses had become so much a part of Baudelaire that it is rare to find a description of them in his works," then it is equally true that the poet fences with this phantom crowd of words as though he were fencing with himself, "parrying his own blows." Language thus serves not only as the field of battle but also as a combatant in a spectral duel that is actually more akin to shadowboxing or to what in German is called *Spiegelfechterei*. Benjamin's approach to Baudelaire's linguistic "mirror fencing" is already anticipated by André Gide, who describes "the interstices between image and idea, word and thing, [as] the real site of Baudelaire's poetic excitation."[30] In Benjamin's reading of Baudelaire, these interstices are not only a site of poetic excitation but also and above all a field of battle.

Perhaps nowhere is this combat more intense than in the very name of Baudelaire. Whereas a fight waged "in the name of" someone usually implies a struggle on his behalf, an effort to plead his cause, and a defense of the principles which that name stands for, here the battle is fought literally in the name of "Baudelaire." This is what the poet himself has to say about the derivation of his name:

> My name is atrocious. . . . In fact, the "badelaire" was a sabre with a short, wide blade and a convex shape [au tranchant convexe] whose point was bent up toward the back of the weapon. It was brought to France by soldiers returning from the crusades and was used in Paris until around 1560 as an executioner's sword. A few years ago, around 1861, they were doing some excavation work near the Pont-au-Change and discovered the badelaire belonging to the executioner of the Grand Chatelet in the twelfth century. Look at it. It's positively frightening. I shudder in thinking that the profile of my face resembles that of the badelaire—"But your name is Baudelaire," replied M. Georges Barral, "not Badelaire."—"Baudelaire, Badelaire . . . it's just a slight alteration," answered the poet. "It's the same thing."[31]

The literalization of this name thus bears witness to a conflict at the very heart of identity which makes of "Baudelaire" something less than a proper name. At this point one begins to appreciate to what extent the poet is obliged to parry his own blows. This *Spiegelfechterei* not only enacts a conflict in the interstices of the word-thing "Baudelaire," it also stages a struggle in the very heart of the creative process. This struggle, it will be recalled, does not simply pit two adversaries against each other—on the one hand, on the other—but instead stages the complicity of writing and erasure— of registering shocks and parrying them. In Benjamin's reading of *Le Soleil,* the scene of the two-handed writing, which we traced in Freud, is reenacted as the poet parries his own styling thrusts as though cutting a path through a phantom crowd of words. Here it would seem that the very defense that was supposed to intercept the shocks of urban life itself turns out to be something that must be defended against. Yet it is equally important to stress how this situation, which rehearses the dilemmas of an instance at odds as much with itself as with another, thereby also stages a rehearsal *for* conflict; that is, this structure of repetition is also a process of habituation and shock training.

It thus becomes increasingly clear that the notion of shock defense is not merely subjective in nature; that is, it is difficult to locate simply within the limits of the self or the individual psyche. By referring to it as a heteroreflexive relationship, I have tried to underscore its original relation to the other and to the play of forces in which the self is enmeshed. As was noted earlier, Benjamin's notion of shock defense is also split in its relationship to time. While its special achievement may, on the one hand, be said to consist in its ability to assign an incident a precise point in time in consciousness, on the other hand, a heightened perception of time is linked to Baudelairean spleen, in which, Benjamin says, "every second finds consciousness ready to intercept *its* shocks" (184).[32] One should not be surprised to learn that these two conflicting valences ascribed by Benjamin to an overly keen perception of time return us once again to the problem of the crowd in Baudelaire. In fact, if, as Benjamin claims, "it is rare to find a description of these crowds in Baudelaire," they do nevertheless reappear both as "a phantom crowd of words" and as something Benjamin suggestively calls "a multitude of seconds [*Schwarm der Sekunden*]." What interests him in *Les Fleurs du mal*'s first poem cycle, *Spleen et Idéal,* is the way that the "ideal" "supplies the power of remembrance," whereas the "spleen" "musters the multitude of the seconds against it. [The Spleen] is their commander, just as the devil is the lord of the flies" (183).

As Benjamin suggests in his critique of Bergson at the beginning of the essay, a heightened awareness of time's passage must be understood in the context of an accelerating process of industrialization in which time increasingly assumes an independent, objectified form.[33] Benjamin further links the increasing precision with which time is measured—hence his focus on the "rhythm of the second-hand"—to an increasing rationalization of the labor process. Thus, he comments, "Marx had good reason to stress the fluid nature of the connection between segments in manual labor [*der Zusammenhang der Arbeitsmomente ein flüssiger ist*]. This connection appears to the factory worker on an assembly line [*Fließband*] in an independent, objectified form" (175).

It is worth dwelling on Benjamin's punning contrast between the relatively loose and fluid (*flüssig*) organization of manual labor with its larger, less regular units of time and the precisely regulated rhythm of the assembly line (*Fließband:* literally, a flowing belt) where workers "learn to co-ordinate their own movements with the uniformly constant movements of an automaton" (175). This transformation of the fluid connections of manual labor into the regimented movement of the *Fließband* also seems to inform Benjamin's thinking about a historical shift in modes of perception from the contemplation of a painting to the "distracted reception" of film.

Bearing in mind the heteroreflexive double binds that structure Benjamin's notion of shock defense, let us turn in conclusion to his essay "The Work of Art in the Age of Mechanical Reproducibility" and his notion of "reception in a state of distraction [*Rezeption in der Zerstreuung*]" (240). As was noted above, Benjamin develops this notion of distraction by setting it off against the contemplative attitude of a spectator standing before a painting. As he says, "The painting invites the spectator to contemplation; before it the spectator can abandon himself to his associations. Before the movie frame he cannot do so. No sooner has his eye grasped a scene than it is already changed. It cannot be arrested" (238).

Thus, whereas the beholder of a painting can still "take time for contemplation" (238), the spectator of film must adapt his or her perception to its "constant, suddenly changing images" (238). Later, in the Baudelaire essay, Benjamin will link "the rhythm of reception in the film" to the "rhythm of production on a conveyor belt" (175). As this language of rhythm and constant, sudden change suggests, the shock effect of film has less to do with the particular content of a perceived image than with a "formal principle" of "perception in the form of shocks" (175). In other words, rather than contemplating an isolated, static, framed image, it is a question of being subjected to the movement of twenty-four frames per second. Here Benjamin's comparison of the rhythm of film reception to that of the conveyor belt is most useful in helping one to gauge the difference between the two processes. For while he claims ·

that "the manipulation of the worker at the machine has no connection with the preceding operation for the very reason that it is
its exact repetition" (177), the rhythm of film reception does not so
much cut off one framed image from another as *cut one into the
other*. As Benjamin says, in film, "the meaning of each single picture appears to be prescribed by the sequence of all the preceding
ones" (226). More generally, as the fluid connections of manual
labor and the relaxed pace of contemplation during which "the
spectator can abandon himself to his associations" are accelerated
in the reception of film, not only is there less time for free association, but more importantly, there is an increasing *interpenetration*
of formerly discrete activities. This is precisely what is implied by
the term "reproducibility" in the title of Benjamin's essay. As he
says in an important footnote:

> In the case of films, mechanical reproduction is not, as with litera-
> ture and painting, *an external condition* for mass distribution. Me-
> chanical reproduction is *inherent in the very technique of film pro-
> duction*. This technique not only permits in the most direct way *but
> virtually causes mass distribution*. It enforces distribution because
> the production of a film is so expensive that an individual who, for
> instance, might afford to buy a painting no longer can afford to buy
> a film. In 1927 it was calculated that a major film, in order to pay its
> way, had to reach an audience of nine million. (244; emphasis added)

Just as on the micro level of the film frame it is a question of
images cutting into one another like a concatenation of signifiers,
so too on the macro level of production, distribution, and con-
sumption what is of interest to Benjamin is an accelerating interpenetration of spheres which had formerly been (and in other arts
still are) connected in a looser and more fluid manner. My reason
for dwelling on this motif of interpenetration is to stress its distance from the Benjaminian notion of aura. As is well known, Benjamin defines aura as a "unique phenomenon of a distance however
close [*nah*] it may be." "Distance," he stresses, "is the opposite of
closeness [*Nähe*]. The essentially distant object is the unapproachable one [*das Unnahbare*]" (243).

With the withering of aura in the age of mechanical reproducibility, the beholder no longer has to leave home or embark on a distant pilgrimage to the site of the original, since technical reproduc-

tion "enables the original to meet the beholder halfway. . . . The cathedral leaves its locale to be received in the studio of a lover of art; the choral production, performed in an auditorium or in the open air, resounds in the drawing room" (220–21).

Here the distant is indeed brought closer and made more familiar as "the reproduction [meets] the beholder or listener in his own particular situation" (221). This movement is taken a step further in the case of film, for not only is there no longer an original to visit *in situ,* but the reproduction now "assails the spectator" instead of simply meeting him. While the essentially distant object may be the unapproachable one, the essentially close projections of film may in turn be ones that are impossible to get a distance on.[34] As was suggested above, post-auratic proximity does not merely bring with it closer contact between discrete surfaces but also involves a cross-coupling and interpenetration of relationships. In temporal terms, this involves not only a shorter distance between one moment and the next as time is subdivided into seconds and split seconds but also an accompanying distension of space; that is, in film the auratic experience of being drawn into the distance is supplanted by an intensified exploration of our nearest and most familiar neighboring spaces, which are dilated—or rather, exploded. As Benjamin says: "Our taverns and our metropolitan streets, our offices and furnished rooms, our railroad stations and our factories appeared to have us locked up hopelessly. Then came the film and burst this prison-world asunder by the dynamite of the tenth of a second, so that now, in the midst of its far-flung debris, we calmly and adventurously go traveling. With the close-up, space expands; with slow motion, movement is extended" (236).

Whereas Benjamin earlier affirms that "distance is the opposite of closeness," the explosive power of film dislocates this opposition by opening new distances in the midst of what is closest to home. The shock it imparts to the familiar is not one of recognition, but rather one of defamiliarization. Indeed, it is no accident that Benjamin introduces these remarks through a reference to Freud's *Psychopathology of Everyday Life,* about which he says: "Fifty years ago, a slip of the tongue passed more or less unnoticed. Only exceptionally may such a slip have revealed dimensions of depth in a conversation which had seemed to be taking its course on the surface. Since the *Psychopathology* . . . things have changed" (235).

Thus, when Benjamin comes to the notion of "reception in a state of distraction" in the final pages of his essay, the apparent lack of attention usually associated with distraction should instead be understood as something akin to the free-floating attention of the psychoanalyst—that is, as a necessarily distracted way of perceiving what emerges in and as the cracks and slips of meaningful communication.[35] As he asserts, this mode of reception "occurs much less through rapt attention than by noticing something in passing or in incidental fashion [*beiläufiges Bemerken*]" (240; trans. mod.). Yet, the significant difference between this notion of distracted reception and the psychoanalytic practice of free-floating attention is to be found in the repetitive character of the former and in the way it serves as a form of defense against shocks. In other words, Benjamin's notion of distraction does not merely represent a means of indirect access to an Other that never appears as such, it also provides a way of averting It. Insofar as these two aspects of distraction inhibit one another, they also make each other possible. They thereby also make of distraction an equivocal mode of reception not unlike the *Ennui* so familiar to the hypocritical readers of Baudelaire. It is not by chance that this passive activity or active form of passivity is linked by Benjamin to a process of habituation and shock training at the conclusion of his essay.

> The tasks which face the human apparatus of perception at the turning points of history cannot be solved by optical means, that is, by contemplation, alone. They are mastered gradually by habit, under the guidance of tactile appropriation.
>
> The distracted person, too, can form habits. More, the ability to master certain tasks in a state of distraction proves that their solution has become a matter of habit. Distraction as provided by art presents a covert control of the extent to which new tasks have become soluble by apperception. . . . Reception in a state of distraction, which is increasing noticeably in all fields of art and is symptomatic of profound changes in apperception, finds in the film its true means of exercise. The film with its shock effect meets this mode of reception halfway. (240)

Here again it would appear that the rehearsal of a conflict serves as a preparation for it—at least insofar as this preparation will have been the very conflict it rehearses.

6

Touché!

From Taboo to Narcissism

Benjamin concludes his essay "The Work of Art in the Age of Mechanical Reproducibility" with a brief discussion of architecture.[1] "Buildings," he says, "are appropriated in a two-fold manner: by use and by perception—or rather, by touch and sight." To illustrate these different modes of reception, he contrasts the attitude of a tourist standing in attentive concentration before a famous building with that of a person who regularly passes by such structures and who takes note of them only in an incidental fashion. The latter's passing attention is what he calls tactile appropriation. As was noted in Chapter 5, this sense of touch is used by Benjamin not only to characterize the peculiarly "distracted" way that city dwellers move through their environment but also and above all to describe the manner in which formerly discrete spaces and seemingly independent spheres of activity increasingly *interpenetrate* one another in the age of mechanical reproducibility.

It is thus no accident that he elaborates the notion of tactile appropriation and its relation to habitual, mechanized behavior in the context of a discussion of architecture. For if he argues that "the ability to master certain tasks in a state of distraction proves that their solution has become a matter of habit" (240), this process of habituation itself involves a twofold transformation of architectural space. What changes here is not merely the shape of buildings or the way one perceives them but, more importantly, the way these spaces pervade those who pass through them.

Furthermore, as I showed previously, the packed cityscapes habitually traversed by urban throngs are not only physical spaces but verbal ones as well. Like the buildings discussed by Benjamin, one dwells amid these linguistic structures only insofar as one is in turn inhabited by them. If these structures are sometimes easy to over-

look and may in fact only be noticed in a passing, distracted manner, it is not because they are hidden like foundations beneath the
level of surface appearances but rather because they are a little too
prominent, habitual, and mundane.[2] Benjamin's notion of tactile
appropriation is introduced precisely as a way of alluding to this
strangeness of the familiar, an uncanny space in which proximity
and distance, surface and depth, are no longer opposable terms.

Returning now to the texts of Freud, I would like to pursue the
issue of tactile appropriation and its relationship to certain verbal
structures through a reading of *Totem and Taboo*. In this text,
which deals at length with the sense of touch, there is an all too
close connection between questions of physical contact and modes
of verbal contamination. These issues are in fact so interrelated
that in discussing the former Freud cannot help but indirectly touch
on the latter. Or to put it another way, issues of verbal contamination and linguistic performance are only addressed by Freud in an
indirect and tangential manner through a discussion of forms of
"contact" (*Berührung*). Reading these interpenetrating concerns in
terms of one another, it becomes possible to understand how infectious modes of "communicability" (such as those discussed in
Chapter 3)—rather than a theory of communication rooted in the
primacy of the signified—inform Freud's thinking about cultural
transmission.

To approach Freud's text in this way is to begin at the point
where *Totem and Taboo* ends—namely, at the place where a different relationship between words and deeds and a shifted order of priority between them is articulated. In closing his treatise with the
famous line from Goethe's *Faust,* "In the beginning was the Deed,"
Freud concludes in a pointedly inconclusive manner; for not only
does he refrain from "laying claim to any finality of judgement,"
literally letting someone else have the last word, but he also ends
with a new beginning.[3] The passage Freud quotes from Goethe is
taken from a scene in which the title character has been trying various ways of translating the opening lines of the Gospel according
to John. After a number of unsatisfying attempts at rendering the
Greek term *Logos,* Faust finally settles on the very radical and very
questionable translation "In the beginning was the Deed." By
placing Faust's creative mistranslation of the Gospel at the inconclusive conclusion of his own text, Freud undoubtedly alludes to

his own questionable account of origins—namely, his account of the primal scene in which the "criminal deed" of collective patricide is said to have been the "beginning of so many things—of social organization, of moral restrictions and of religion" (*S.E.*13, 142). Yet, the quotation from *Faust* also summarizes a different approach to the relationship of words and deeds developed in the course of *Totem and Taboo*. It is this relationship and above all the performative power of words *as* deeds which forms my own point of departure. These issues will in turn lead to a reexamination of Freud's account of the primal scene in particular and the question of cultural transmission in general.

As is well known, the sense of touch plays a central role in Freud's search for points of agreement linking "primitive" taboo prohibitions to the self-imposed restrictions of modern obsessive neurotics.[4] Thus, he finds that restrictions applying to various kinds of contact constitute the principal prohibition of many taboo observances as well as the nucleus of neuroses sometimes known as "touching phobia," or *délire du toucher*. In the latter case,

> the prohibition does not merely apply to immediate physical contact [*direkte Berührung mit dem Körper*] but extends as wide as the metaphorical use of the phrase "to come into contact with" [*in Berührung kommen*]. Anything that directs the patient's thoughts to the forbidden object, anything that brings him into intellectual contact with it [*eine Gedankenberührung hervorruft*] is just as much prohibited as direct physical contact. This same extension also occurs in the case of taboo. (*S.E.*13, 27; trans. mod.)

It is worth noting that the locution translated by Strachey as "the metaphorical use of the phrase" appears in the German as *"die übertragene Redensart."* While in this particular case the term *übertragen* is used to describe the figurative extension of a literal sense of touch, more typically in the second section of *Totem and Taboo* it is employed in passages dealing with the transmission and communicable spread of some form of contagion. For example, Freud speaks of persons and things being charged with a "dangerous power which can be transferred [*übertragen*] through contact with them, almost like an infection" (*S.E.*13, 21). His use of the same term in these separate but related instances further suggests that the contact mentioned here may be *verbal* as well as physical or intellectual. In such cases, the metaphorical extension of a literal sense of touch would not only *describe* a shift from one form of contact to another but would itself be the very medium through which this shift occurs. In other words, the overdetermination of the verb *übertragen* in this text suggests that language itself be understood as an infected and infectious carrier of certain forms of contamination. It is in this susceptibility and even hospitality of language—both literal and figurative—to certain "dangerous powers" that one should search for a connection between the various senses of *Übertragung* used in *Totem and Taboo*.

In order to explore these connections, it may be useful to follow Freud's discussion of touching phobia. Such phobias, he says, usually have their roots in very early childhood and may be traced to a time when the child shows a strong desire to "touch itself"—that is, to play with its own genitals—a desire that is promptly met by an external prohibition.[5] This interdiction is accepted (*aufgenommen*), since it finds support from powerful internal forces, namely the child's loving relationship to those persons who impose the prohibition. Nevertheless, in consequence of the child's primitive psychical constitution, the prohibition does not succeed in abolishing the drive but only in repressing it. Thus, Freud says, "both the prohibition and the drive persist" (*S.E.* 13, 29).

Because I am concerned with the interaction of these opposing forces, I quote Freud's description of this struggle at length.

> The prohibition owes its strength and its obsessive character precisely to its unconscious counterpart, the concealed and undiminished desire—that is to say, to an internal necessity inaccessible to conscious inspection. The ease with which the prohibition can be transferred and extended [*Die Übertragbarkeit und Fortpflanzungsfähigkeit des Verbotes*] reflects a process which is in keeping with the unconscious desire and is greatly facilitated by the psychological conditions that prevail in the unconscious. The desire is constantly shifting in order to escape from the impasse in which it finds itself and endeavors to find surrogates—substitute objects and substitute acts—in place of the prohibited ones. In consequence of this, the prohibition itself shifts about as well, and extends to any new aims which the forbidden impulse may adopt. (*S.E.* 13, 30; trans. mod.)

Reading these remarks in conjunction with Freud's earlier description of a prohibition against touching, which "extends as wide as the metaphorical use of the phrase 'to come into contact with,'" it becomes clear that this process of extension is anything but neutral. Instead, it involves a movement of forbidden desire and a ceaseless displacement of psychical conflict. Freud's remarks further suggest that the shift from literal to figurative sense discussed above does not so much extend or add on to what is already there as supplement what is missing or wanting. In other words, the literal and physical sense of touch is not so much lengthened as prosthetically extended by other senses. Just as a prosthesis artificially replaces a severed limb or a seriously impaired organ, so too do these surrogate senses supplement the reach of an unconscious desire cut off from forbidden sources of pleasure while at the same time displacing the field of conflict onto substitute objects and metaphorical activities.

Whereas Freud tends to describe the constant shifting of desire as an attempt "to escape from the impasse in which it finds itself," its volatility may also indicate a certain ambivalence inherent in it. That is, this forbidden desire may be internally conflicted at the same time that it is at odds with an equally volatile prohibition to which it is at least in principle opposed. A second look at the so-called imposition of a parental prohibition against masturbation may help to elaborate this relationship. Whereas the prohibition against "touching oneself" is said to be imposed from without, its efficacy ultimately depends upon the child's willingness to accept it. Thus, Freud speaks of "the support from powerful *internal* forces," namely the child's loving relation to the authors of the prohibition.[6] What appears at first to be an interpersonal conflict turns out to be an intrapersonal one as well—that is, as much a question of an ambivalent desire on the part of the child to satisfy two wishes simultaneously (both to please its parents and to obtain onanistic pleasure) as a conflict between one's own desires and prohibitions imposed from without. Similarly, in terms of the role language plays in such conflicts, it may be said that the metaphorical does not merely overtake, supplant, or transform the literal from without. Instead, room will have already been made for it within the body of the literal[7]—precisely insofar as the conflicts that are repeated and dislocated in the shift from literal to figurative language already dislocate and alienate the so-called original from within.

There are a number of reasons for dwelling on the linguistic dimension of Freud's discussion of the sense of touch in general and the supplementarity of an *übertragenen Redensart* in particular. First, it helps account for his interest in the term "taboo" itself. Rather than describing it as a one-sided prohibition, Freud approaches "taboo" as a kind of dynamic—as what he calls the *Kompromißsymptom des Ambivalenzkonfliktes,* "the symptom of an ambivalence, the compromise struck between conflicting impulses ambivalently joined together" (*S.E.*13, 66; trans. mod.). In opposition to Wundt, who claims that "taboo" did not originally possess the two meanings of "sacred" and "unclean," Freud argues that "the word . . . had a double meaning from the very first and that it was used to designate a particular kind of ambivalence and whatever arose from it." He adds significantly that "'taboo' is itself an ambivalent word and one feels on looking back [*nachträglich*] that the well-attested meaning of the word should alone have made it possible to infer . . . that the prohibitions of taboo [*das Tabuverbot*] are to be understood as consequences of an emotional ambivalence" (*S.E.*13, 67).

In short, Freud suggests that the word itself is touched and contaminated by the very conflicts in which it is embroiled. Elsewhere he implies that as these conflicts diminish over time or "spread to other, analogous relations" (*S.E.*13, 67), the word "taboo," or rather, the words analogous to it, such as the *sacer* of the Romans, the ἄγος of the Greeks, and the *kadesh* of the Hebrews lose their specificity, become associated with only one side of the ambivalence, or simply fall out of use.

A second reason for concerning ourselves with the question of touch is that Freud relates it not only to forms of verbal contamination, but also to questions of linguistic performance. "Touching," he says, "is the first step towards obtaining any sort of power over [*Bemächtigung*], or attempting to subject a person or object to one's control [*dienstbar zu machen*]" (*S.E.*13, 33–34). At this point, one should not be surprised to learn that the form of contact he has in mind has less to do with touching in the literal and immediate sense of laying one's hands on some object or physically overpowering some person than with contact in an extended sense, touching at a certain distance, and forms of remote control. Or, to put it more accurately, when Freud turns to the practices of magic and sorcery and the development of an animistic system of thought in the third section of *Totem and Taboo,* the aforementioned distinction between proximity and distance, literal and extended sense, does not really apply. As E. B. Tylor notes in a remark cited by Freud, the principle on which magical action is based is simply the "mistaking [of] an ideal connection for a real one" (*S.E.*13, 79).[8] Thus, as Freud comments in a footnote, to compel a spirit one need only have control over its name (*sich seines Namens bemächtigen*).

That Freud wishes to have his earlier characterization of touching (described as "the first step towards obtaining any sort of power over") resonate in his discussion of animism may be inferred from the way he introduces this subject: "It is not to be supposed that men were inspired to create their first global system [*Weltsystem*] by pure speculative curiosity. The practical need for controlling the world around them [*sich der Welt zu bemächtigen*] must have played its part. So we are not surprised to learn that, hand in hand with the animistic system, there went a body of instructions upon how to obtain mastery over men, beasts and things — or rather over their spirits. These instructions go by the names of 'sorcery' and 'magic'. . . and may be described as the 'technique' rather than the 'strategy' of animism" (*S.E.*13, 78; trans. mod.).

One has the impression that Freud uses the locution "hand in hand [*Hand in Hand geht*]" in this passage solely in order to have it echo two sentences later in the term *behandelt.* There he explains how "sorcery is essentially the art of influencing spirits by treating them in the same way as one would treat [*behandelt*] men in like circumstances" (*S.E.*13, 142). This heavy-handed wordplay not only helps him stress the continuity between a literal sense of manhandling the world and a more spiritualized technique of obtaining control over it, it also invites the reader to take an interest in the repetitions and play of Freud's own language.[9] Nowhere are these repetitions more conspicuous than in Freud's plays on the word "play" (*Spiel*) in the third section of *Totem and Taboo.*

> From the vast number of magical acts having a similar basis [as those using effigies] I will only draw attention to two more, which

have played [*gespielt*] a large part among primitive peoples of every age . . . that is, rituals for producing rain and fertility. Rain is produced magically by imitating it or the clouds and storms which give rise to it. It is almost as though one were "playing 'it's raining'" [*"regnen spielen"*]. In Japan, for instance, "a party of Ainos will scatter water by means of sieves, while others will take a bowl, fit it up with sails and oars as if it were a boat, and then push or draw it about the village and gardens." In the same way, the fertility of the earth is magically promoted by staging for its benefit a play in which human intercourse is performed [*indem man ihm das Schauspiel eines menschlichen Geschlechtsverkehrs zeigte*]. Thus, to take one example [*ein Beispiel*] from a countless number of instances, "in some parts of Java, at the season when the bloom will soon be on the rice, the husbandman and his wife visit their fields by night and there engage in sexual intercourse" to encourage the fertility of the rice by their example [*Beispiel*]. (*S.E.*13, 80; trans mod.)

If one subtracts the statements appearing within quotation marks from this citation, the insistence of the signifier *Spiel* in Freud's commentary becomes even more striking. The games, dramatic productions, and examples (*Spiele, Schauspiele,* and *Beispiele*) to which he refers are not only performances but also and above all performatives in the Austinian sense of the term. That is, their function is not to inform, describe, or depict, but rather to accomplish an act through the very processes of playing, staging, and exemplifying. What matters is not whether these performances are true or false, faithful or inaccurate representations, but rather whether they are successful or unsuccessful operations.[10] These performances are, in short, the very infected and infectious carriers of the activity which those who perform them wish to see repeated.[11] In other words, they partake of the action their participants wish to impart in exactly the same way that the sons who take part in the murder and especially in the devouring of the primal father are said to partake of the latter's strength. We will return to this relationship and the very literal sense of parasitism implied in it in Chapter 7.[12]

For the moment it is sufficient to note that the stress Freud places on the sense of touch in *Totem and Taboo* generally has to do with a subtle shift in accent from constative to performative speech acts and from a theory of communication based on the priority of the signified to modes of communicability and infectiousness which accord a childish and primitive significance to relations obtaining among the signifying elements themselves. Thus, Freud asserts that "relations which hold between the representations [Vorstellungen] of things are assumed to hold equally between the things themselves" (S.E. 13, 85). While this formulation might in turn suggest some kind of parallelism between things and their representations and therefore some kind of fundamental difference between them, the very next sentence precludes just such a difference and distance in the case of magic. "The world of magic," Freud says, "has a telepathic disregard for spatial distance and treats past situations as though they were present" (S.E. 13, 85). The effect of this disregard for distance is of course to make direct contact, influence, and contamination possible. It is therefore no accident that Freud now returns to the matter of touch.

> It is further to be noticed that the two principles of association—similarity and contiguity—[according to which the aforementioned representations are linked] are both included in the more comprehensive concept of "contact." Association by contiguity is contact in the literal sense; association by similarity is contact in the metaphorical sense. The use of the same word for the two kinds of relation is no doubt accounted for by some identity in the psychical process concerned which we have not yet grasped. We have here the same extension [Umfang] of meaning of the concept of "contact" as we found in our analysis of taboo. (S.E. 13, 85)

What is articulated here is a representational praxis in which the representative partakes of and is in contact with the "represented" in such a way that the former cannot be considered secondary, inferior, or logically subordinate to the latter. Furthermore, if, as we have seen, Freud returns repeatedly to the question of touch in Totem and Taboo, he does so precisely in order to recathect the seemingly neutral space separating the representative from the represented in traditional theories of representation.[13] In doing so, he does not so much collapse this space as recharge it, thereby cathecting it as a highly contaminated and ambivalent field of force.

As one might expect, the question of "contact" and all that it implies has relevance beyond the exceptional cases involving children, so-called primitives, and neurotics discussed here precisely because these "special cases" are not as easy to isolate and quarantine as one might at first assume. While in *Totem and Taboo* Freud does not discuss more "normal" instances in which issues of contact and spacing are at issue, he does return briefly to the question in *Inhibitions, Symptoms, Anxiety*.[14] There he introduces the notion of isolation, a technique used primarily by obsessional neurotics but which is also linked to the "normal phenomenon of concentration." Freud explains that when something unpleasant has happened to an obsessional neurotic or when the person himself has done something that has significance for his neurosis, "he interpolates an interval during which nothing further must happen — during which he must perceive and do nothing." Here "the experience is not forgotten, but is instead deprived of its affect, and its associative connections are suppressed or interrupted so that it remains as though isolated" (*S.E.*20, 120).

The technique of isolation thus consists in an interpolation of the very kind of neutral space so foreign to magical, animistic thinking. And as alien as this distancing mechanism is to the various forms of *Spielen* discussed earlier, it is to the same degree typical of more familiar, normal modes of thought. As Freud says, "Even a normal person uses concentration to keep away not only what is irrelevant or unimportant, but above all, what is unsuitable because it is contradictory. He is most disturbed by those elements which once belonged together but which have been torn apart in the course of his development. . . . Thus, the ego has a great deal of isolating work to do in its function of directing the current of thought" (*S.E.*20, 121).

As though the question of touch had all this time been covertly informing Freud's thinking about isolation, he now brings this connection explicitly to the fore.

> But in thus endeavoring to prevent associations and connections of thought, the ego is obeying one of the oldest and most fundamental commands of obsessional neurosis, the taboo on touching. If we ask ourselves why the avoidance of touching, contact, or contagion should play such a large part in this neurosis and should become the subject-matter of complicated systems, the answer is that touching and physical contact are the immediate aim of the aggressive as well

as the loving object-cathexes. Eros desires contact because it strives to make the ego and the loved object one, to abolish all spatial barriers between them. But destructiveness, too, which (before the invention of long-range weapons) could only take effect at close quarters, must presuppose physical contact, a coming to grips. (*S.E.*20, 121–22)

The parenthetical mention of long-range "arms" in this passage again draws attention to the limited scope of a literal sense of touch and its connection to direct, physical aggression. Yet it also reintroduces in a very concrete and graphic way the issue of prosthetic extension and the supplementary reach of an *übertragenen Redensart*, discussed earlier.[15] Rather than pursuing these issues in *Inhibitions, Symptoms, Anxiety*, Freud focuses instead on the question of isolation and the constant state of watchfulness which the ego must maintain in order to enforce a taboo against touching. Whereas this later text focuses primarily on the ego's defenses, on questions of anxiety and *Angstbereitschaft*, *Totem and Taboo* is more concerned with the interaction—or rather, the mutual contamination—of the defenses and what they defend against. In this text, it is not merely a question of isolation per se, but rather of the compromises struck between the opposing moments of isolation and contamination, moments that, to paraphrase Freud, perhaps once belonged together but that have been torn apart in the course of development.[16] When dealing with these compromises, it is no longer possible to treat touching either simply as the object of a prohibition or as the aim of a particular desire, for here it names the very problem that arises whenever the prohibition and the prohibited become so entangled with each other that it is difficult to distinguish one from the other.

Freud leads the reader into and through these entanglements in an indirect way—namely, by adducing examples of taboos attaching to enemies and rulers. While these sections of *Totem and Taboo* merely bring together material drawn from other sources, the manner in which the information is organized and presented merits close scrutiny. For just as Freud argues that dreams reproduce logical connections by simultaneity in time, so too do the examples adduced here trace a certain movement of thought by virtue of their juxtaposition and metonymic contact.

Freud thus begins by describing the purification rituals that returning warriors must first perform and the periods of isolation they must endure before being accepted back into their communities. "In Timor," for example, "the leader of the expedition is forbidden 'to return at once to his own house. A special hut [*Hütte*] is prepared for him, in which he has to reside for two months, undergoing bodily and spiritual purification. During this time he may not go to his wife nor feed himself; the food must be put into his mouth by another person'" (*S.E.*13, 39).

From this straightforward sense of physical quarantine associated with a "special hut," Freud turns shortly thereafter to a more complicated, two-sided process of isolation. Again citing Frazer, who is quoted on this rare occasion both in German in the body of the text and in English in a footnote, he says, "rulers 'must not only be guarded, they must also be guarded against' [*Man muß sich vor ihnen hüten, und man muß sie behüten*]" (*S.E.*13, 41). The verbs *hüten* and *behüten,* which are used here to translate the two forms of guarding mentioned in the English, retain the sense of sheltered isolation evoked earlier by the term *Hütte.* Yet whereas in the previous instance the place of internal exile was located on the fringes of society, in the present case the neutral zone shifts to the very center of the community, where it acts as a two-way buffer. As Freud says, taboos upon the ruler, on the one hand, protect the subjects against a "dangerous magical power which is transmitted by contact like an electric charge," while, on the other hand, they protect the ruler against his own subjects.

Because the life of the sovereign is valuable only so long as he discharges the duties of his position in a way that benefits his people, as soon as he fails to do so, the care, devotion, and religious homage that his people had hitherto lavished on him cease. "He is banished in disgrace and may be thankful if he escapes with his life. . . . A king of this sort lives walled in [*eingemauert*], as it were, behind a system of ceremonies and rules of etiquette, ensnared [*eingesponnen*] in a network of prohibitions and observances, the intention of which . . . is to restrain him from conduct which, by disturbing the harmony of nature, might involve himself, his people, and the universe in one common catastrophe" (*S.E.*13, 44; trans. mod.).

As these remarks make clear, the strictures designed to assure a certain harmony between the interlocking spheres of natural and social existence only protect the chief against the wrath of his subjects by making him a veritable prisoner of his position of power. These privative aspects of privilege are, according to Freud, a little too systematic to be merely a matter of chance. He therefore argues that such taboos upon rulers must have been intended from the very first to function not only as doubly neutralizing buffers but also and above all, as highly charged vehicles of an insidiously double-edged form of aggression. It is precisely the "double meaning" revealed by these ceremonials—which persecute as they protect and deprive as they empower—that suggests a connection to the ritual practices of obsessional neurotics. "Here," Freud says, "we have an exact counterpart of the obsessional act in the neurosis, in which the suppressed impulse and the impulse that suppresses it find simultaneous and common satisfaction. The obsessional act is *ostensibly* a protection against the prohibited act; but *actually* it is a repetition of it" (*S.E.* 13, 50).

These examples of taboo observances thus move from a case involving a single hut that isolates a certain contagion within its walls to a two-way buffer providing protection for and against a ruler and thence to a double-edged form of defense which performs the very act it is supposed to prevent. In the juxtaposition of these examples, Freud takes the reader from specific taboos against touching to the more diffuse, equivocal kind of contact obtaining between the seemingly opposed moments of isolation and contamination—or rather, between the act of prohibiting and the repetition of a prohibited act.

It is important to note here that Freud's use of the term "repetition" in the passage cited above has more to do with the rehearsal of a conflict in which the prohibiting and prohibited impulses are engaged than with a one-sided return of the repressed. This distinction is worth emphasizing, since it mirrors a shift in Freud's understanding of transference, which, as Harold Bloom argues, was undergoing an important revision at this time.[17] In the postscript to *An Analysis of a Case of Hysteria,* Freud initially defines the transferences simply in terms of a return of the repressed. "They are new editions or facsimiles of the tendencies and phantasies which are aroused and made conscious during the progress of the analysis; but they have the peculiarity . . . that they replace some earlier person by the person of the physician. To put it another way: a whole series of psychological experiences are revived not as belonging to the past, but as applying to the person of the physician at the present moment" (*S.E.*7, 116).

By contrast, in "The Dynamics of the Transference," published the same year as parts of *Totem and Taboo,* Freud now stresses the role of resistance and the compromises that transference strikes.

> In following a pathogenic complex from its representation in the conscious . . . to its root in the unconscious, we shall soon enter a region in which the resistance makes itself felt so clearly that the next association must take account of it and appear as a compromise between its demands and those of the work of investigation. It is at this point . . . that transference enters on the scene. . . . the transference-idea has penetrated into consciousness in front of any other possible association because it satisfies the resistance. . . . Over and over again, when we come near to a pathogenic complex, the portion of that complex which is capable of transference is first pushed forward into consciousness and defended with the greatest obstinacy. (*S.E.*12, 103–4)

It is precisely around questions of repetition and transference that Freud develops the less obvious *temporal* aspects of touching and the related issue of remote control in *Totem and Taboo.* While numerous passages bear witness to an approach that places equal stress on spatial and temporal considerations, the following remark brings this dual perspective clearly into focus: "Since the matter of distance presents no particular problem for thinking in general — that is, since what lies at the furthest distance in space or belongs to a completely different period of time is easily gathered and thought together in a single act of consciousness — so too does the world of magic show a telepathic disregard for spatial distance and treat past situations as though they were present" (*S.E.*13, 85; trans. mod.).

Treating a past situation as though it were present is of course the way an analysand acts when transferring portions of a repressed complex onto the person of the analyst. More generally, in *Totem and Taboo* Freud is concerned not only with the revival (*Wiederbelebung*) of past psychological experiences in present situations but also with the survival (*Weiterleben*) of certain primitive modes of thought in the contemporary "scientific view of the world." Thus, his aim in presenting a sketch of "the evolution of human views of the universe" is twofold. On the one hand, he stresses that the scientific *Weltanschauung* can no longer accommodate a belief in human omnipotence, since men of science are obliged to confess their insignificance (*Kleinheit*) and submit resignedly to death as well as to the other necessities of nature. On the other hand, he adds, "nonetheless some of the primitive belief in omnipotence still survives in the trust one places in the power of the human mind and its ability to take into account the laws of reality" (*S.E.* 13, 88). As one might expect, Freud's interest lies in pursuing implications deriving from the latter case. [18] The survival of a "primitive belief in omnipotence" bears witness to a psychological tendency to hold on to experiences and forms of thought which flatter one's sense of power and feelings of importance in the world.

In short, Freud is gradually drawn to the issue of narcissism and the difficulties one has in renouncing any portion of it. Yet, the question that arises at this point is whether narcissism itself is to be understood as a primitive mode of thinking which survives in the scientific period as a phase of early childhood through which every person still must pass or whether a primitive belief in the omnipotence of thought and all that it implies is itself to be traced back to the narcissism of early childhood. As Freud would say, the question must be answered with a *non liquet,* for not only can the case not yet be decided, but, for reasons that will soon become apparent, it is of necessity undecidable.

Rather than locating the origin of certain primitive beliefs in the narcissism of early childhood (or vice versa), Freud instead attempts to establish parallels between the childhood of an individual and that of mankind in general. That is, he compares the stages of an individual's libidinal development to phases in the evolution of human views of the universe. Here the general phase of animism is said to correspond to the individual stage of narcissism "both chronologically and in its content" (*S.E.* 13, 90). While this comparison places narcissism and animism on an equal footing, it also suggests a dubious equation between children and so-called primitives. Not only does this equation effectively turn the cultural Other into a familiar and necessarily immature version of oneself, but in the process it turns Freud's own investigation of narcissism into an example of the very problem it purports to analyze.

Yet, as has been suggested on numerous occasions, the radicality of Freud's thinking is to be sought less in such facile equations than in those places where the terms of his comparison stand slightly out of line and the phases he compares remain just out of sync. Perhaps the best way to gauge this asynchronous margin of difference between an atavistic survival of animism and the persistence among primitive adults of childhood narcissism is to begin by examining Freud's difficulties in locating narcissism as an "intermediate phase" somewhere between the libidinal stages of auto-erotism and object-choice: "Manifestations of the sexual drives," he says, "can be observed from the very first, but to begin with they are not yet directed towards any external object. The separate drive components of sexuality work independently of one another to obtain pleasure and find satisfaction in the subject's own body. This stage is known as that of auto-erotism and it is succeeded by one in which an object is chosen" (*S.E.*13, 88).

Thus, in this first phase the sexual drives not only lack unity but, like workers without a union or like brothers driven from the primal horde by a jealous father, they are as yet unorganized. As Freud says, they "work [*arbeiten*] independently of one another to obtain a margin of pleasure [*auf Lustgewinn*]" (*S.E.*13, 88; trans. mod.). Only at a later stage, which is not yet that of object-choice, will these unorganized drives (*Triebe*), like the banished (*ausgetriebene*) brothers, get their act together and become unified.[19] When exactly this will occur is difficult to say, and the conspicuous hedging of Freud's subsequent remarks makes this difficulty all the more apparent.

> Further study has shown that it is expedient and indeed indispensable to insert a third stage between these two, or, if you will, to divide the first stage of autoerotism into two [*in zwei zu zerlegen*]. At this intermediate stage, the importance of which is being made more and more evident by research, the previously scattered sexual drives have already come together into a single unity [*haben die vorher vereinzelten Sexualtriebe sich bereits zu einer Einheit zusammengesetzt*] and have also found an object; this object, however, is not an external one, extraneous to the individual, but is his own ego, which has been constituted at about this same time. Bearing in mind the pathological fixations of this new stage, which become observable later, we have given it the name of "narcissism." (*S.E.*13, 88–89; trans. mod.)

Freud makes no attempt to conceal his uncertainty about where to locate the peculiar betweenness of narcissism. He describes this intermediate phase as a "third stage," but one that does not come after stages one and two. Instead, it will have taken place halfway between them "or, if you will," will have taken its place only by splitting the first in two. The sense of betweenness that emerges in this description thus seems to indicate a certain instability within the notion of narcissism.

While *Totem and Taboo* describes this notion both as an intermediate phase wedged between the stages of autoerotism and object-choice and as a cleaving of the former from itself, a year later in Freud's formal "introduction" of this psychoanalytic concept it is narcissism itself that is described as being divided in two and split into primary and secondary narcissism. Yet, the introduction of this supplementary split does not so much divide narcissism into two separate and successive stages as underscore the fragmentary nature of a phase of development radically *out of phase* with itself. As we will see, this asynchronous structure—which appears to be as divided as it is divisive—cannot be plotted on a continuum of libidinal development but instead must be understood as a mode of repetition and as an act of transference. What I am suggesting is that if narcissism is so difficult to locate in the first place, this is due to the fact that *primary narcissism,* like transference, may only be experienced indirectly and vicariously through an ineluctible relation to another.

Needless to say, *Totem and Taboo* makes no distinction between primary and secondary narcissism, nor does the passage cited above or the discussion that follows attempt to link narcissism to issues of transference or modes of indirect experience. At best, it suggests that certain problems arise when attempting to locate this interphase either as a stage of libidinal development or as a period in the evolution of human views of the universe. Nevertheless, if one is prepared to read *Totem and Taboo* in a kind of future perfect tense and to insert another, seemingly later stage of Freud's own thinking between the lines of what is said here, one can begin to gauge just how out of sync with itself the Freudian concept of narcissism really is.

7

Acknowledgments

Narcissism, Taboo, and the
Generational Nexus

Original sin, the old injustice committed by man, consists in
the complaint unceasingly made by man that he has been the
victim of an injustice, the victim of original sin.

Kafka

In a recent essay dealing with Freud's paper "On Narcissism: An
Introduction," the Argentine psychoanalyst R. Horacio Etchegoyen observes that "the proposition of a primary narcissism as
the starting point of psychic life is at the root of the fundamental
controversies of psychoanalysis today."[1] As Etchegoyen explains,
"There are those who maintain that narcissism is primary, object
relations coming only later, and those who maintain that mental
life begins with the relation to the object, narcissism being only a
turning back and therefore always secondary."[2] The debate over
the primariness of narcissism in general is further complicated by
disagreements over the exact definition of the term "primary narcissism" in psychoanalytic discourse. As the authors of *The Language of Psychoanalysis* observe, this notion

> undergoes extreme variations in sense from one author to the next.
> The problem here is the definition of a hypothetical stage in the de-
> velopment of the infantile libido, and there are complex debates
> over the way such a state should be described as well as over its
> chronological position, while for some theorists its very existence is
> debatable.
>
> In Freud's work primary narcissism refers in a general way to the
> first narcissism—that of the child who takes itself as its love-object
> before choosing external objects. This kind of state is said to corre-
> spond to the child's belief in the omnipotence of its thoughts.[3]

Laplanche and Pontalis further point to the difficulties involved in ascertaining the exact moment of the establishment of this state. For not only are there a variety of views on the subject, but Freud himself places this phase at different points in time at different stages in his thinking. According to these authors, Freud's works of the period 1910-15 place primary narcissism between the phases of primitive autoerotism and object-love, thus apparently making it "contemporaneous with the first emergence of a unified subject— in other words, of an ego." Later on, however, with the elaboration of the second topography, Freud uses the term to mean instead a first state of life, prior even to the formation of an ego, which is epitomized by life in the womb.[4] The problem with this latter view, Laplanche and Pontalis rightly observe, is that "it is difficult to see just *what* is supposed to be cathected here." In other words, "this approach loses sight of the reference to an image of the self or to a mirror-type relation which is implicit in the etymology of 'narcissism.'"

It is the question of this mirror-type relation and its status in primary narcissism that returns us to Freud's 1914 essay. For the question raised between the lines of this text is, whose self-image are we dealing with in the case of primary narcissism? Is this image simply and primarily that of the child? Toward the end of the second section of his paper Freud states that "the primary narcissism of the child which is assumed by us [*von uns supponierte Narzißmus*] and which forms one of the hypotheses [*Voraussetzungen*] in our theories of the libido, is less easy to grasp by direct observation than to confirm by deduction [*Rückschluß*] from another consideration" (*S.E.*14, 90; trans. mod.). Thus, in contrast to secondary narcissism, which is plainly visible in the withdrawal of libido from external love-objects and its redirection back onto the subject's own ego, the existence of primary narcissism is merely a matter of conjecture, hypothesis, and deduction. Why, then, is primary narcissism not accessible to direct observation? Freud's surprising response, which itself must be deduced from his remarks about the parents of "His Majesty the Baby," is that this narcissism is primarily that of another—that is, of another whose own narcissism can only be owned up to and indirectly experienced in a transferential relation to another.

In a crucial passage whose rhetorical verve and free indirect style are very much a part of its argument, Freud remarks:[5]

If we look at the attitude of doting parents towards their children, we have to recognize [erkennen] it as a revival and reproduction [Wiederaufleben und Reproduktion] of their own, long since abandoned narcissism. The trustworthy pointer constituted by over-estimation, which we have already come to appreciate as a narcissistic stigma in the case of object-choice, dominates, as is well known, this emotional attitude [diese Gefühlsbeziehung]. Thus they are under a compulsion [So besteht ein Zwang] to ascribe to the child all manner of perfections which sober observation would not confirm, to gloss over [verdecken] and forget [vergessen] all his shortcomings—a tendency with which, indeed, the denial [Verleugnung] of infantile sexuality is connected. Moreover, they are inclined to suspend in the child's favor the operation of all those cultural acquisitions whose acknowledgement has come at the cost of their own narcissism [deren Anerkennung man seinem Narzißmus abgezwungen hat] and to renew in his person the claims for privileges which were long ago given up by themselves. The child shall have things better than his parents; he shall not be subject to the necessities which they have recognized [erkannt] as dominating life. Illness, death, renunciation of enjoyment, restrictions on his own will, shall not touch him; the laws of nature, like those of society, shall be abrogated in his favor; he shall once more really be the center and core [Kern] of creation—"His Majesty the Baby," as once we fancied ourselves to be [wie man sich einst selbst dünkte]. The child [Es] shall fulfill those wishful dreams of the parents which they never carried out, to become a great man and a hero in his father's stead, or to marry a prince as a tardy compensation to the mother. At the touchiest point of all in the narcissistic system, the immortality of the ego, which is so hard pressed by reality, security is achieved by taking refuge in the child. Parental love, which is so moving and at bottom so childish [Die rührende, im Grunde so kindliche Elternliebe], is nothing other than the reborn narcissism of the parents which, though transformed into object-love, nevertheless reveals its former character in no uncertain terms. (S.E.14, 90–91; trans. mod.)[6]

Thus, narcissism may be said to be primary only insofar as it is associated with an image of perfection which is primarily imposed upon the child. Like the Lacanian theory of the mirror stage, the Freudian hypothesis of primary narcissism paradoxically locates the constitution of the ego *outside the self*—in an exterior, however, which is not yet that of object-choice but rather the cathected interspace of an "as if": that is, a dimension of fictionality and a relation to a seemingly faultless mirror image.[7] Yet, whereas Lacan emphasizes the *child's* identification with a perceived image of wholeness that contrasts sharply with its own bodily experience of faulty motor control, deficiency, and dependency, Freud stresses the *parents'* transferential identification with the child.[8] In Freud a certain mirror image is *involuntarily* impressed upon the child in the sense of being both compulsively passed on by the parents and passively received by the infant. As he says, the parents "are compelled [*So besteht ein Zwang*] to ascribe to the child all manner of perfections which sober observation would not confirm." Ultimately, then, the deluded self-image — the mirage — of primary narcissism will never have been one's own except in a "fictive" identificatory relation to another.[9]

Furthermore, like the parental prohibition against "touching oneself," this externally imposed self-image cannot simply be accepted or rejected by the child. For what is imposed upon it is an image that is as impossible to live up to as it is to renounce. As in the case of the touching taboo, the child is put in the position of having to accommodate two incompatible desires, and once again it responds by displacing the conflict as a way of temporizing it. Before attempting to follow this movement of displacement through an examination of Freud's mirrorlike pairing of the terms "ideal-ego" and "ego-ideal" in section 3 of "On Narcissism," it is important to stress the fact that the transferences and displacements I am tracing are themselves the very divided and divisive media in which narcissism will primarily have taken place. In other words, being out of sync is not a transitory, anomolous, or correctable situation in the case of narcissism, but rather its primary condition of possibility and its slightly but decisively disjointed temporal framework.

As was suggested earlier, narcissism cannot be understood either simply as a primitive mode of thinking which survives in the scientific period as a phase of early childhood or as a childish system of thought which persists among so-called primitive adults. For, as Freud's essay makes clear, it is parental love that is the most childish — and the most primitive — at least insofar as this transference-love acts out narcissistic desires, which from the first will have been the desire of another. That is to say, such desires will never have been the original property of some particular other or primal parent precisely because this asynchronous structure of desire dislocates the very notions of parentage and linear descent. The desire of the Other only insists insofar as it is *disowned* from generation to generation — that is, insofar as it is compulsively passed *between* generations like a metastasizing contagion.

This unconscious transmission of the very privileges that parents have been obliged to forgo in the process of acculturation is also fraught with a certain ambiguity. For just as the taboos upon rulers discussed earlier ensconce the leader in an unrivaled position of power within the community while at the same time making him a veritable prisoner of his place of privilege, so too does the narcissism of parental love place the child in an untenable position. The flattering self-image with which "His Majesty the Baby" is invested proves to be as difficult to surrender as it is to measure up to. It is precisely this dilemma that leads Freud to link a distorted and "secondarily revised" narcissistic image imposed upon the child to a discussion of the ethical standards a subject imposes on him- or herself. That these issues are meant to be raised in relation to each other is suggested by Freud's use of the terms "ideal-ego" and "ego-ideal" in section 3. Not only does each term literally repeat the other in displaced form, but each also serves as the inverted mirror image of the other.

Before examining the relationship of these terms, it is important to stress that just as the idealization of the child involves an element of compulsion on the part of the parents, so too does the self-imposition of ethical ideals have less to do with a striving to meet conscious goals than with a compulsive need to obey certain unconscious imperatives.[10] As a way of emphasizing this contrast, Freud plays off the German term *Anerkennung* against what he describes as *eine bloß intellektuelle Kenntnis*. Whereas the former is associated with an unconscious acknowledgment of and an involuntary submission to these ethical ideals, the latter involves "a merely intellectual knowledge" of them (*S.E.* 14, 93).

Returning now to Freud's mirrorlike pairing of the terms ideal-ego and ego-ideal, he says that the former serves as a kind of standard against which the subject measures his actual ego. "To this ideal-ego [*Idealich*] is now directed the self-love [*Selbstliebe*] which the real ego enjoyed in childhood" (*S.E.* 14, 94; trans. mod.). At the risk of belaboring a point that should be obvious by now (but which is sometimes obscured by Strachey's translation), it should be noted that the *Selbstliebe* enjoyed here is as much that of the parents as of the infant. While the abandoned self-love of the former is "reborn," as Freud says, and transferentially reenacted as object-love directed toward the child, this narcissistic self-love will also have been the infant's own — at least insofar as the child's ego is also structured by a mirror stage in which it will have identified with the totalized image presented to it by the parents' own narcissism.[11] Freud continues:

> The narcissism seems to be now displaced onto this new ideal ego [*ideale Ich*], which, like the infantile ego, is found to possess every kind of perfection.[12] As always where the libido is concerned, here again man has shown himself incapable of giving up a gratification he has once enjoyed. He is not willing to forgo the narcissistic perfection of his childhood; and if, as he develops, he is disturbed by the admonitions of others and by the awakening of his own critical judgement, so that he can no longer retain [*festhalten*] that perfection, he seeks to recover it in the new form of an ego-ideal [*Ich-ideal*]. That which he projects before him as his ideal [*als sein Ideal vor sich hin projiziert*] is the substitute for the lost narcissism of his childhood — the time when he was his own ideal. (*S.E.* 14, 94; trans. mod.)

Thus, in the space of a paragraph the term "ideal ego" (*das ideale Ich,* written as two separate words in contrast to the previous mention of an *Idealich*) is replaced by the term "ego-ideal." While Freud never explicitly draws attention to this terminological shift, it does seem to reflect certain changes in the status of the ego outlined in the last section of the essay. These changes are described not only as the ego's fall from an ideal state in which it first existed but also as a subsequent attempt to refind that lost paradise in a substitute form — namely in a ideal projected into the future and as an image placed before it with which it can identify. As in other myths of original presence, this fall from an ideal state is attributed to the intervention of certain outside forces. "The development of the ego," Freud writes, "consists in a departure [*Entfernung*] from primary narcissism and gives rise to a vigorous attempt to recover that state. This departure [*Entfernung*] is brought about by means of the displacement of libido on to an ego-ideal imposed from without [*von außen aufgenötigtes Ichideal*]; and satisfaction is brought about from fulfilling this ideal" (*S.E.*14, 100).

As was suggested above, this purportedly scientific description of the ego's development reads like a narrative told from the invested and idealized perspective of the ego itself. It is as though the account given here were written in a kind of free indirect style in which the narrator, Freud, has taken on the speech of the subject discussed. Or, to put it a little differently, the ego addressed in this passage appears to speak through the voice of the seemingly detached observer. Yet, superimposed on this very traditional story line is another version of narcissism whose primariness, I have argued, will have always already been slightly but decisively out of phase with itself — and with more familiar narratives of libidinal development and the evolution of human views of the universe. This other version — like primary narcissism itself — is not directly presented in Freud's text but instead must be read between the lines — or rather in the exaggerated coherence and secondary revision — of the idealized plots that are put forward.

As was noted earlier, Freud's use of the term *Anerkennung* in this essay suggests a different mode of cognition whose specificity is described only in negative terms — that is, as something other than "a merely intellectual knowledge" of the existence of certain ideas. It may further be said that this term tends to appear in those places in his text where the reader herself is compelled to acknowledge another dimension of discourse which exceeds the "merely intellectual knowledge" provided by the manifest level of the account given. Such passages sometimes go so against the grain of normal cognitive expectations that certain mistakes in translation come to exemplify the very process of secondary revision which concerns us here. Consider, for example, Cecil Baines's translation of a passage from "On Narcissism" in which Freud takes up the question of how "conscience" may be known.

> It would not surprise us if we were to find a special institution [*Instanz*] in the mind which performs the task of seeing that narcissistic gratification is secured from the ego-ideal and that, with this end in view, it constantly watches the real ego and measures it by that ideal. If such an institution [*Instanz*] does exist, it cannot possibly be something which we have not yet discovered; we only need to recognize [*agnoszieren*] it, and we may say that what we call our *conscience* has the required characteristics. Recognition [*Anerkennung*] of this institution enables us to understand the so-called "delusions of observation" or, more correctly, of *being watched,* which are such striking symptoms in the paranoid diseases.[13]

According to Baines, the institution of conscience "cannot possibly be something which we have not yet discovered." And yet, what Freud actually says is that "if such an instance exists, we are fated never to discover it [*so kann es uns unmöglich zustoßen, sie zu entdecken*]; we can *only acknowledge* it as such [*wir können sie nur als solche agnoszieren*]" (emphasis added). Freud's point is that the functioning of what we call our "conscience" is not directly available to conscious scrutiny. That it may be approached only in a highly indirect manner is suggested by Freud's own avoidance of terms that could be translated as "recognition" and his use in their stead of the verb *agnoszieren* and the noun *Anerkennung*. Not only are these terms employed in explicit contrast to merely intellectual modes of cognition, but in the present case the verb *agnoszieren* in particular evokes the doctrine of agnosticism and in general draws attention to the limits of what is consciously knowable.

Thus, while Freud remarks in *Totem and Taboo* that "in some languages the words for 'conscience' and 'conscious' can scarcely be distinguished," the essay "On Narcissism" teaches us to be especially wary of family resemblances. For here the unconscious Other is not merely outside the conscious Self, but is instead its uncanny and hauntingly familiar double. In its intimate relationship to conscience, the ego is put in the alienating and untenable position of having to ward off the very instance that wards over its ideal.[14] This position is both alienating and untenable insofar as the ego, which guards itself against an instance standing guard over its very sense of self, is threatened not by another but rather by the essential otherness of its "own" self-image.

Like Freud's other psychical guardians such as censorship, repression, and *Angstbereitschaft,* the instance of conscience ultimately is something of a double agent. As keeper of the ego-ideal, it does not simply attempt to retain—or even to reattain in displaced form—the exalted image the ego once had of itself, as Freud sometimes contends. Instead, it holds in abeyance an interspace of desire and a dimension of fictionality in which the identity of the ego will always already have been that of another. In other words, the relationship of conscience, ego, and ego-ideal does not so much link three distinct instances as rehearse in a displaced form the conflicts that inhabit, structure, and drive the ego from the very first. If there is ultimately any movement in "On Narcissism," it is one of inversion, repetition, and superimposition rather than a process of evolution, succession, or linear development.

The terminological displacement from "ideal-ego" to "ego-ideal" in a sense simply shifts the focus from a certain narcissistic *self-image* that transferentially passes between generations to the movement of the gaze itself. Yet in focusing on this gaze, on the figure of the watchman (*Wächter*), and on the various delusions of being observed discussed in the final section of "On Narcissism," Freud merely refocuses attention on the adoring gaze of the narcissistic parents and adds to it a critical edge that will have already been there in the first place.[15] For just as the image of perfection presented to "His Majesty the Baby" by the parents' own "reborn narcissism" imposes a standard that is as difficult to measure up to as it is to relinquish, so too is the narcissistic regard in which the child is held primarily double-edged. What returns as the watchfulness of conscience in the latter part of this essay is merely the critical view of the child, which is acknowledged without quite being recognized in the observation of its faultlessness.

It is important to add that conscience is not merely the inheritor of a certain way of looking but its legator as well. For insofar as primary narcissism is always the desire of the Other and only insists insofar as it is *disowned* from generation to generation, it cannot simply be traced back to a desire originating in the parents. As Freud's discussion of parental love makes clear, the compulsion to recognize one's "own" abandoned narcissism in the projected, idealized image of a future generation is itself driven by an acknowledgment of the demands that conscience places on the egos of a previous generation. What this essay thus elaborates is an overlapping temporal structure in which conscience demands acknowledgment of that which narcissism seeks to deny. Not only does each mirror the other in inverted form, but the very movement of inversion keeps the two slightly but decisively out of sync.

Whereas Freud's essay often speaks of "the child" and "the parent" as though it were basing a universal understanding of intergenerational relationships on the experience of modern Western nuclear families, Freud's aim, I would argue, is less to apply the terms of his analysis to other cultures and time periods (a gesture that would be narcissistic in the extreme) than to emphasize the way one's view of the world is inevitably shaped by powerfully insistent narcissistic compulsions. His use of free indirect style in this essay as well as his discussion of the survival of a belief in the omnipotence of thought within the "scientific world-view" in *Totem and Taboo* at the very least suggest that his own seemingly demystified scientific discourse cannot help but be contaminated by the very desires it wishes to get a hold—and a distance—on. Just as the Freudian notion of primary narcissism has been shown to be out of phase in a way that is not merely transitory, anomalous, or correctable, but rather primary and constitutive, so too does his use of terms like *agnoszieren* and *Anerkennung* suggest an approach that is ineluctibly indirect. This indirection, I have argued, is itself dictated by an object of study which is at once divided and divisive and which will only have been "itself" in and as a movement of displacement. Thus, instead of simply circling around an impenetrable object of study, Freud's discourse is implicated in and contaminated by a movement of conflictual desire.

As we return now to *Totem and Taboo,* it might be recalled that the notion of "taboo" has less to do with a particular prohibition than with a certain *dynamic;* it is, according to Freud, the "symptom of an ambivalence, the compromise struck between conflicting impulses ambivalently joined together" (*S.E.*13, 66). Furthermore, as has been suggested, what is passed on in this movement of conflict is a certain disowning of knowledge. Thus, when Freud says that "to us [taboo prohibitions] are incomprehensible [*unverständlich*], while to those who are dominated by them they are self-evident [*selbstverständlich*]" (*S.E.* 13, 18), the outsider's ignorance is not contrasted with the privileged access of a knowing insider but rather compared to another kind of blindness, which in this case is the result of things being a little too self-evident. More generally, it might be said that *Totem and Taboo* does not so much *apply* the findings of individual psychology to the fields of anthropology and the history of religion as move from one relation of incomprehension to another, reading one form of miscognition through the filter of another. My own aim in reading *Totem and Taboo* through the filter of "On Narcissism" has been twofold: first, to identify a certain compulsion to misconstrue and "secondarily revise" reality in the structure of primary narcissism; second, to suggest that understanding how such compulsions and misconstructions are disowned from one generation to another may help us to make sense of related structures of repetition elaborated in Freud's famous account of the sons' murder of the primal father.

As was mentioned in the preceding chapter, there are a number of parallels between *Totem and Taboo*'s description of narcissism and the account it provides of the unification of the patricidal sons. While Freud's brief discussion of the transition from autoerotism to the intermediate phase of narcissism refers to "hitherto dissociated sexual drives [*bisher dissoziierte Sexualtriebe*]," the protagonists of the primal scene are described as scattered brothers who had been driven out (*ausgetrieben*) of the primal horde. While the former are said "to come together into a single whole," the latter are described as "one day having come together [*Eines Tages taten sich . . . zusammen*]." The problems involved in locating the peculiar betweenness of the narcissistic phase are at least partially echoed in Freud's way of beginning his account of the primal scene with the locution *Eines Tages,* which Patrick Mahoney describes as "one of the most famous of all fictional formulas."[16] Also, Freud's parenthetical suggestion that "some cultural advance, perhaps command over some new weapon" is what gives the brothers the sense of superiority needed to bring them together at this point in time seems so implausible that it tends to highlight the problem it is supposed to resolve. If anything, this suggestion subtly reintroduces the issues of contact, long-range arms, and prosthetic extension with which I began.

When the "previously scattered" sexual drives come together into a single unity, Freud says that they "cathect the ego as an object." Yet this object, he insists, has a strangely borderline status, for it stands over against the subject without being external to it. Its liminality thus repeats in spatial terms the temporal betweenness of narcissism described as an interphase wedged between autoerotism and object-choice "or, if you will," a cleaving of autoerotism from itself. Similarly, the banished brothers are described as coming together "around an envied and feared *Vorbild*" (*S.E.*13, 142). Whereas Strachey translates this term as "model," more literally it means "an image placed before or out in front." The literality of the term is worth emphasizing, since it clearly anticipates Freud's later description of the ego-ideal as an image that is not merely projected into the future but moreover placed before the subject as a model with which to identify. This projected image does not simply compensate the subject for "the lost narcissism of its childhood," as Freud sometimes claims, but instead constitutes the very medium of identity—or rather, the medium of an ongoing and conflictual process of *identification*. Understood in this way, the sons' ambivalent attitude toward this *Vorbild* foreshadows Freud's subsequent discussion of the double-edged quality of the narcissistic image in his essay of 1914.

Like the hypothesis of primary narcissism, *Totem and Taboo*'s hypothetical primal scene is certainly less easy to grasp by direct observation than to confirm by deduction from other considerations.[17] Thus, Freud attempts to reconstruct the scene by drawing on contemporary research and by attempting to build on the speculations of Atkinson, Darwin, and Robertson Smith.[18] Here, then, is Freud's famous analytic "construction":

> One day the brothers who had been driven out came together [*Eines Tages taten sich die ausgetriebenen Brüder zusammen*], killed and devoured their father and made an end of the patriarchal horde. United, they had the courage to do and succeeded in doing what would have been impossible for them individually. (Some cultural advance, perhaps command over some new weapon, had given

them a sense of superior strength.) Cannibal savages, as they were, it goes without saying that they devoured their victim as well as killing him. The violent primal father had doubtless been the feared and envied model [*Vorbild*] of each one of the company of brothers: and in the act of devouring him they accomplished their identification with him, and each one acquired a portion of his strength. The totem meal, which is perhaps mankind's earliest festival, would thus be a repetition and a commemoration of this memorable and criminal deed, which was the beginning of so many things—of social organization, of moral restrictions and of religion. (*S.E.*13, 141–42)

No sooner is this account presented than its claims to veracity are undercut. Freud immediately appends a long footnote, which concludes: "The lack of precision in what I have written in the text above, its abbreviation of the time factor and its compression of the whole subject-matter, may be attributed to the reserve necessitated by the nature of the topic. It would be as foolish to aim at exactitude in such questions as it would be unfair to insist upon certainty" (*S.E.*13, 142–43).

Freud further argues that the scene he has described need not even have actually taken place in order to produce the moral reaction that created totemism and taboo. "The mere hostile *impulse* against the father, the mere existence of a wishful *phantasy* of killing and devouring him," he says, "would have been enough" (*S.E.*13, 159–60). The distinction between committing a real act of murder and merely *wishing* to do so in this case has as little relevance as the difference between a thing and its representation in the case of magic and sorcery. That is, both the parricidal wish and the magical representation performatively act out the desires they wish to see realized rather than simply depicting or re-presenting them. As Freud states as early as 1897, "The unconscious contains no clue of reality, so that we cannot distinguish truth from fiction charged with affect." In other words, these unconscious fictions are not isolated by a neutral interval from some signified reality considered to be both temporally and logically prior to them but are instead the highly cathected, infected, and incontinent carriers of desires which they stage "as statements of fact."

Or as Freud argues at the conclusion of *Totem and Taboo*,

neurotics are so inhibited in their actions that with them "thought is a complete substitute for the deed." "Primitive men," on the other hand, are so uninhibited that "with them it is rather the deed that is, so to speak, a substitute for the thought" (*S.E.*13, 161). While the inverted symmetry of these remarks makes neurotics and so-called primitives into inverted versions of each other, this linguistic mirroring also and above all suspends the normal order of representation which places the signified before the signifier, the model before the image, and the word or thought (*Logos*) before the deed.[19] Moreover, in suspending this representational order, Freud also suspends the normal order of generational succession in which a child comes after its parent in the way that a copy takes after an original. Freud thereby also invites the reader to consider a logical, historical, and representational framework in which a moral *re*action is not merely produced by a preceding act of parricide, be it real or fantasized, but is instead cofounded and confounded with it in a movement of repetition which is ultimately and of necessity *unfounded*.

As critics have often pointed out, Freud's account of the criminal deed that was to have been "the beginning of social organization, of moral restrictions, and of religion" is patently circular in its reasoning. Thus, Lévi-Strauss criticizes the way *Totem and Taboo* describes "a vicious circle deriving the social state from events which presuppose it," while Derrida argues that the primal scene "in fact, inaugurates nothing since repentance and morality had to be possible before the crime."[20] Yet, the apparent failure of *Totem and Taboo* to account for the origin of complex social, moral, and religious institutions is nevertheless commensurate with its success in describing these institutions as the transferential and compulsively repetitive structures they will always already have been.[21] In other words, Freud's failure to provide a linear account of the origin of morality itself points to the necessity of approaching the seemingly isolated and successive moments of desire and its prohibition—the deed and its retraction—as mutually contaminating, *cofounding* impulses at once parent and child of each other.

Moreover, because it is a question here of impulses and "overvalued psychical *acts*" (*S.E.*13, 159) rather than of thoughts and their modes of expression, Freud tends to focus more on forms of verbal contamination than on the transmission of signified contents, more on performative speech acts than on constative ones. In short, his discussion comes to center increasingly on the issue of transference and, more specifically, on the way transferences act out the conflictual and ambivalent *relationship* linking an act of prohibition to a prohibited act.

It is for this reason that I insisted earlier that the Freudian notion of *Übertragung* be understood in a threefold sense: as an *übertragene Redensart,* or metaphorical way of speaking; as a form of (linguistic) contagion; and as the rehearsal of a conflict between a resistance and its overcoming. It was further argued that in focusing on the question of "contact" in this text, Freud draws attention both to forms of verbal contamination and to questions of linguistic performance. Thus, it is through his own plays on the signifier *spiel* that attention is drawn to the activities of playing, staging, and exemplifying, which serve as the infected and infectious carriers of the activities that those who perform them wish to see repeated.

The final sections of *Totem and Taboo* return to the issue of linguistic performance. Only now it is not merely a question of rehearsing activities that the participants wish to see repeated, but rather a matter of restaging conflicts they cannot help but take part in and moreover cannot avoid imparting to others. That this involuntary way of imparting psychic conflicts is related to questions of transference is suggested by a statement made toward the conclusion of *Totem and Taboo* which Bloom reads as an indication that "we have already made the crossing to the dynamics of transference."[22] There Freud says, "We may safely assume that no generation is able to conceal any of its more important mental processes from its successor. For psycho-analysis has shown us that everyone possesses in his unconscious mental activity an apparatus which enables him to interpret other people's reactions, that is, to undo the distortions which other people have imposed on the expression of their feelings" (*S.E.* 13, 159).

Freud does not spell out precisely how unconscious interpretation involves the undoing of distortions or how this occurs from one generation to the next. He merely affirms that "an unconscious understanding such as this of all the customs, ceremonies and dogmas left behind by the original relation to the father may have made it possible for later generations to take over their heritage of emotion." In contrast to this linear sense of transmission and inheritance, I have proposed a reading of "On Narcissism" in which I have tried to suggest that some of the "more important mental processes," as Freud calls them, are imparted only insofar as they remain in a certain sense uninterpreted—that is, insofar as they are perpetually *disowned as the desire of the Other* from generation to generation.

Rather than transmitting psychical contents, primal memories, or inherited dispositions, this disowned legacy transferentially restages a conflict within desire itself—at least insofar as desire will have always already been overdetermined and at odds as much with itself as with certain similarly ambivalent prohibitions. Both *Totem and Taboo* and "On Narcissism" suggest that this rehearsal of unconscious conflict will have taken place primarily on another scene—as a divided and divisive interphase out of sync with itself—and in the highly charged interspace that *is* the generational nexus. I have argued that this nexus involves an irreducible dimension of fictionality, be it that of the secondarily revised narcissistic image; the feared and envied *Vorbild* of the primal father; the "hypotheses" of primary narcissism and the primal scene; the suspension of the logico-temporal priority of model over copy, parent over child, thought over deed; or the notion of transference itself, which Freud describes as "a kind of intermediary region between illness and real life" (*S.E.* 12, 154).

Finally, as a way of indicating the transferential dimension of Freud's own text and its own infectious way of passing on that which it cannot contain as a discrete diegetic content or particular object of study, I would suggest that one follow the insistence of the signifier *teil* in the final sections of *Totem and Taboo*. Take, for example, the following passage:

> Kinship implies participation [*Anteil . . . haben*] in a common substance. It is therefore natural that it is not merely based on the fact that a man is a part [*Teil*] of his mother's substance, having been born of her and having been nourished by her milk, but that it can be acquired and strengthened by food which a man eats later and with which his body is renewed. If a man shared [*Teilte man*] a meal with his god he was expressing a conviction that they were of one substance; and he would never share [*teilte*] a meal with one whom he regarded as a stranger. (*S.E.* 13, 135)

While the signifier *teil* appears with unusual frequency in this and other passages having to do with sharing one's food or being part of a common substance, more generally its insistence draws attention to the part which remains in a sense *undigested* and unassimilable. It is the part imparted from generation to generation — or rather *between* generations — through a restaging of unconscious conflicts and a transferential disowning of the desires of the Other.

The signifier *teil* thus functions in these passages as a kind of linguistic parasite which not only inhabits key terms of Freud's discussion but in a sense also feeds on them. In the process it signifies an internal alteration of Freud's language and brings to the fore an altered sense of linguistic participation which will be discussed at length in Chapter 8.

Before concluding, then, with Freud that "In the beginning was the Deed," we should recall that Faust, in pronouncing these words which (mis)translate the opening of the Gospel according to John, himself (mis)performs a *linguistic* deed, committing a significant parapraxis which Freud's own act of citation strangely repeats. For in retranslating the opening of the Gospel, Faust not only reads, writes, and narrates aloud what he is doing but, in speaking the words "In the beginning was the Deed," also seems inadvertently to summon the devil himself onto the scene. Although Mephistopheles had in a sense already made his entrance disguised as a poodle at the very beginning of the *Studierzimmer* episode, it is only Faust's (mis)speech that at this point works like an ironical exorcism to free him from the canine shape he was initially forced to assume.

Insofar as literary citation is itself a kind of summons, Freud's repetition of Faust's words cannot help but participate in the diabolically sorcerous parapraxis to which it alludes. In his own way, then, Freud summons the devil to appear — or least to appear to appear — at the pointedly inconclusive conclusion of *Totem and Taboo.* As though conjured by the very last words of the text, the devil enters as the text closes. Never quite closed in or shut out, never appearing as such, Mephistopheles appears spellbound at the threshold of Freud's text — once again, it seems, in need of "the sharp tooth of a rat [*eines Rattenzahns*]" to cut him free. It is thus to the devil summoned by Freud's citation of *Faust* that we leave the last word, which, needless to say, is also in its own way a first one:

Faust

> You call yourself a part, yet whole you stand in view?
> [*Du nennst dich einen Teil, und stehst doch ganz vor mir?*]

Mephistopheles

> I speak a modest truth for you.
> Whereas your Man, that microcosmic fool,
> Regards himself an integer as a rule,
> I am but part of the part that at first was all
> [*Bescheidne Wahrheit sprech' ich dir.*
> *Wenn sich der Mensch, die kleine Narrenwelt,*
> *Gewöhnlich für ein Ganzes hält—*
> *Ich bin ein Teil des Teils, der anfangs alles war*]

The Sense of an *Unding*

Kafka, Ovid, and the
Misfits of Metamorphosis

Is impossibility, then, a stone wall?
Dostoevsky, *Notes from Underground*

In a letter to his friend Max Brod, written in June 1921, Franz
Kafka placed his literary production under the sign of a fourfold
impossibility: "the impossibility of not writing, the impossibility
of writing German, the impossibility of writing differently," and
finally even "the impossibility of writing" itself.[1] As other parts of
the letter make clear, the sense of impossibility that is intoned with
a kind of percussive insistence in these lines conveys more than a
feeling of frustration. For while the writer may indeed be confronted by obstacles at every turn, the impossibilities mentioned
here are by no means mere impediments; they are instead, as we
shall see, the very twists, turns, and interlocking holds of an ineluctible double bind. Each mention of a particular "impossibility"
is nothing more or less than an attempt to seize an inextricable
knot by one of its constituent threads, an attempt to display an
overdetermined and ever-mutating problem in a number of its
determinate permutations.

This problem, it should be stressed, is not primarily psychological in nature—at least not in this case and certainly not in the
more restricted, personal, intrapsychic sense of the term. Indeed,
Kafka's enumeration of the manifold impossibilities of writing is
prompted by reflections on the current state of German-Jewish *linguistic* relations and, more specifically, on a particular mode of linguistic performance known as *mauscheln*. "This *mauscheln*," he
says, "taken in the broadest sense, the only sense in which it should
be taken, consists in a bumptious, tacit, or painfully self-critical

appropriation of another's property, even though there is no evidence of a single solecism. . . . It is an organic compound of bookish German and pantomime."[2]

Throughout the letter, Kafka is exercised by the question of why Jewish writers should be "so irresistibly drawn" to the German language. Gradually, he is led to formulate a response that comes close enough to Freudian theories of generational conflict to elicit a defensive gesture on his part.

> Psychoanalysis lays stress on the father-complex and many find the concept intellectually fruitful. In this case I prefer another version, where the issue revolves around the father's Jewishness. Most young Jews who began to write German wanted to leave Jewishness behind them, and their fathers approved of this, but vaguely (this vagueness was what was outrageous to them). But with their hind legs they were still glued [*klebten sie noch:* they still adhered] to the father's Jewishness and with their waving front legs they found no new ground. The ensuing despair became their inspiration.

In this magnificent image of generational conflict, the Jewish sons are captured rearing their front legs, suspended in the very gesture of revolt. And while this prolonged suspension perhaps potentiates the uprising movement of rebellion, it also conveys a sense of flailing filial impotence. Such gestures, I would suggest, define Kafka's own four-legged writing and its inspiration born of despair. "An inspiration," Kafka continues,

> as honorable as any other, but on closer examination showing certain sad peculiarities. First of all, the product of [the sons'] despair could not be German literature, though outwardly it seemed to be so. They existed among three impossibilities, which I just happen to call linguistic impossibilities. It is simplest to call them that. But they might also be called something entirely different. These are: The impossibility of not writing, the impossibility of writing German, the impossibility of writing differently. One might also add a fourth impossibility, the impossibility of writing.

With the enumeration of these impossibilities, Kafka's letter ceases to move forward in a progressive, linear fashion. Instead, as was suggested earlier, it appears to falter at every step as though mired in the very sense of despair and futile necessity it speaks about. In such circumstances the only possible step to be taken, the only way to gain time and room to maneuver, the only way to negotiate the double binds articulated here is, paradoxically, to write. Thus, he adds a comment that, it seems, could only have been advanced in the suspension of a parenthetical aside: "(since the despair could not be assuaged by writing, is an enemy both of life *and* of writing, writing is here only a moratorium [*ein Provisorium*], as for someone who is writing his will shortly before he hangs himself—a moratorium that may well last a whole life)" (trans. mod.).

Like Kafka's own last-minute proviso appended to the preceding list of linguistic impossibilities, "writing" here functions as the very spacing—the indispensable temporizing movement—of deferral.

Getting One's Bearings: Benjamin on Kafka

While it is doubtful that Walter Benjamin ever had access to this letter, his essay "Franz Kafka: On the Tenth Anniversary of His Death" focuses on just this connection between writing, dying, and dilatory expedients. To do justice to the complexity of Benjamin's essay would obviously require a separate chapter.[3] In what follows I propose merely to treat those aspects of his text that bear on the issues mentioned above. Such an approach, however, is complicated by the fact that Benjamin's essay is an "interpretation" of Kafka in both the hermeneutic and performative senses of the term. His essay must be read both as a theoretical discourse, whose primary aim is to elucidate and unfold the complexities of the texts it treats, and also as a transferential repetition and creative displacement of the stresses and gestures of those texts.

Benjamin himself alludes to the necessity of such an approach when speaking about the "unfolding [*Entfaltung*] of the parable" in Kafka. "It is the reader's pleasure," he says, "to smooth it out so that he has the meaning on the palm of his hand [*so daß ihre Bedeutung auf der flachen Hand liegt*]" (122).[4] Benjamin's own pleasure, by contrast, lies elsewhere: not on the palm of the hand, where differences are ironed out and everything appears, as it were, as clear as day (*auf der Hand*), but rather in the indelible creases of the palm, whose mysteries are reserved for the skilled chiromancer. In reading the flat of the hand, Benjamin suggests, it is necessary not only to trace the furrowed lines of the palm but also and above all to follow the silent writing—the *gestural movements*—of the hands themselves. This mute language is compared in his essay to Chinese theater, "one of the most significant functions" of which, he says, "is to dissolve happenings into their gestic components" (120). As though to emphasize the gestural twists and turns of this graphic art—whose adverse effects are legible in the very squirming of those written upon—Benjamin links it in section 3 of his essay to a kind of ornamental *writing on the back* (such as one finds in "The Penal Colony") rather than to more traditional modes of handwriting. If, as he says of this writing, "it is thus the back on which it lies, the back on which everything depends [*Es ist also der Rücken, dem es aufliegt*] and it was always this way with Kafka [*Und ihm liegt es bei Kafka seit jeher auf*]" (133), the stress here lies not only on the back but also on the verb *aufliegen*. In other words, to say that everything lies on the back rather than on the palm of the hand, as clear as day, is to turn the seemingly self-evident gesture of meaningful presentation back on itself, reposing it as a question and interrogating the very gesture by which meaning presents itself as the smoothing out of a complication, the elucidation of an enigma, or the parabolic illustration of a truth. Implicated in this movement of reversion, the reader is thus invited to turn back on Benjamin's own text the question it poses to the would-be expositors of Kafka's parables: "But do we have the doctrine which [these] parables interpret and K.'s postures and the gestures of his animals clarify? It does not exist; all we can say is that here and there we have an allusion to it. Kafka might have said that these are relics transmitting the doctrine, although we could regard them just as well as precursors preparing the doctrine" (122).

Whether it is because they come too early or too late, Kafka's parables—like Benjamin's essay—fail to present any doctrine. Rather than dissolving into a semantically transparent means of instruction, they remain cloudy and opaque.[5] As Werner Hamacher has observed,

> The mark of failure in Kafka's prose is what Benjamin calls on three different occasions the "cloudy spot" [*wolkige Stelle*] in his parables. In connection with the Potemkin anecdote toward the beginning of his essay he writes, "The enigma which beclouds it is Kafka's enigma." Later, he writes about the parable "Before the Law,"

"The reader who encountered it in 'A Country Doctor' may have been struck by the cloudy spot in its interior." And in the third section of his essay, Benjamin again takes up this strange metaphor: "For Kafka, there was always something that could only be grasped in the gesture. And this gesture, which he did not understand, constitutes the cloudy region of the parables [*die wolkige Stelle der Parabeln*]. From it emerges Kafka's literature."

Curiously enough, it is precisely by means of these "cloudy spots," which obscure more than they clarify, that Benjamin gets his bearings in Kafka's text. Through them, he is drawn not into heretofore uncharted regions but rather more deeply and ineluctibly into the very question of *bearings* itself; this term, it should be stressed, is to be understood in this context not only in the sense of a fixed point of orientation but also in the related sense of a supportive, weight-bearing structure.[6] As a way of gesturing to the fact that it is this particular question on which the entire essay bears, the text opens by invoking the stationary figure of Atlas shouldering the globe and closes with the moving image of a man on horseback: "Whether it is a man or a horse is no longer so important, if only the burden is removed from the back" (140). The strategic placement of these framing figures at the outset and end of Benjamin's text seems to suggest that the essay does not so much *pose* the question of bearings as *mobilize* it. The shift is worth emphasizing, since what is at stake is a particular volatilization of the question. Once set in motion, it is no longer posed in the static oppositional terms of bearer and borne. Instead, as it takes flight, there is a slight but decisive shift in accent from the back upon which everything is said to lie and depend to the pointedly ambiguous verb *aufliegen,* which itself begins to sound more like *auffliegen:* to fly up; such shifts are in turn accompanied by a gradual blurring of the distinction between Atlas and the globe he is supposed to carry. Mobilized, this spinning orb now sweeps its bearer up in its revolutionary flight through space. It is no doubt for this reason that Benjamin is drawn to the world of the "assistants" in Kafka, whom he describes as "falling outside the circle" of the family.[7] "None has a firm place in the world, firm inalienable outlines. There is not one that is not either rising or falling, none that is not trading qualities with its enemy or neighbor, none that has not completed its period of time and yet is unripe, none that is not deeply exhausted and yet is only at the beginning of a long existence. To speak of any order or hierarchy is impossible here" (117).

Here again it appears that as the question of bearings becomes increasingly volatile, imposing itself more massively and with an ever-increasing sense of urgency, identities come unhinged and in their place clouds of unstable, mercurial figures begin to form.[8] As these clouds gather, the question of bearings itself becomes more nebulous. Yet, as was stated earlier, it is paradoxically by means of these "cloudy spots" that Benjamin orients himself in Kafka's text—orients himself, that is, in the direction of a demanding revolutionary practice of perpetual disorientation. Needless to say, there is more to this practice than simply losing one's bearings in an otherwise stable structure, for it is a practice that also and perhaps above all involves listening to the stresses and accents, the props, supports, and weight-bearing structures of Kafka's text as they shift about and give way to unsettling movements of displacement.

With Benjamin's "interpretation" of Kafka as our guide, I would now like to return to the relationship of writing, death, and dilatory expedients with which I began and then move eventually to a reinterpretation of Kafka's *Metamorphosis,* which I propose to read as a singular metamorphic dislocation not only of Ovid's *Metamorphoses* but, moreover, of the very notion of metamorphosis.

Managing a Stagnant Economy

In section 3 of his essay, Benjamin observes that "in the stories which Kafka left us, narrative art regains the significance it had in the mouth of Scheherazade: to postpone the future [*das Kommende hinauszuschieben*]" (129). Before continuing this citation, it is not irrelevant to note that Benjamin here takes up the question of postponement as a way of introducing the life and death issues involved in the writing and execution of Kafka's own last will and testament—a document that, as is well known, was to have sentenced his unpublished literary offspring to destruction.[9] Benjamin continues:

> In *The Trial* postponement is the hope of the accused man only if the proceedings do not gradually turn into the judgement. The patriarch himself is to benefit by postponement, even though he may

have to give up his place in tradition for it. "I could conceive [Kafka writes] of another Abraham — to be sure, he would never get to be a patriarch or even an old-clothes dealer — an Abraham who would be prepared to satisfy the demand for sacrifice immediately, with the promptness of a waiter, but would be unable to bring it off because he cannot get away [*weil er von zuhause nicht fort kann*], being indispensable; the household needs him, there is always something or other to take care of, the house is never ready; but without having his house ready, without having something to fall back on, he cannot leave — this the Bible also realized, for it says: "He set his house in order." (129)

While Benjamin allows this passage to speak for itself, what draws him to it is apparently the connection made here between the house Abraham is preparing to leave and the economy (from the Greek *oikos:* house) of deferral which provisionally shelters the patriarch's offspring from the execution of the death sentence he is prepared to carry out. Here, as Benjamin implies, it is not only the judgment but "The Judgment" that is adjourned through the postponements of *The Trial,* through a singular recitation of the "trial" of Abraham. In Benjamin's reading of Kafka, deferral (*Aufschub*) thus seems to have two related components: first and more obviously, it involves a process of temporal postponement which, however, "may well last a whole life," as Kafka writes to Brod of the man sitting down to write his will shortly before hanging himself; second, and perhaps more importantly, it implies a suspension of narratives and narrative citations — in short, of *récits* — into and through one another.[10] To put it a little differently, deferral here involves a suspension within narrative of elements that effectively interrupt and relay each other in a way that upsets the order of the house, postpones closure, and manages a stagnating economy.

It is this very particular sense of stagnation as deferral and suspension that leads Benjamin to assert that Kafka's "novels are set in a swamp [*spielen in einer Sumpfwelt*]" (130). This remark is justified not only by the observation that "Kafka did not consider the age in which he lived as an advance over the beginnings of time" (130) but moreover by the way in which the very sense of narrative and historical progress is altered in Kafka's writings. Curiously enough, evidence of this alteration is to be found both in passages

Benjamin cites from Kafka *and* in the odd narrative progression of his own text. Consider, then, the following sequence, which is adduced in support of Benjamin's claim that what is forgotten is not merely absent but rather is *actual* by virtue of this very oblivion: "An experience deeper than that of an average person can make contact with it. 'I have experience,' we read in one of Kafka's earliest notes, 'and I am not joking when I say that it is a seasickness on dry land.' It is no accident that the first 'Meditation' was made on a swing. And Kafka does not tire of expressing himself on the fluctuating [*schwankende*] nature of experiences. Each gives way and mingles with its opposite" (130).

Is it unreasonable to suggest that the final words of this citation refer both to the fluctuating experiences mentioned in the preceding sentence and to the very movement of the passage itself? Does the text, in other words, at this point stage a mode of experience which, because it is closer to the swamp of oblivion than to the ordered progress of conscious thought, actually present itself in a different narrative manner? As though moving through a number of determinate alterations of a muddled and indeterminate relationship, the passage proceeds from a particular experience of instability described as a seasickness on dry land, to an experience set in the shifting frame of a swing, to finally a reflection on the unstable, fluctuating nature of experiences. Rather than providing a sense of narrative progression, the passage has a way of turning back on itself as each momentary consolidation of this swamplike experience gives way to, mingles with, and becomes mired in the others.

Such a reading is supported by Benjamin's own subsequent analysis of the following lines from Kafka's "Knock at the Manor Gate," which follow directly on the heels of the passage cited above: "With my sister I was passing [*kam . . . vorüber*] the gate of a great house on our way home. I don't remember whether she knocked on the gate out of mischief or in a fit of absent-mindedness, or merely shook her fist at it and did not knock at all" (130).

Benjamin comments that the "very possibility of the third alternative [*Vorgang*] puts the other two [*die vorangehenden*], which at first seemed harmless, in a different light. It is from the swampy soil of such experiences that Kafka's female characters rise. They are swamp creatures" (130). Not only is much of the wit of Benjamin's commentary lost in Zohn's otherwise competent translation, its very point is obscured. For just as Kafka's text is concerned with what transpires as the narrator and his sister proceed past a particular gate, Benjamin is interested in the steps involved in a certain logical procedure. Slipping from the noun *Vorgang* to the etymologically related verb *vorangehen* in this passage, Benjamin playfully suggests that the footing gets especially slippery when the "alternative" — or more literally, the *procedure* — mentioned in the third place (*des an der dritten Stelle erwähnten Vorgangs*) allows the *preceding* ones (*die vorangehenden*) to *step forth* in a different light (*in ein anderes Licht treten*). What Benjamin refers to as the "swampy soil of such experiences" is precisely the absence of progress here, the inability of the reader to move through the competing versions mentioned and establish some order of priority, plausibility, or sense of temporal succession. So long as one is unable to order the alternatives presented in terms of a rational sequence, this swampy soil will remain a logical quagmire. Similarly, the swamp creatures who emerge from this soil are autochthonous heroines only insofar as they spring from a promiscuous mingling of opposites giving way to each other. Or as Benjamin suggests, they rise out of "the dark, deep womb, the scene of the mating 'whose untrammeled voluptuousness,' to quote Bachofen, 'is hateful to the pure forces of heavenly light and which justifies the term used by Arnobius, *luteae voluptates*'" (131).

Elsewhere, Benjamin remarks, "Not to find one's way in a city may well be uninteresting and banal. It requires ignorance — nothing more. But to lose oneself in a city — as one loses oneself in a forest — that calls for quite a different schooling."[11] If losing one's footing in the muddle of experiences described above is itself to metamorphose an uninteresting and commonplace sense of stagnation into a creatively altered mode of experience, one must learn how to proceed differently through logical alternatives that so obviously contradict and exclude one another. Felman's reading of the knotty figure of the dream navel in Freud, discussed in Chapter 3, and my own discussion of the kettle logic of dream censorship in Chapter 2 should prepare us to deal with these alternatives as threads of experience which run into and through one another in such a way as simultaneously to implicate, displace, and "unfold" each other as they go.

Learning how to trace the passage of these alternatives through one another certainly mires one more deeply in the *Sumpfwelt* of Kafka's novels. Yet, it also enables one to see how Kafka, who, as Benjamin says, "could understand things only in the form of a gesture," used such gestures to break through stable frames of reference into more fluid, unfamiliar spaces. Consider in this regard the unusually violent language Benjamin employs when describing the power of the gesture in Kafka: "Just as this bell [described by Werner Kraft in a commentary on 'A Fratricide'], which is too loud for a doorbell, rings out toward heaven, the gestures of Kafka's figures are too powerful [*zu durchschlagend*] for our accustomed surroundings [*die gewohnte Umwelt*] and break out into wider areas [*brechen in eine geräumigere ein*]" (121).

A little further down, Benjamin adds: "What Kafka could see least of all was the *gestus*. Each gesture is an event—one might even say, a drama—in itself. The stage on which this drama takes place is the World Theater which opens up toward heaven. On the other hand, this heaven is only background; to explore it according to its own laws would be like framing the painted backdrop of the stage and hanging it in a picture gallery. Like El Greco, Kafka tears open the sky behind every gesture [*reißt hinter jeder Gebärde—wie Greco—den Himmel auf*]" (121).

This paragraph then concludes: Kafka "divests [*nimmt*] the human gesture of its traditional supports [*die überkommenen Stützen*] and then has a subject for reflection without end [*die kein Ende nimmt*]" (122). As the reader will have noticed, in each of these three passages the violence is directed against some kind of support—be it the stable, orienting frame of familiar surroundings, the props and painted backdrop of the stage, or the traditional mainstays of the human gesture. In doing violence to these structures, which are apparently as burdensome as they are weight bearing, Kafka's gestures break—or rather tamper—with the very laws of gravity. They provisionally suspend these laws and, in doing so, open a different kind of space, one whose dimensions, Benjamin implies, can be measured only in negative and relativistic terms as particular movements of dislocation, distortion, and disorientation. The violence associated with these gestures is thus double-edged: for the very gesture that "breaks into wider areas," "tears open the sky," and "takes away traditional supports" is also the one that enables Kafka to grope his way in the unbearable lightness of such nebulous regions. I would suggest that it is Benjamin's incomparable feel for the tentativeness of these gestures that leads him to the paradoxical observation that "for Kafka, there was always something that could only be grasped in the gesture. And this gesture which he did not understand constitutes the cloudy part of the parables" (129).

The Metamorphosis

The gestures of Kafka's text thus provide a very particular sense of disorientation. For while they perhaps help one to lose one's bearings, they also supply in their stead — and in lieu of more familiar modes of cognition — a grasp that is not that of understanding, a grasp that instead dislocates understanding from within and makes of this creative *misunderstanding* a means by which to get a different hold on things. Nowhere in Kafka's work does this sense of disorientation or the question of bearings in general make itself felt with greater urgency than in the text of *The Metamorphosis*. Kafka's story abruptly begins with the famous words, "When Gregor Samsa woke up one morning from unsettling dreams [*aus unruhigen Träumen*], he found himself changed in his bed into a monstrous vermin" (3).[12] As though to emphasize the primacy of questions of orientation in this text, the calming effect and sense of reassurance which recognizably familiar surroundings may provide, and even the power of such surroundings to dissipate the hazy sense of inquietude left in the wake of unsettling dreams, Kafka draws an explicit contrast in the second paragraph between Gregor's dreams — his *unruhige Träume* — and the "room, a regular human bedroom, a little on the small side" which "lay tranquilly [*ruhig*] between the four familiar walls" (3).

Whereas readers of *The Metamorphosis* generally tend to focus on the fate of its central character; his sudden transformation from man to animal; and the altered relationship of this "vermin" to his profession, family, and self, I believe that before taking up such weighty issues it is necessary to dwell first on the more mundane matter of the text's physical setting. The stakes of such preliminary reflections are considerable. For, as I hope to demonstrate, it is only by orienting oneself in relation to the shifting spatial and temporal coordinates of Kafka's story that one can begin to discern another process of metamorphosis, one in which the very notion of transformation is metamorphosed from within—without, however, being changed into something else. It is this internal dislocation of metamorphosis, I will argue, that emerges only through an examination of the manner in which the seemingly tranquil setting of Kafka's text is repeatedly unsettled and upset. To appreciate the ways in which Kafka's singular *Metamorphosis* effects a displacement of more familiar notions of transformation and mobilizes the resources of metamorphic tradition only in order to deplete and divert them, it may be useful at this point to compare certain aspects of his text to Ovid's *Metamorphoses*.

In Ovid one finds no one definitive account of origins or sources. Indeed, precisely because there are so many competing creation stories presented in his text, it is impossible to find one string by which to pull all the others. In the absence of any single guiding thread, the reader is left to wind his or her way through stories of intricately woven tapestries, delicate webs, and sturdy nets. In lieu of any one cosmic weaver, there is only an incessant interlacing of connections, an endless spinning of yarns, and a fabulously self-reflexive fabrication of texts. Weaving mythical narratives into and through one another, Ovid's *Metamorphoses* raise and answer questions of motivation and causality by telling self-legitimating stories; that is, they present narratives that, in accounting for the existence of gods, mortals, and natural phenomena, also account for themselves. They contain their self-justification in their own telling—not in any one narrative but instead in the overall interconnectedness of narratives, in the fabric of their mutual and ever-mutating relations. Such a textual production as Ovid's *Metamorphoses,* or rather such processes of textual autoproduction, underwrite their own birth certificate as authorship and authority become effects the text itself produces.

In contrast to the plurality, heterogeneity, and interconnectedness of Ovid's *Metamorphoses,* the title of Kafka's text speaks of metamorphosis in the singular. As was noted earlier, its first line describes how a certain Gregor Samsa "woke up one morning from unsettling dreams, and found himself changed in his bed into a monstrous vermin" (3). In describing Gregor's change so immediately, Kafka seems to drain his metamorphosis of all the pathos and drama that typify Ovid's metamorphoses. Here it seems as if the metamorphosis—both Kafka's and Gregor's—had already come to an abrupt end by the conclusion of the first sentence.[13]

Whereas in Ovid transformations occur for some particular reason, Kafka's *Metamorphosis* simply begins with the inexplicable and unmotivated transformation of Gregor Samsa into a monstrous vermin. Yet, who is this person, and what indeed is a monstrous vermin? While some critics have attempted to domesticate this monstrosity by describing it in positive terms either as a gigantic cockroach or as an enormous dung beetle—Nabokov even tried to draw a picture of it in his essay on Kafka—the German text significantly calls it an *ungeheures Ungeziefer*.[14] As critics have often noticed, both terms begin with the negation *un-*. Moreover, unlike the detachable nose of Gogol's famous story, this prefix cannot be separated from the terms to which it adheres, since in German there is no such thing as a *geheuer* or a *Geziefer*.[15] Removing the negative prefixes from these signifiers does not restore them to some prior positive form, nor does doubling these negatives by combining them in the phrase *ungeheures Ungeziefer* yield any stable positive identity. Instead, the product of such a combination is only a kind of redoubled negativity. Etymologically, the noun *Ungeziefer* derives from a term formerly used to designate an unclean animal unsuited for sacrifice.[16] The adjective *ungeheuer*, which is rendered in English translations of *The Metamorphosis* as "gigantic" or "monstrous," also has the sense of something boundless, enormous, outrageous, and uncanny.[17]

Just as it is a little too easy to say that in rendering Kafka's *ungeheures Ungeziefer* as "monstrous vermin" much is lost in translation, it is equally misleading to imply that German is the only language that could accommodate such a doubly negative monstrosity.[18] For if we understand anything about Kafka's *Metamorphosis,* it is that this *Unding,* this monstrosity (formerly a traveling salesman), is not at home especially when in its own home— among family and familiar surroundings. It is significant in this regard that Gregor literally cannot even speak in his own mother tongue. Instead, his thoughts are communicated only through the medium of a narrator, about whom much remains to be said.

It seems, then, that this *ungeheures Ungeziefer* may be lost in translation even before it is explicitly translated from one positive language to another. Translation in a sense only redoubles its negativity. Recall that whenever Gregor tries to communicate directly, without the intervention of a narrator, translator, or interpreter, his voice is almost immediately engulfed in static noise—"as if from below, an insistent distressed chirping intruded, which left the clarity of his words intact only for a moment really, before so badly garbling them as they carried, that no one could be sure if he had heard right" (5).

Lost in translation, always in need of an interpreter, always a mistranslation in need of retranslation, the double negative that Gregor has become may itself be a creature *lost in metamorphosis*.[19] For just as there are unclean animals unsuited for sacrifice, so too perhaps are there monstrosities unfit for metamorphosis—for example, monstrous vermin that prey on the host body of a text or narrative contents that cannot be contained within the borders of a frame narrative. What I am suggesting is that certain monstrous forms of parasitism and incontinence here inhabit the very notion of metamorphosis and transform it from within. Yet, as was suggested earlier, they do so not by changing it into something else but instead by corrupting and corroding it. Like Gregor's fasting, this corrosion at the center of metamorphosis consumes and displaces the text from the inside out. One might consider in this regard the following entry from Kafka's diary written approximately ten months before he set to work on *The Metamorphosis:*

> When it became clear in my organism that writing was the most productive direction for my being to take, everything rushed in that direction and left empty all those abilities which were directed toward the joys of sex, eating, drinking, philosophical reflection and above all music. I atrophied [*magerte ab*] in all these directions. This was necessary because the totality of my strengths was so slight that only collectively could they even halfway serve the purpose of my writing. Naturally, I did not find this purpose independently and consciously, it found itself, and is now interfered with only by the office, but that interferes with it completely. . . . My development is now complete and, so far as I can see, there is nothing left to sacrifice; I need only throw my work in the office out of this complex in order to begin my real life.[20]

In *The Metamorphosis,* it is the verminous Gregor Samsa who grows thin through fasting. As his body parasitically feeds on itself, it loses volume and flattens out. More generally, it may be observed that in the course of the narrative the focus also shifts from three dimensions to two: from the interior space of Gregor's "regular human room, a little on the small side lying tranquilly between the four familiar walls" to the two-dimensional space of the walls themselves. In other words, as Gregor begins to climb the walls and ceiling, the emphasis shifts from voluminous interiors to flat, planar surfaces. In order to appreciate the full significance of these shifts, it is important to bear in mind the ways in which other related issues cluster around these coordinates. For example, it is no accident that at the beginning of the story there is a close relationship between the "four familiar walls" used by Gregor to get his bearings in space and the quarter-hour divisions of the clock by which he locates himself in time. This carefully calibrated coordination of time and space at the outset of the story is best captured in the numerous references to trains (where distance is but a relation of speed and time) and railway timetables (which, as his mother says, Gregor studies even on his days off). The precision with which these relationships may be measured and translated into each other is at this point also linked to the sharpness of the narrative eye. For instance, when describing Gregor's numerous little legs, which never stopped waving in all directions and which he could not control in the least, the narrator adds: "If he wanted to bend one [*Wollte er eines einmal einknicken*], the first thing that happened was that it stretched itself out; and if he finally succeeded in getting this leg to do what he wanted, all the others in the meantime, as if set free, began to work in the most intensely painful agitation" (7).

Here the futile effort to gain control over each individual leg and to coordinate its movements with those of the others is reflected on the level of the signifier through an emphatic repetition of the morpheme *ein*. As though sounding out the stresses and strains of individuation, the *ein* in *Beinchen* here insists in the phrase *Wollte er eines einmal einknicken*. Such details would hardly be worth mentioning were it not for the fact that, later on, the very same signifier is repeated in terms used to describe a movement in the opposite direction: a movement in which oppositions are neutralized as sharp contours blur and everything fades into a hazy shade of gray. This movement is summed up in a vision Gregor has at his window of "a desert [*eine Einöde*] where the gray sky and the gray earth were indistinguishably fused [*sich vereinigten*]" (29).[21]

What is important to bear in mind is the way issues of depth perception—in particular Gregor's ability to see things in relief as they stand out individually from their surroundings—are related to the matter of Gregor's own physical volume ("his domelike brown belly") and especially to his position relative to *his* surroundings—both physical and familial—at the outset of the story. It is not by chance, for instance, that Gregor's mother, father, and sister—each standing at a different door of his centrally located bedroom—communicate with each other through his space. Gregor may at this point be unable to take part in the conversation, but he is still the principal object of discussion, just as his room is literally the medium through which communication takes place.[22]

By contrast, when Gregor dies, his body is described as being "completely flat and dry" (55). This literal loss of volume reflects not only an atrophying interest in the world outside but also a decrease in the attention paid to him by others. Moreover, it accentuates an evacuation of the very opposition between inside and outside as the focus increasingly shifts to the tenuous borderland of writing and to a different, less stable articulation of spatio-temporal relationships. Here it should be recalled that even before Gregor is positively attracted to flat, planar surfaces, before he distracts himself by crawling over the walls and ceiling of his room, he begins to experience three-dimensional space—both the volume of his room and that of his own body—as oppressive. Thus, toward the beginning of the second section, the narrator describes in a kind of free indirect style how "the empty high-ceilinged room in which he was forced to lie flat on the floor made him nervous, without his being able to tell why—since it was, after all, the room in which he had lived for the past five years—and turning half unconsciously and not without a slight feeling of shame, he scuttled under the couch where, although his back was a little crushed and he could not raise his head any more, he immediately felt very comfortable" (23).

Gregor's agoraphobia, which one might describe as an anxiety about being in a voluminous, open space, is accompanied by a significant decrease in his field of vision: "from day to day he saw things even a short distance away less and less distinctly; the hospital opposite, which he used to curse because he saw so much of it, was now completely beyond his range of vision, and if he had not been positive that he was living in Charlotte Street—a quiet but still very much a city street—he might have believed that he was looking out of his window into a desert where the gray sky and the gray earth were indistinguishably fused" (29).

One can almost picture the horizons of visibility closing in on Gregor here as his myopia increases.[23] It is important to note, however, that the shallowing of his depth of vision and the weakening of his sense of sight is to some degree compensated for by a hyper-developed sense of smell and touch. More important, and something typical of Kafka's text, is the fact that Gregor's decreasing capacity to see shapes clearly and distinctly is accompanied by the increasing dissolution of his own shape. Long before his bodily space is literally violated when he is kicked through doorways or bombarded with apples, Gregor's space is defined not simply by the palpable contours of his body but by everything with which he comes into contact. Thus, for example, his sister does not dare touch the utensils used for feeding him. When, at the beginning of section 2, she retrieves a bowl of milk from his room, she "picks it up immediately—not with her hands of course but with a rag" (24). This touching taboo also extends to Gregor's very name, which is almost never used to contact him, and which is later replaced by the pronoun "it" when his sister exclaims, "I won't pronounce the name of my brother in front of this monster, and so all I say is: we have to try to get rid of it" (51). In short, as Gregor becomes more dependent upon his antennae and sense of touch, the taboo against touching *him* extends to almost everything with which he has come into contact. Such things can only be touched indirectly, if at all.

It is important to note, moreover, that what Gregor loses in clarity, depth of vision, and volume, he gains in extension and two-dimensional spread. In order to give him room to spread out and range across the floor and walls, his sister even attempts to remove all the furniture from his room. What comes increasingly to define Gregor are not so much his palpable physical contours or proper name, but everything he has touched and thereby contaminated. The dissolution of the protagonist as a particular three-dimensional character might thus be described as a movement from the space of Gregor, that is, his literal physical body, to Gregor's space, his room and whatever he comes in contact with, to finally something like Gregorian space, which might be defined as the *way* people move through space and the ways in which they posture and position themselves.[24] Gregorian space is defined not by *where* things are positioned but instead by certain gestures—by how they "assume the position," so to speak. Taking one example among many, consider the following description of Gregor's father. Notice in particular the upward mobility of the passage.

> Was this the same man who in the old days used to lie wearily buried in bed when Gregor left on a business trip; who greeted him on his return in the evening, sitting in his bathrobe in the armchair, who actually had difficulty getting to his feet but as a sign of joy only lifted up his arms; and who, on rare occasions when the whole family went out for a walk, on a few Sundays in June and on the major holidays, used to shuffle along with great effort between Gregor and his mother, who were slow walkers themselves, always a little more slowly than they, wrapped in his old overcoat, always carefully planting down his crutch-handled cane, and, when he wanted to say something, nearly always stood still and assembled his escort around him? Now, however, he was holding himself very erect, dressed in a tight-fitting blue uniform with gold buttons . . . ; above the high stiff collar of the jacket his heavy chin protruded.

And a little further down:

> He probably did not know himself what he had in mind; still he lifted his feet unusually high off the floor, and Gregor staggered at the gigantic size of the soles of his boots. (37–38)

Here the erect father stands in stark contrast to the totally prostrate son.[25] The two could not be farther apart, nor could their contrary fates be more graphically described. Nevertheless, for all the father's apparent superiority, he still stands, paradoxically, under the shadow of what lies below him. Certainly the roles have been reversed between father and son, but the *terms* of the opposition remain the same and are still Gregorian.[26] As if to hint at this state of affairs, the erect father in a way seems to be held up only by virtue of a kind of exoskeleton not unlike Gregor's own armorlike exterior. Not only is he corseted by his tight-fitting blue uniform, but the only thing keeping his "protruding chin" up is the high stiff collar of his jacket.[27]

Thus, as Gregor literally gets flatter and lower, his existence in the family and his influence over it become more insidious and indirect, more nebulous and diffuse. His reduction to the pronoun "it," while certainly depersonalizing him in the extreme, at the same time assures, or at least confirms, his absorption into — and contamination of — the very language of the text. Like a fresco that fades into the wall on which it was painted, so too does Gregor's image fade into the surface of the narration. And just as his weakened vision and insomnia diminish his ability to differentiate dark from light as everything turns into an indistinct and monotonous "desert where the gray sky and the gray earth were indistinguishably fused" (29), and just as Gregor's initial attempts to e-nun-ci-ate clearly fail as his words are engulfed in a "persistent horrible twittering sqeak . . . which . . . rose up reverberating around them to destroy their sense," so too are the black islands of print in a sense absorbed into the white background of the page. In short, as the spacing shifts, the monstrous vermin becomes increasingly illegible as a particular unique mark or distinct unit of meaning. He or "it" instead merges into the walls of the text, the flatness of the page, and the surface of everyday language.

Finally, just as Gregor flattens out as he cleaves to the two-dimensional surfaces described in the text, so too does the text itself metamorphose into a wall. It is no coincidence in this context that the German word for wall, *eine Wand,* is at the center of the word for metamorphosis, *eine Verwandlung.* In the context of all the shifts from three to two dimensions which we have been following — *and only in light of these displacements* — can one read the title a little differently: as a becoming-wall of metamorphosis. This sounding out of the *Wand* in *Verwandlung* is emblematic of the way Kafka's text metamorphoses metamorphosis — not by turning it into something else, but by dislocating it from within, exposing the resounding wall in its midst.

Music of the Masonry

To readers of Ovid, this becoming-wall of metamorphosis should come as no surprise. For, as is well known, at the very center of

The Metamorphoses, in the eighth book of a text consisting of fifteen books, Ovid places the story of another great wall, namely the convoluted enclosure of the Minoan labyrinth.[28] Returning to inspect the walls of book 8, one finds, in addition to the maze designed by Daedalus on the isle of Crete, the musical walls of the city of Alcathous to which King Minos had laid siege. Ovid describes these ramparts as follows: "Winged victory had long been hovering between the two sides, undecided. There was a tower belonging to the king, built on to those tuneful city walls where Leto's son, they say, laid down his lyre, so that its music was imparted to the masonry. Often in the days of peace Nisus' daughter had been in the habit of climbing up there, and flinging pebbles against the stones to make them ring."[29]

Without dwelling on these melodious walls or the various ways in which they continue to resonate throughout book 8, one might nevertheless recall how Scylla, Nisus' daughter, purportedly out of love for Minos, decides to open up the city gates to him, instead of waiting for his military strength to breach the city's fortifications. The obvious sexual imagery is made even more explicit later on, as Pasiphae, Minos's wife, opens up her gates to a bull through a hole in a walled enclosure constructed for her by Daedalus. It might also be recalled in this regard that Minos himself is said to be the offspring of an affair involving Zeus disguised as a bull and the mortal Europa. The tension here between real bulls and just a lot of bull, between literal and figurative language, between true and fictive accounts of one's origins, is compounded when the shunned Scylla questions Minos's own pedigree, claiming that his father was not Zeus masquerading as a bull, but in fact a real one. While the woman who had hoped to give herself so completely to Minos is left behind by him and is transformed into a bird known as a *ciris* by the father whom she has "castrated," her impertinent questions have an uncanny way of staying with the Cretan king. Like stowaways, these questions somehow manage to lodge themselves in his inner ear, where they continue to hover and fly about, unanswered and perhaps unanswerable. Unwittingly bearing these questions back home with him, Minos is confronted upon his return with the Minotaur, "the strange hybrid creature that revealed his wife's love affair. He determines to rid his home of this shameful sight, by shutting the monster away in an enclosure of elaborate and involved design, where it could not be seen. Daedalus, an arch-itect famous for his skill, constructed the maze, confusing the usual marks of direction, and leading the eye of the beholder astray by devious paths winding in different directions" (183).

At this point in his description of the means by which an ob-server's eye may be led astray, Ovid curiously introduces nothing less than a visual aid for the reader as he goes on to compare this maze to the river Meander: "Just as the playful waters of the Me-ander in Phrygia flow this way and that, without any consistency, as the river, turning to meet itself, sees its own advancing waves, flowing now towards its source and now towards the open sea, always changing directions, so Daedalus constructed countless wandering paths and was himself scarcely able to find his way back to the entrance, so confusing was the maze" (183).

The irony of Ovid's image is striking, since what this compari-son helps one to visualize is not so much a particular path as the devious ways by which the eye may be led astray. In other words, as a way of aiding the beholder of his text to picture an optical illu-sion, Ovid playfully offers the reader another one. One is thus left to consider whether this doubling of one *trompe l'oeil* by another actually helps to correct our vision, helps us to see through the illu-sion, or whether it merely redoubles the deception under the pre-tense of giving us a clearer picture of it.

In the guise of providing the reader with two images of a laby-rinth, the passage instead seems to wander circuitously through labyrinthine figures. Instead of two pictures, the reader beholds an extremely convoluted *picture frame* — and a family picture frame at that. For just as the river Meander flows without any consistency and doubles back on itself, so too does the scandal involving the Minotaur flow back one or two generations, redound to Minos, and put his own pedigree in question. If Minos does not simply remove the monster by sending him away but instead keeps him in a kind of internal exile at home in the labyrinth, it may be because the king can neither adequately distance himself from nor suffi-ciently accustom himself to this stereophonic questioning of the legitimacy of his paternal line.

Beyond simply containing a Minotaur, the convoluted corridors of the labyrinth figure a crisis in lineage. At this point in book 8, both the story line and the paternal line double back on themselves, greatly disorienting the reader. Not only do the city walls of Alcathous resonate in all of Daedalus's walled constructions, but all of Scylla's questions regarding Minos's origins, which had formerly lodged themselves in the cochlea of his inner ear, seem once again to echo through the endless passageways of the labyrinth. Nevertheless, as complicated and convoluted as these labyrinthine walls may be, they do seem just barely to contain the Minotaur. They do give Minos just enough distance. Daedalus is just barely able to find his way back to the entrance, just as Theseus hanging by a thread is just barely able to do so later. Ovid is just barely able to contain this labyrinthine tale as the literal centerpiece and Medusalike aegis of his *Metamorphoses*. In Ovid, it seems, just barely is just enough.

In many ways, Kafka's singular *Metamorphosis* can be read as an unfolding of certain unresolved questions in Ovid. As in its predecessor, Kafka's *Verwandlung* literally has a wall, or *Wand,* in its midst. Yet, whereas in Ovid the walls of the labyrinth center his *Metamorphoses* and actually emblematize the complex interconnectedness of the many convoluted frame narratives that comprise the text, the walls of Kafka's *Metamorphosis* are labyrinths one enters without warning—just as Joseph K. awakens one morning to find himself ensnared in a seemingly endless web of legal complications in *The Trial*. If the Minoan labyrinth is a place of internal exile, a place recognizably foreign within a domestic setting, what is so disorienting about Kafka's *Metamorphosis* is the strange familiarity of it all. Here one finds no labyrinth as such, no clearly marked entrance or exit, and no real drama attached to it. What is so disconcerting is the familiar, everyday, utterly prosaic tone of it all.[30] There are no visible signs of labyrinthine walls, only an insistent shift from three- to two-dimensional space, only an increasing sense of claustrophobia, of invisible walls closing in, of myopia. In place of a maze, confusing the usual marks of direction, there is only a general sense of futility, of gray, unbroken monotony, the kind that makes one forget one was once human.

Whereas in Ovid the eye of the beholder is deceived by optical illusion, "by confusing the usual marks of direction," in Kafka's myopic world the spectator is not so much led astray as absorbed into a spectacle observed at dangerously close range. Here one might recall the scene Kafka stages in which Grete decides to remove all the furniture from her brother's room. Nowhere in the story does Gregor bear a greater resemblance to Ovid's Minotaur. While Grete clears the room, Gregor remains hidden under a couch, covered over with a cloth whose abundant folds conceal his hideous frame in the same way that the manifold walls of the Cretan labyrinth hide the Minotaur. Yet while the Minoan hybrid is literally half-man, half-bull, Kafka's *ungeheures Ungeziefer* is neither human nor animal. Instead, he or it is but a double negative suspended in metamorphosis. Were Grete to remove all the furniture, Gregor reflects, "he would be able to crawl around unhampered in all directions but at the cost of simultaneously, rapidly, and totally forgetting his human past. Even now he had been on the verge of forgetting, and only his mother's voice, which he had not heard for so long, had shaken him up" (33).

Gregor thus decides to break out of his semi-oblivion and salvage at least the souvenirs of his human existence. Yet in doing so, he attempts to rescue not just the memories of his human past but also and above all the activity of memory itself. As the *sound* of his mother's voice (which literally shakes him up) reminds him, he must remember to remember if he is to preserve anything of his human identity. Linking past and present, it is memory that makes possible the sense of continuity over time which conditions one's sense of self. By contrast, animal-like forgetfulness—at least in Nietzsche's parable of *On the Advantage and Disadvantage of History for Life*—involves a leaping from one present moment to another. "These animals," says Nietzsche, "do not know what yesterday and today are but leap about, eat, rest, digest and leap again."[31] Gregor's semi-oblivion is not a return to this "lost paradise" of discontinuous jumps from "now" to "now" but rather the unpunctuated, gray continuity of quotidian existence. Thus, Gregor finds that it was "the monotony of family life, combined with the fact that not a soul had addressed a word directly to him, [that] must have addled his brain in the course of the past two months" (33). Here in addition to seeing how monotony erodes memory as it "addles the brain," we also notice how the use of apostrophe actively calls its addressee to life. Thus, it is not by chance that the scene we are considering climaxes in Gregor's being directly addressed by his sister for the first and only time since the very beginning of the story. After breaking out from under the couch, he changes direction four times, not knowing what to salvage first, "then he saw hanging conspicuously on the wall, which was otherwise bare already the picture of the lady all dressed in furs, hurriedly crawled up on it and pressed himself against the glass which gave a good surface to stick to and soothed his hot belly. At least no one would take away this picture, while Gregor completely covered it up. He turned his head toward the living-room door to watch the women when they returned" (35).

Whereas Corngold's translation tells of how the glass "gave a good surface to stick to," in the German it is the glass that "had a firm hold" on Gregor and "held him fast [das Glas, das ihn festhielt]." In flattening himself against the glass, Gregor finds himself flush up against another two-dimensional creature, namely the picture cut out of an illustrated magazine of a lady whose fur-clad forearm is raised toward the spectator.[32] Here picture, frame, and an incredibly myopic beholder seem to merge in the flat, transparent fifth side of the frame, namely the glass.[33] The spectator is literally absorbed in an image that catches his eye and draws him in. As if following out the logic of this merger, the absorbed spectator in turn makes a spectacle of himself. For just as the lady in fur is said to gesture toward the viewer (dem Beschauer einen schweren Pelzmuff entgegenhob), so too does Gregor turn his head toward the doorway and cross glances with a subsequent spectator, his sister Grete, who in turn raises her fist toward the spectacle on the wall and cries out, "You, Gregor!" To which the narrator immediately adds, "these were the first words she had addressed to him since his metamorphosis" (36). Needless to say, both the fist raised toward Gregor and the calling out of his name repeat the ways in which the spectacle gestures toward the beholder. Grete's involuntary repetition of these gestures in turn absorbs her in the spectacle, which, like the glass of the picture frame, seems to have a firm hold on her as she beholds it. Thus, in contrast to the convoluted shape of Ovid's labyrinth, in which the eye of the beholder is led astray by devious and winding paths, Kafka's labyrinth is constructed as a flat, transparent surface, into which spectator and spectacle are mutually absorbed.

As was noted earlier, the actual metamorphosis of Gregor Samsa into an ungeheures Ungeziefer is described as a fait accompli in the very first sentence of the text. Yet, as Corngold argues, "in the process, it appears to accomplish still another change: it metamorphoses a common figure of speech. This second transformation emerges in the light of the hypothesis proposed in 1947 by Günther Anders."[34] According to Anders,

> All that Kafka has to work with is the common possession of ordinary language. . . . More precisely: he draws from the resources on hand, the figurative nature [*Bildcharakter*] of language. He takes metaphors at their word [*beim Wort*].
>
> For example: Because Gregor Samsa wants to live as an artist [i.e. as a *Luftmensch*—one who lives on air, lofty and free-floating], in the eyes of the highly respectable, hard-working world he is a "nasty bug [*dreckiger Käfer*]": and so in *The Metamorphosis* he wakes up as a beetle whose ideal of happiness is to be sticking to the ceiling.[35]

In claiming that Kafka "takes metaphors at their word [*beim Wort*]," Anders and others who have attempted to build on his hypothesis often fail to appreciate the extent to which Kafka also takes *words* at their word.[36] That is, in addition to literalizing metaphors, he literally disarticulates the signifying matter itself. This is apparent not only in the becoming-wall of *Verwandlung* but also in a term central to Anders's reading of Gregor's desire to live as a free-floating *Luftmensch*: namely, the word "ceiling." In the German text, Kafka uses the more common term *Decke* as well as the loanword *Plafond,* borrowed from French. Thus, he writes in the passage to which Anders's analysis refers,

> Eating soon stopped giving him the slightest pleasure, so, as a distraction [*zur Zerstreuung*], he adopted the habit of crawling criss- cross over the walls and the ceiling [*Plafond*]. He especially liked hanging from the ceiling [*Decke*]; it was completely different from lying on the floor; one could breathe more freely; a faint swinging sensation went through the body; and in the almost happy absent-mindedness [*Zerstreutheit*] which Gregor felt up there, it could happen to his own surprise that he let go and plopped onto the floor. . . . His sister immediately noticed the new entertainment Gregor had discovered for himself—after all, he left behind traces of his sticky substance wherever he crawled—and so she got it into her head to make it possible for Gregor to crawl on an altogether wider scale by taking out the furniture which stood in his way. (31–32)

Using the synonymous terms *Decke* and *Plafond* in this passage, Kafka is able to avoid unnecessary repetition. Yet, more importantly, his use of the less common loanword *Plafond* in conjunction with his mention of the walls of Gregor's room marks a pivotal moment in the text. For just as the term *Plafond* condenses the roots *plat* and *fond* into a kind of oxymoron of profound superficiality, so too at this point is there a marked shift from the not so roomy interior of Gregor's bedroom and the shrinking volume of his body ("eating soon stopped giving him the slightest pleasure") to the flat surfaces of the ceiling and walls themselves. In order to gauge the extent of this shift, it might be recalled that Gregor's room is initially described as "a regular human room lying tranquilly [*ruhig*] between the four familiar walls" (3). The tranquillity of these walls, it might be remembered, stands in stark contrast to the agitation of Gregor's unsettling [*unruhige*] dreams. When Gregor becomes increasingly restless—perhaps haunted again by the dreams from which he first awoke—the walls in turn lose their familiarity.³⁷ No longer the four compass points by which he might orient himself in space, the walls and ceiling merely provide increased surface area for his "almost happy absentmindedness [*Zerstreutheit*]" (32).

While Corngold's translations of *Zerstreutheit* as "absent-mindedness" and *Zerstreuung* as "distraction" are certainly legitimate, taking these words at their word one also hears in them etymological resonances of "dispersion" and "dissemination," which are particularly relevant in this context. Repeating these signifiers in close proximity to one another, the text foregrounds a certain mode of fertilization—a kind of cloud seeding—as it sounds out yet another link to Ovid's *Metamorphoses* and the sexual overtones of its musical masonry. Whereas in Ovid Scylla opens her city's gates instead of waiting for Minos to breach its fortifications, and Pasiphae copulates with a bull through a hole in the wall of a device constructed for her by Daedalus, in Kafka it is the walls themselves, papered over in a floral pattern, that are clouded over and volatilized as Gregor absentmindedly leaves behind "traces [*Spuren*] of his sticky substance" (32). Rather than copulating *through* the walls, Gregor disseminates himself in them, thereby making himself into wall (*sich verwandeln*) as more walls are made. The scene thus anticipates the mutually absorbing spectacle later enacted on the fifth transparent side of the picture frame, on "the glass which gave a good surface to stick to and soothed [Gregor's] hot belly." If the sexual practices alluded to here are, to say the least, a little bizarre, it is perhaps because a different sense of pleasure and of reproduction is being articulated. As Corngold says, "In this story, writing reproduces itself, in the mode of allegory, as metamorphosis, literality, death, play, and reduction—the whole in a negative and embattled form."[38]

Losing One's Bearings: On the Plafond

For all its strangeness, Kafka's *Metamorphosis* is still very much a story of the workaday world. Indeed, the narrative has often been read as a gradual metamorphosis of the home into a workplace—as if it were not one already. In this sense, *The Metamorphosis* has always already taken place, for it takes place repeatedly, monotonously, senselessly without ever really taking place as such. The development the narrative traces is but a retracing. Thus, when Grete stands up at the end and stretches her young body, one has the sense that she is finally prepared to become what Gregor had been before the beginning—perhaps not a traveling salesman, but at least someone who could bring another meal ticket into the family. A good husband is what her parents seem to feel she is ready for.

As a traveling salesman, Gregor had ventured far from home for days at a time. When one morning he can no longer leave for work, the office suddenly comes to him with a vengeance in the person of the manager, whose presence occasions some of the funniest and most sardonic exchanges in the story. Soon after the initial crisis, all the familiar family roles are reversed as Gregor stays home while the other three go out to work. Mother and daughter even bring work home with them, while the father never even takes off his uniform. Indeed, the more the workplace enters the domestic space, the more the father's work clothes come to resemble the old bathrobe he never took off while staying at home. Finally, the family's living quarters do indeed become a second workplace when the three boarders move in.

The former center of the family, Gregor, through whose room the others literally communicated with each other at the beginning, is now displaced more and more to the periphery and served cold leftovers, while the strangers in the midst of the family are regaled with music and hot, steaming meats. Indeed, Gregor becomes so peripheral that by the end the family practically forgets to forget him. It could in fact be argued that he finally dies only in order to be remembered. His death seems to be almost a direct response to Grete's question, "But how can it be Gregor? If it were Gregor, he would have realized long ago that it isn't possible for human beings to live with such a creature, and he would have gone away of his own free will. Then we wouldn't have a brother, but we'd be able to go on living and honor his memory" (52).

As was noted earlier, Gregor's death is described as another loss of volume, another shift from three to two dimensions. As the narrator says, "Then, without his consent, his head sank down to the floor, and from his nostrils streamed his last weak breath" (54). "Gregor's body was completely flat and dry" (55).

As I have tried to suggest, the scene of metamorphosis, the becoming-wall of *Verwandlung,* is played out on a number of uncannily "deep surfaces" ranging from the glass of the picture frame to all the floors, ceilings, and walls of the text, to the surface of everyday language, the plane of the printed page, and the general shift from three to two dimensions. To conclude, I would like to focus briefly on the narrating surface itself. If Gregor is a creature lost in translation and a mistranslation always in need of retranslation, a character who is almost never directly spoken to and one who never speaks for himself, it is the narrator who repeatedly translates, interprets, and speaks for him. The narrator, however, does not simply have another voice. For if he is the one who is most intimately in touch with Gregor, his voice is also the one most contaminated. Indeed, it is contaminated to the point where the reader often cannot distinguish Gregor's thoughts from the narrator's own editorializing comments.[39]

While the text is replete with examples of this fusion and confusion of voices, consider the following passage, in which the narrator describes Gregor's reaction to the cleaning woman's exclamation, "Look at that old dung beetle!"

> To forms of address like these Gregor would not respond but remained immobile where he was, as if the door had not been opened. If only they had given this cleaning woman orders to clean up his room every day, instead of letting her disturb him uselessly whenever the mood took her. (45)

Like the transparent glass of the picture frame in which spectator and spectacle are mutually absorbed, Kafka's frequent use of free indirect style confuses the unspeakable thoughts of an *ungeheures Ungeziefer* with the disembodied voice of a faceless narrator. And if we as readers, as beholders of *The Metamorphosis,* look closely and read myopically, we may in turn find ourselves absorbed in a narrative that from beginning to end is profoundly superficial. As such, Kafka's *Metamorphosis,* unlike Ovid's Minoan labyrinth, never quite lets one in — or out.

NOTES

Chapter 1. The Other Hand

1. Cited in Michael Werner, "Der politische Schriftsteller und die (Selbt-) Zensur: Zur Dialektik von Zensur und Selbstzensur in Heines Berichten aus Paris, 1840–1844 ("Lutezia")," in *Heine Jahrbuch* 1987 (Hamburg: Hoffman and Campe, 1987), 44; translation mine.

2. See in this regard Jürgen Habermas's essay "Heinrich Heine and the Intellectual in Germany," in *The New Conservatism: Cultural Criticism and the Historians' Debate,* ed. and trans. Shierry Weber Nicholsen (Cambridge: MIT Press, 1990), 71–99.

3. For an excellent general introduction to the notion of censorship, viewed in a historical and comparative context, see Annabel Patterson's article "Censorship," in *The Encyclopedia of Literature and Criticism,* ed. Matthew Coyle et al. (London: Routledge, 1990), 901–14. Patterson's suggestions for further reading include a number of important case studies. Also see her *Censorship and Interpretation: The Conditions of Writing and Reading in Early Modern England* (Madison: University of Wisconsin Press, 1984). For a discussion of what has been described as the "new" censorship, see Richard Burt's introduction to *The Administration of Aesthetics,* ed. R. Burt (Minneapolis: University of Minnesota Press, 1994).

4. Heine's description of the self-censoring writer as a kind of smuggler has led many critics to search for an encoded, contraband subtext of his work. While such an approach clearly has its merits, it often leads one to view self-censored writing in the overly static terms of exoteric façade versus hidden esoteric truth. See in this regard Leo Strauss's *Persecution and the Art of Writing* (Glencoe, Ill.: Free Press, 1952).

5. Obviously, such questions have already been raised and extensively discussed by Barthes, Foucault, Derrida, and others. It is not that Heine scholars are unaware of this body of literature, but rather that they choose to disregard it. As one critic, who describes his book as a "look into Heine's workshop reaching from the smallest textual elements to the genesis of whole works and their partial destruction through self-censorship," remarks, "graphological-psychologizing considerations played no part in this study." Erhard Weidl, *Heinrich Heines Arbeitsweise* (Hamburg: Hoffmann und Campe, 1974), 8; translation mine.

6. Sigmund Freud, *The Standard Edition of the Complete Psychologi-*

cal Works of Sigmund Freud, trans. James Strachey (London: Hogarth Press, 1953), 4: 308. Further references to the standard edition (*S.E.*) appear in parentheses in the body of the text.

7. "The gesture sketched out by Freud [*Le geste esquissé par Freud*]," Derrida asserts, "opens up a new kind of question about metaphor, writing, and spacing in general." *Writing and Difference,* trans. Alan Bass (Chicago: University of Chicago Press, 1978), 199.

8. I would further suggest that one read Derrida's analysis of the plurality of hands at work in Freud's text in juxtaposition with Strachey's description of his single-handed English translation of Freud: "When the *Standard Edition* was first planned," he says, "it was considered that it would be an advantage if a single hand has carried out the greater part of the work of translation, and even where a former version has been used as a basis it was found that a large amount of remodelling has been imposed. This unfortunately has involved the discarding, in the interests of this preferred uniformity, of many earlier translations that were excellent in themselves" (S.E. 1, xviii–xix).

9. Shoshana Felman, "On Reading Poetry," in *The Purloined Poe: Lacan, Derrida, and Psychoanalytic Reading,* ed. John P. Muller and William J. Richardson (Baltimore: Johns Hopkins University Press, 1988), 152–53.

10. Shoshana Felman, "To Open the Question," in *Literature and Psychoanalysis: The Question of Reading: Otherwise,* ed. Shoshana Felman (Baltimore: Johns Hopkins University Press, 1982), 5. Further references to this essay appear in parentheses in the body of the text.

11. Agreeing with Felman, Peter Brooks adds that the "reference to psychoanalysis has traditionally been used to close rather than open the argument, and the text." Brooks, "Psychoanalytic Literary Criticism," in *The Trial(s) of Psychoanalysis,* ed. Françoise Meltzer (Chicago: University of Chicago Press, 1987), 147.

12. See Theodor Reik, *Listening with the Third Ear: The Inner Experience of a Psychoanalyst* (New York: Grove Press, 1948), and Jacques Lacan, "Seminar on 'The Purloined Letter,'" in Muller and Richardson, *The Purloined Poe,* 53. In Lacan, this mode of receptiveness has everything to do with reading one's *implication* in the text—that is, with reading the ways in which one is enfolded, textualized, and emplotted by it in an "intersubjective modulus of repetitive action" (32). Needless to say, in "The Purloined Letter" these repetitions are not confined to the action described in the text. They are also and perhaps above all *transacted between* the text and its would-be interpreters.

13. Thus, for example, Meltzer observes that "literature is not alone in

its uneasy status with respect to psychoanalysis — quite the contrary. To all of the other disciplines psychoanalysis has visited, invaded, and (at times) colonized, it assigns the same 'place' as it does to literature." *Trial(s) of Psychoanalysis,* 3.

14. I return to the specific figure of the dream navel in Chapter 3.

15. Stanley J. Coen, "How to Read Freud: A Critique of Recent Freud Scholarship," *Journal of the American Psychoanalytic Association,* no. 36 (1988): 483. In this review Coen discusses recent work by Bettelheim, Masson, Mahoney, Felman, and Weber. Further references to this article appear in parentheses in the body of the text.

16. Ibid., 487.

17. Freud to Fliess, December 6, 1896, in *The Complete Letters of Sigmund Freud to Wilhelm Fliess,* trans. and ed. Jeffrey Moussaieff Masson (Cambridge: Harvard University Press, 1985), 208.

18. See the recent collection of essays edited by Darius Gray Ornston, Jr., M.D., *Translating Freud* (New Haven: Yale University Press, 1992); of particular interest in this regard is the essay contributed by the editors of a new French edition of Freud's work, 135–90.

19. Samuel Weber, *The Legend of Freud* (Minneapolis: University of Minnesota Press, 1982), xvi.

20. Of relevance here is Lacan's description of Freud's modus operandi in *"Du sujet enfin en question:"* "What is distinctive about [this] operation," he observes, "is that it clearly articulates the status of the symptom with the status of its own discourse, for it constitutes precisely the very *operation proper to the symptom,* in both senses of the word." Lacan, *Ecrits* (Paris: Editions du Seuil, 1966), 234. The passage is cited in English in Shoshana Felman, *Jacques Lacan and the Adventure of Insight: Psychoanalysis in Contemporary Culture* (Cambridge: Harvard University Press, 1987), 63.

21. Weber, *Legend of Freud,* xvi.

22. Coen, "How to Read Freud," 509. A similar point is made by Joel Whitebook in his review of Paul Robinson's *Freud and His Critics.* There Whitebook describes "the proponents of a so-called literary Freud, deriving largely from Lacan and Derrida" as "the avant-garde of Freud's reception in the academy" and as a group that does "not constitute part of the solution but part of the problem. Despite their enthusiasm for Freud," he continues, "this school reads Freud *against* Freud precisely to subvert his modernist intentions and appropriate him for their position." Joel Whitebook, "Freudian Slip," review of *Freud and His Critics,* by Paul Robinson, *New York Times Book Review,* September 12, 1993, 31.

23. Ibid., 485.

24. See in particular Weber's chapter "Observation, Description, Figurative Language," in *The Legend of Freud*, 17–31, and Felman's essay "What Difference Does Psychoanalysis Make: or, The Originality of Freud," in *Jacques Lacan and the Adventure of Insight* (Cambridge: Harvard University Press, 1987), esp. 61–67.

25. Felman, "On Reading Poetry," 147.

26. To put it another way, what needs to be *repeatedly rediscovered* is that dimension of Freud's thought which is *incessantly being repressed:* its literary dimension, to be sure, but also, as Lacan says, that which Freud himself "discovered and rediscovers with a perpetually increasing sense of shock"—namely, "that the displacement of the signifier [i.e., of a dead letter, a letter in sufferance] determines the subjects in their acts, in their destiny, in their refusals, in their blindness, in their end and in their fate, their innate gifts and social acquisitions notwithstanding, without regard for character or sex, and that, willingly or not, everything that might be considered the stuff of psychology, kit and caboodle, will follow the path of the signifier." Lacan, "Seminar on 'The Purloined Letter,'" 43–44.

27. It is certainly no accident in this regard that the reader of Poe's story has no direct knowledge of the "contents" of the letter, which is first purloined by the minister and then stolen in turn by Dupin. Indeed, at the very moment in the narrative where the reader expects to be given "an accurate description of the letter," the text suddenly switches from direct quotation to paraphrase, thereby dramatizing a more general shift away from the signified contents of "The Purloined Letter" toward its various forms of speech and modes of "delivery." As Barbara Johnson observes, "What is paraphrased is thus the description of the letter the story is about. And, whereas it is generally supposed that the function of paraphrase is to strip off the form of a speech in order to give us only its contents, here the use of paraphrase does the very opposite: it withholds the contents of the Prefect's remarks, giving us only their form. And what is swallowed up in this ellipsis is nothing less than the contents of the letter itself. The fact that the letter's message is never revealed, which will serve as the basis for Lacan's reading of the story, is thus negatively made explicit by the functioning of Poe's text itself." Barbara Johnson, "The Frame of Reference," in Muller and Richardson, *The Purloined Poe*, 216.

28. As Derrida has shown, Lacan's own text, while certainly drawing attention both to the literary *in* analysis and to the interimplication of psychoanalysis and literature, is itself at times guilty of using Poe(try) to illustrate certain psychoanalytic truths. Derrida points, for example, to the following passage in Lacan:

Which is why we have decided to illustrate for you today the truth which may be drawn from the moment in Freud's thought under study—namely, that it is the symbolic order which is constitutive for the subject—by demonstrating in a story the decisive orientation which the subject receives from the itinerary of a signifier.

It is that truth, let us note, which makes the very existence of fiction possible.

As Derrida notes, "Literary writing, here, is brought into an *illustrative* position; 'to illustrate' here meaning to read the general law in the example, to make clear the meaning of a law or of a truth, to bring them to light in striking or exemplary fashion." Derrida, "The Purveyor of Truth," in Muller and Richardson, *The Purloined Poe*, 177.

29. Weber, *Legend of Freud*, 27.

30. For other discussions of metaphor in Freud, see Bertram D. Lewin, "Metaphor, Mind, and Manikin," *Psychoananalytic Quarterly* 40 (1971): 6–39; Leon Wurmser, "A Defense of the Use of Metaphor in Analytic Theory Formation," *Psychoanalytic Quarterly* 46 (1977): 466–98; Jacob A. Arlow, "Metaphor and the Psychoanalytic Situation," *Psychoanalytic Quarterly* 48 (1979): 363–85; Jonathan T. Edelson, "Freud's Use of Metaphor," *Psychoanalytic Study of the Child* 38 (1983): 17–59; and Donald L. Carveth, "The Analyst's Metaphors: A Deconstructionist Perspective," *Psychoanalysis and Contemporary Thought* 7 (1984): 491–560.

31. On Strachey's questionable translation of *Deckerinnerung* as "screen memory" rather than as "cover memory," see Orston's excellent essay, "Improving Strachey's Freud," in *Translating Freud*, esp. 15–16.

32. Jane Gallop's readings of Freud have been particularly attentive to the ways in which a pursuit of resemblances, congruences, and conformities can effectively repress important differences and dissymmetries in the text. For example, in her discussion of the analogy that Freud discovered between the jokework and the dreamwork in *Der Witz,* she observes that there "seems to be some guilty pleasure in this analogical gratification, homological acquisition. For Freud, analogy is dangerously seductive: 'Shall we not *yield to the temptation* to construct [the formation of a joke] on the analogy of the formation of a dream?' He repeatedly defends himself against the imagined complaint that 'under the influence of the model' he is abusing the material, 'looking only for techniques of joking which fitted in with it, while others would have proved that this conformity [*Übereinstimmung*] is not invariably present." Freud's nervously defensive rhetoric suggests to her that his analogies may indeed serve to conceal more than they reveal. Her reading thus applies interpretive pressure to German terms like *Übereinstimmung* and *Gleichnis* (translated here as

"conformity" and "analogy") in order to disclose another, less assimilable dimension of the text. See Gallop, "Why Does Freud Giggle When the Women Leave the Room?" in *Psychoanalysis and . . .* , ed. Richard Feldstein and Henry Sussman (New York: Routledge, 1990), 49–53. See also her chapter "The Father's Seduction," in *The Daughter's Seduction* (Ithaca: Cornell University Press, 1982), esp. 68–69.

33. Weber, *Legend of Freud,* 28.

34. Ibid., 28–29.

35. Weber's critical strategy thus recalls Derrida's own polemic with "Lacan" in "The Purveyor of Truth." Reading the epigraph of Derrida's text (a quote from Baudelaire about Poe, which begins, "They thank him for the great truths he has just proclaimed") as an allusion to *Lacan*'s disciples, Barbara Johnson claims that "Derrida argues, in effect, not against Lacan's *text* but against Lacan's *power*—or rather, against 'Lacan' as the apparent cause of certain effects of power in French discourse today. Whatever Lacan's text may *say,* it functions, according to Derrida, as if it said what *he* says it says. The statement that a letter always reaches its destination may be totally undecipherable, but its assertive force is taken all the more seriously as a sign that Lacan himself has everything all figured out." Johnson, "The Frame of Reference," 227.

36. Weber, *Legend of Freud,* 82.

37. Jean-Luc Nancy and Philippe Lacoue-Labarthe, *The Title of the Letter: A Reading of Lacan,* trans. François Raffoul and David Pettigrew (Albany: State University of New York Press, 1992), xx–xxi.

38. John Bender and David Wellbery, *The Ends of Rhetoric: History, Theory, Practice* (Stanford: Stanford University Press, 1990), 31.

39. Samuel Weber, *Return to Freud: Jacques Lacan's Dislocation of Psychoanalysis,* trans. Michael G. Levine (Cambridge: Cambridge University Press, 1991), 38.

40. Cited in Ernest Jones, *The Life and Work of Sigmund Freud* (New York: Basic Books, 1953), 1: 196.

Chapter 2. Freud and the Scene of Censorship

1. *The Complete Letters of Sigmund Freud to Wilhelm Fliess,* trans. and ed. Jeffrey Moussaieff Masson (Cambridge: Harvard University Press, 1985), 371. Letter dated September 11, 1899.

2. Ibid., 373–74. Letter dated September 21, 1899.

3. Jacques Derrida, *Writing and Difference,* trans. Alan Bass (Chicago: University of Chicago Press, 1978), 199. Further references to this essay appear in parentheses in the body of the text.

4. On the history of the term *censorship* in Freud's writings, see Wil-

liam J. McGrath, *Freud's Discovery of Psychoanalysis* (Ithaca: Cornell University Press, 1986) 165, 245–46.

5. There is only a passing reference to Freud's comparison of censorship to a kind of *Strahlenbrechung:* a refraction or more literally a breaking of the ray (215). Such passages would have to be read in conjunction with Derrida's discussion of pathbreaking elsewhere in the essay. See especially 229.

6. See in this regard Marx's discussion of the levels of censorship in *"Bemerkungen über die neueste preussische Zensurinstruktion"* (1842), in *Marx Engels Werke* (Berlin: Dietz Verlag, 1956), 1: 3–25.

7. Mikkel Borch-Jacobsen, *The Freudian Subject,* trans. Catherine Porter (Stanford: Stanford University Press, 1988), 3.

8.   Die Schere klirrt in seiner Hand,
            Es rückt der wilde Geselle
            Dir auf den Leib—Er schneidet ins Fleisch—
            Es war die beste Stelle

What is lost in the English translation of these lines is precisely the economy effected through Heine's use of the term *Stelle,* which refers both to the best part of the body and to the most interesting passage in the text. The incision made by the censor's scissors is thus double—not merely because it inflicts two discrete wounds, but rather because it opens an interspace in which text and body transpierce each other in such a way that violence done to the one will have been experienced as a mutilation of the other.

9. Of particular relevance in this regard is the description that Heine himself provides, in the preface to the French edition of *Lutezia,* of the methods he used in his journalistic writings to slip sensitive material past the censors. These include such techniques as disguising personal opinions as objectively reported statements of fact; shifting the speaker to have another give voice to one's own views; feigning a tone of indifference; and the use of a parabolic style. While Freud never explicitly refers to the passage in question, his extensive knowledge of Heine's work and personal biography suggests that he may well have been familiar with it.

10. I return to this relationship in Chapter 3.

11. Borch-Jacobsen, *The Freudian Subject,* 3.

12. Cf. Jacques Lacan, "Censorship Is Not Resistance," in *The Seminar of Jacques Lacan,* book 2, *The Ego in Freud's Theory and in the Technique of Psychoanalysis, 1954–1955,* trans. Sylvana Tomaselli (New York: Norton, 1991), 123–33.

13. This problem is taken up again in the essay "The Unconscious," where Freud distinguishes between what he calls the functional hypothesis

and the topographical hypothesis: "When a psychical act (let us confine ourselves here to one which is in the nature of a representation [*Vorstellung*]) is transposed from the system Ucs. into the system Cs. (or Pcs.), are we to suppose that this transposition [*Umsetzung*] involves a fresh record—as it were, a second registration—of the representation in question which may thus be situated as well in a fresh psychical locality, and alongside of which the original unconscious registration continues to exist? Or are we rather to believe that the transposition consists in a change in the state of the representation, a change involving the same material and occurring in the same locality?" (*S.E.* 14, 174).

14. As Freud remarks in the section entitled "The Forgetting of Dreams," "The modifications to which dreams are submitted under the editorship of waking life are . . . associatively linked to the material which they replace, and serve to show us the way to that material, which may in its turn be a substitute for something else" (*S.E.* 5, 515).

15. Freud further illustrates these foregrounding effects in the following examples: "In preparing a book for the press, I have some word which is of special importance for understanding the text printed in spaced or heavy type; or in speech I should pronounce the same word loudly and slowly and with special emphasis. . . . Art historians have drawn our attention to the fact that the earliest historical sculptures obey a similar principle: they express the rank of the persons represented by the size [*Bildgröße*]. A king is represented twice or three times as large as his attendants or as his defeated enemies. A sculpture of Roman date would make use of subtler means for producing the same result. The figure of the Emperor would be placed in the middle, standing erect, and would be modelled with special care, while his enemies would be prostrate at his feet; but he would no longer be a giant among dwarfs. The bows with which inferiors greet their superiors among ourselves today are an echo of the same ancient principle of representation" (*S.E.* 5, 595–96).

16. "It begins to dawn on us that it is more expedient and economical to allow the unconscious wish to take its course, to leave the path to regression open to it so that it can construct a dream, and then to bind the dream and dispose of it with a small expenditure of preconscious work—rather than to continue keeping a tight rein on the unconscious throughout the whole period of sleep. It was indeed to be expected that dreaming, even though it may originally have been a process without a useful purpose, would have procured itself some function in the interplay of mental forces. . . . Dreaming has taken on the task of bringing back under control of the preconscious the excitation in the Ucs. which has been left free; in so doing it discharges the Ucs. excitation, serves as a safety valve [*Ventil*] and at the same time preserves the sleep of the preconscious in return for a

small expenditure of waking activity. Thus, like all the other psychical structures in the series of which it is a member, it constitutes a compromise; it is in the service of both of the two systems, since it fulfills the two wishes insofar as they are compatible with each other [i.e., the unconscious wish and the preconscious wish to sleep]" (*S.E.* 5, 578–79).

17. Samuel Weber, *Return to Freud: Jacques Lacan's Dislocation of Psychoanalysis,* trans. Michael G. Levine (Cambridge: Cambridge University Press, 1991), 81.

18. Samuel Weber, *The Legend of Freud* (Minneapolis: University of Minnesota Press, 1982), 12.

19. Ibid., 14.

20. It might be noted in passing that Weber's description of the way systematic thought is driven "to fill in the 'gaps and cracks' in the edifice of the universe" is an allusion to Freud's own characterization of secondary revision in *The Interpretation of Dreams.* "This function," he says, "behaves in the manner which the poet maliciously ascribes to philosophers: it fills up the gaps in the dream-structure with shreds and patches." As Strachey notes, the poet alluded to here is Heine, who in poem LVIII of *The Homecoming* writes, *"Mit seinen Nachtmützen und Schlafrockfetzen, / Stopft er die Lücken des Weltenbaus."* ("With his nightcaps and rags of gown / He stops up the gaps of the universe.") Curiously, Freud's decision to paraphrase Heine rather than quote him directly allows a second, more distant intertextual echo to be heard. Whereas in Heine the gaps in the edifice of the universe are stopped by "nightcaps and rags of gowns," in Freud they are filled with *"Fetzen und Flicken,"* correctly translated by Strachey as "shreds and patches." The passage thus echoes Hamlet's description of his father's ghost as "a king of shreds and patches" in act 3, scene 4. That an allusion to Heine should inadvertently summon the ghost of *Hamlet* is perhaps no coincidence. For, as we shall see in the next chapter, Heine himself refers to the "marvelous prince of Denmark" in his discussion of self-censorship in *The Romantic School.* It might be interesting to compare Heine's comments about Hamlet cited on p. 43 to the following lines of *The Interpretation of Dreams:* "Dreams, then, are often most profound when they seem most crazy. In every epoch of history those who have had something to say but could not say it without peril have eagerly assumed a fool's cap. The audience at whom their forbidden speech was aimed tolerated it more easily if they could at the same time laugh and flatter themselves with the reflection that the unwelcome words were clearly nonsensical. The Prince in the play, who had to disguise himself as a madman, was behaving just as dreams do in reality; so that we can say of dreams what Hamlet said of himself, concealing the true circumstances under a cloak of wit and unintelligibility: 'I am but mad north-north-west:

when the wind is southerly, I know a hawk from a handsaw!'" (480–81).

21. For a discussion of overinterpretation in Freud's text, see Jean-Michel Rey's essay "Freud's Writing on Writing," in *Literature and Psychoanalysis: The Question of Reading: Otherwise,* ed. Shoshana Felman (Baltimore: Johns Hopkins University Press, 1982), esp. 303–11.

22. The relationship between "censorship" and "repression" is discussed in Chapter 4.

23. Carl E. Schorske, *Fin-de-Siècle Vienna: Politics and Culture* (New York: Vintage Books, 1981), 183.

24. Ibid., 187. For a further discussion of Freud's response to the Austro-Hungarian political situation and in particular to the 1897 crisis surrounding the language ordinances put forward by the government of Count Badeni, see William McGrath, *Freud's Discovery of Psychoanalysis.*

25. Schorske, *Fin-de-Siècle Vienna,* 203.

Chapter 3. Heine and the Dream Naval

1. *The Prose and Poetical Works of Heinrich Heine,* trans. C. G. Leland (New York: Crosscup and Sterling, 1920), 10: 354–55 (trans. mod.).

2. For discussions of Heine's censorship battles, see H. H. Houben, *Verbotene Literatur von der klassischen Zeit bis zur Gegenwart,* vol. 1 (Berlin: Rowolt; Bremen: Schünemann, 1924, 1928. Reprinted Hildesheim: Olms, 1965); Ute Radlik, *"Heine in der Zensur der Restaurationsepoche,"* in Jost Hermand, *Zur Literatur der Restaurationsepoche, 1815–1848: Forschungsreferate und Aufsätze* (Stuttgart: Metzler, 1970); Jochen Zinke, *Autortext und Fremdeingriff* (Hamburg: Hoffmann and Campe, 1974); Erhard Weidl, *Heinrich Heines Arbeitsweise* (Hamburg: Hoffmann and Campe, 1974); Norbert Altenhofer, *"Harzreise in die Zeit: Zum Funktionszusammenhang von Traum, Witz und Zensur in Heines früher Prosa"* (Düsseldorf: Heinrich Heine Gesellschaft, 1972).

3. Michael Werner, "Das Augsburgische Prokrustesbett," in *Cahier Heine* (Paris: Presses de l'Ecole Normale Supérieure, 1975), 49; translation mine.

4. Michael Werner, "Der politische Schriftsteller und die (Selbst-) Zensur: Zur Dialektik von Zensur und Selbstzensur in Heines Berichten aus Paris, 1840–1844 ("Lutezia"), in *Heine Jahrbuch* 1987 (Hamburg: Hoffmann and Campe), 44; translation mine.

5. Ibid., 49.

6. Shoshana Felman, "Postal Survival, or The Question of the Navel," in "The Lesson of Paul de Man" (Special Issue), *Yale French Studies,* no. 69 (1985): 66.

7. See in this regard Samuel Weber, "The Meaning of the Thallus," in

The Legend of Freud (Minneapolis: University of Minnesota Press, 1982): 65–83.

8. Felman, "Postal Survival," 69.

9. Jeffrey Sammons, *Heinrich Heine: A Modern Biography* (Princeton: Princeton University Press, 1979), 185.

10. Sammons, *Heine,* 186.

11. While the translations of Heine are largely my own, references to C. G. Leland's *The Prose and Poetical Works of Heinrich Heine,* vol. 1 (New York: Crosscup and Sterling, 1920) will be provided in the body of the text.

12. This form of salvation is generally acknowledged to be Heine's original contribution to the legend.

13. Manfred Frank, *Die unendliche Fahrt: Ein Motiv und sein Text* (Frankfurt am Main: Suhrkamp Verlag, 1979), 78.

14. Ernest J. Lovell, Jr., "Irony and Image in *Don Juan,*" in *Twentieth Century Interpretations of Don Juan,* ed. Edward E. Bostetter (Englewood Cliffs, N.J.: Prentice Hall, 1969), 28.

15. For an excellent discussion of the narrative interruptions of Plato's *Symposium,* see Michel Serres, *The Parasite,* trans. Lawrence Scher (Baltimore: Johns Hopkins University Press, 1982). See also Weber's discussion of the navel of that text in *The Legend of Freud,* 148–64. It might further be noted that the process of forming a navel, which Aristophanes significantly compares to the drawing together of the strings of a purse (190E), also provides a figure for the very movement of Plato's dialogue. For when the round of speeches delivered in praise of love is about to come full circle and is ready to draw to a close, there is an interruption, an intrusion, a change in the seating order, and a prolongation of the discussion. The dialogue thus ends as open-endedly as it begins. As in Freud, the navel not only figures this movement, it is also woven into it; that is, instead of simply tying up the loose ends and centering both the body and the text, the navel winds corporeal and textual figures through one another and knots them together. In this way, Aristophanes' description of the navel is but a prefiguration of the inconclusive conclusion of *The Symposium,* a text whose unending ending is itself only the inverted mirror image of its deferred beginning *in media res.* The significant difference between Plato's navel and that of *Schnabelewopski* is that the navel of the former is ultimately a figure of mediation, whereas in the latter it is associated with exile and suspension.

16. Consider in this regard Lacan's remark in his "Seminar on 'The Purloined Letter,'" in *The Purloined Poe: Lacan, Derrida, and Psychoanalytic Reading,* ed. John P. Muller and William J. Richardson (Baltimore: Johns Hopkins University Press, 1988): "The plurality of subjects, of

course, can be no objection for those who are long accustomed to the per-
spectives summarized by our formula: *the unconscious is the discourse of
the Other.* And we will not recall now what the notion of the *immixture
of subjects,* recently introduced in our reanalysis of the dream of Irma's
injection, adds to the discussion" (32). See also Lacan, *Le Séminaire, Livre
II: Le moi dans la théorie de Freud et dans la technique de la psychanalyse*
(Paris: Editions du Seuil, 1978), 177–204.

17. It is, of course, not by chance that the landlord makes hernia belts
(*Bruchbände*) for a living.

18. It should be noted at this point that the *Schnabel* of Schnabelewopski is not merely a *beak* closely tied to the human organ of speech by idi-
omatic expressions like *"Halt den Schnabel"* ("Shut your trap"), but in
light of the nautical motifs of the text is also to be thought of as a ship's
prow (Schnabel)—the kind that not only cuts through water but also
breaches a path through dreams, causing them to cut into and through one
another. On the "question of style," its involvement with "the weight or
examen of some pointed object" used to attack but also as protection
against the threat of such an attack, and its comparison to "the prow . . .
of a sailing ship, its *rostrum,* the projection of the ship which surges ahead
to meet the sea's attack and cleave its hostile surface," see Jacques Derrida,
Spurs: Nietzsche's Styles / Eperons: Les Styles de Nietzsche, trans. Barbara Harlow (Chicago: University of Chicago Press, 1978), 37–47. As I
have attempted to argue throughout, Heine's styling *Schnabel*—like the
Damoclean sword of (self-)censorship—tends to cut both ways.

19. As critics have often pointed out, the figure of "little Samson . . .
born in the free city of Frankfurt" is a barely veiled allusion to Ludwig
Börne. For more on Heine's relationship to Börne, see his monograph
Heinrich Heine über Ludwig Börne.

20. The significance of this event was in no way lost on Freud. In the
section of his book *Der Witz* dealing with the subjective determinants of
jokes, he remarks (in reference to *The Baths of Lucca*): "There are not a
few passages in which the poet himself seems to be speaking, under a thin
disguise, through the mouth of Hirsch-Hyacinth, and it soon becomes a
certainty that this character is only a self-parody. Hirsch explains his reasons for having given up his former name and why he now calls himself
'Hyacinth.' He goes on: 'There's the further advantage that I already have
an "H" on my signet, so that I don't need to have a new one cut.' But Heine
himself effected the same economy when, at his baptism, he changed his
first name from 'Harry' to 'Heinrich.'" Freud, *Jokes and Their Relation
to the Unconscious (S.E.8,* 141). For a highly illuminating discussion of
Freud as reader—and reciter—of Heine, see Sander Gilman, *The Jew's
Body* (New York: Routledge, 1991), 150–68; see also Jane Gallop, "Why

Does Freud Giggle When the Women Leave the Room?" in Richard Feldstein and Henry Sussman, eds., *Psychoanalysis and* . . . (New York: Routledge, 1990), 49–53.

21. Sammons, *Heine,* 108.

22. *Heines Sämtliche Werke,* ed. Ernst Elster (Leipzig: Bibliographisches Institut, 1887–1890), 7:407; cited in Sammons, *Heine,* 109.

23. Heine to Moser, January 9, 1826, in *Heinrich Heine Säkularausgabe,* ed. Nationale Forschungs- und Gedenkstätten der klassischen deutschen Literatur in Weimar and Centre National de la Recherche Scientifique in Paris (Berlin and Paris: Akademie-Verlag and Editions du CNRS, 1970–), 21:95; cited in Sammons, *Heine,* 109.

24. Heinrich Heine, *Historisch-kritische Gesamtausgabe der Werke* (Düsseldorfer Ausgabe), ed. Manfred Windfuhr et al. (Hamburg: Hoffmann and Campe, 1973–), 6:581, 134; cited in Sammons, *Heine,* 109.

Chapter 4. *Halt!*

1. While the metaphor of the prosthesis imposes itself here as a metaphor of metaphor, the prosthetic powers of figurative language in turn produce an appearance of naturalness as the most artificial effect of self-dissimulating artifice. I will return to the privileged relationship of prostheses and figurative language in the context of a reading of *Totem and Taboo* in chapters 6 and 7.

2. Obviously, such processes of naturalization and incorporation also involve relations of *power,* as Nietzsche suggests in *On the Advantage and Disadvantage of History for Life.* There he describes these processes in terms of a conflict of natures and, moreover, as a naturalization of conflict: "At best we may bring about a conflict between our inherited, innate nature and our knowledge, as well as a battle between a strict new discipline and ancient education and breeding; we implant a new habit, a new instinct, a second nature so that the first nature withers away." To which he adds, "this first nature also was, at some time or other, a second nature . . . every victorious second nature becomes a first." Nietzsche, *On the Advantage and Disadvantage of History for Life,* trans. Peter Preuss (Indianapolis: Hackett Publishing, 1980), 22. See also François Roustang's chapter "Freud's Style," in *Psychoanalysis Never Lets Go,* trans. Ned Lukacher (Baltimore: Johns Hopkins University Press, 1983), 1–25, as well as Patrick Mahoney's very fine chapter "The Resources of Figurative Language," in his *Freud as a Writer* (New York: International Universities Press, 1982), 133–60.

3. See in this regard Harold Bloom, "Freud: Frontier Concepts, Jewishness, and Interpretation," *American Imago* 48, no. 1 (1991): 135–52.

4. Freud employs these abbreviations for the systems "unconscious"

(Ucs), "consciousness" (Cs), and "preconscious(consciousness) (Pcs[Cs])" when attempting to describe them from a dynamic rather than a topological perspective. See section 2 of "The Unconscious." Also see Nicolas Abraham's discussion of the significance of Freud's use of abbreviations in "The Shell and the Kernel," trans. Nicolas Rand, *Diacritics* (Spring 1979): 16–28.

5. As we will see, this shift is already anticipated in "The Unconscious," where anxiety also functions as a signal and serves the interests of psychic defense.

6. It is also worth noting in this regard the proximity of the static image of a screen memory to the more dynamic notion of a transference idea. In "The Dynamics of Transference," Freud describes how in following "a pathogenic complex from its representation in the conscious . . . to its root in the unconscious, we shall soon enter a region in which the resistance makes itself felt so clearly that the next association must take account of it and appear as a compromise between its demands and those of the work of investigation. It is at this point . . . that transference enters on the scene. When anything in the complexive material . . . is suitable for being transferred on to the figure of the doctor, that transference is carried out; it produces the next association, and announces itself by indications of a resistance—by a stoppage, for instance. *We infer from this experience that the transference-idea has penetrated into consciousness in front of any other possible association because it satisfies the resistance. . . . Over and over again, when we come near to a pathogenic complex, the portion of that complex which is capable of transference is first pushed forward into consciousness and defended with the greatest obstinacy"* (*S.E.* 12, 103–4; emphasis added).

7. Freud discusses these issues at length in "The Psychical Mechanism of Forgetting" and in *The Psychopathology of Everyday Life*. For a discussion of the forgetting of "Signorelli" from a Lacanian perspective, see Anthony Wilden, "Freud, Signorelli, and Lacan: The Repression of the Signifier," *American Imago* 23 (1966): 332–66, and Samuel Weber, *Return to Freud: Jacques Lacan's Dislocation of Psychoanalysis,* trans. Michael G. Levine (Cambridge: Cambridge University Press, 1991), 91–97. See also Freud's early paper "On Screen Memories."

8. Here I have translated the German term *Vorstellung* as both "representation" and "idea." Strachey usually employs the latter. Needless to say, this term plays a crucial role in Freud's writings on repression, since what often determines the qualitative character of a certain quantum of affect is its attachment to a particular *Vorstellung*. It is important to note that in addition to altering the quality of an affect, a particular *Vorstellung* may

also serve as a dissimulating front for another representation and for the affect associated with it. Here a *Vor-stellung* would function literally as something placed before or set forth in front. A story recounted in *Jokes and Their Relation to the Unconscious* bears witness to Freud's sensitivity to the play of literal and figurative sense in this term: "'What do these statues *vorstellen* [represent or put forward]? [*Was stellen diese Statuen vor?*]' asks a stranger to Berlin of a native of the city, looking at a row of monuments in a public square. 'Oh, well,' the other responds, 'either their right leg or their left'" (*S.E.*8, 38–39).

9. Here and in the quotations that follow in this chapter (except where otherwise noted) I cite Cecil M. Baines's translation of Freud, which Philip Rieff has chosen to include in his widely circulated paperback edition of Freud's metapsychological writings, entitled *General Psychological Theory* (New York: Macmillan, 1963). I have chosen to cite Baines rather than Strachey for the following reasons: first, in order to take issue with Rieff's selection of a translation that is, on the whole, significantly inferior to Strachey's; second, in order to suggest the ways in which the very deficiencies of Baines's translation may serve to highlight (by contrast and overstatement) certain nuances in Freud's German. More generally, I want to argue that the problems one encounters in English translations of Freud have their roots not simply in the idiosyncrasies or particular talents of any one translator but rather in the fundamental strangeness of Freud's thought. The reading that follows is therefore to be construed not merely as an attempt to correct particular mistranslations (though it is also that) but also and above all as an effort to make contact *via these distortions* with certain conflicts and tensions in Freud's thinking. For the sake of comparison, reference in the following will be made to both Baines's and Strachey's translations and will appear as follows: Baines, 104; *S.E.*14, 146.

10. Here I follow Laplanche in translating Trieb as "drive" rather than as "instinct." See Jean Laplanche, *Life and Death in Psychoanalysis,* trans. Jeffrey Mehlman (Baltimore: Johns Hopkins University Press, 1990), 9–18.

11. Baines, 104; *S.E.*14, 146.

12. Derrida uses the feint of an allegedly missed encounter couched in the future perfect (which turns out to introduce a roundabout way of getting at a topic that is impossible to approach directly) in the opening lines of *Spurs: Nietzsche's Styles,* trans. Barbara Harlow (Chicago: University of Chicago Press, 1979), 34–35. It is also important to consider in this regard Freud's use of the term *Nachträglichkeit,* which appears throughout his work at those points (most notably around the issue of trauma) where a different relationship to time is being articulated. The French and English translations of this term as "deferred action," "belatedness," or *après coup* tend to accentuate the ways in which certain traumas are expe-

rienced less as positive, lived events than as a haunting series of disruptive aftereffects. Here the element of a missed and missing encounter combined with the necessity of indirect experience through anxiety dreams and repetition compulsions must be stressed. In short, the future perfect tense should be understood in these cases less in terms of a positive temporal framework than as a modality of missing in which the present tense and more direct modes of presentation will of necessity have been bypassed. See in this regard Cathy Caruth's essay "Unclaimed Experience: Trauma and the Possibility of History," *Yale French Studies* 79 (January 1991): 190–92, as well as her introduction to "Psychoanalysis, Culture, and Trauma" (Special Issue), *American Imago* 48 (Spring 1991): 1–12.

13. Jacques Derrida, "Freud and the Scene of Writing," in *Writing and Difference,* trans. Alan Bass (Chicago: University of Chicago Press, 1978), 215.

14. Ibid., 219.

15. Baines, 104; *S.E.*14, 146.

16. Baines, 105; *S.E.*14, 147. Here it seems as if a consciousness unable to accommodate contradiction were compelled to split itself.

17. Ibid.

18. Baines 127, *S.E.*14, 179.

19. While the problem of maintenance primarily involves the precariousness of repression's hold on the repressed, Derrida also alludes to a temporal dimension of the problem in his discussion of Freud's "Note on the Mystic Writing-Pad," in "Freud and the Scene of Writing." There he writes: "it is less a machine than a tool. And it is not held with only one hand. This is the mark of its temporality. Its *maintenance* is not simple. The ideal virginity of the present (in French, *maintenant*) is constituted by the work of memory. At least two hands are needed to make the apparatus function" (226). We will return to the temporality of this scene of writing, which, needless to say, is also a scene of censorship, in Chapter 5.

20. Baines, 129; *S.E.*14, 180.

21. For an extended commentary on this passage, see Samuel Weber, *The Legend of Freud* (Minneapolis: University of Minnesota Press, 1982), 70–83.

22. Baines, 128; *S.E.*14, 179.

23. Baines, 130; *S.E.*14, 181.

24. Baines, 130; *S.E.*14, 182.

25. Baines, 130–31; *S.E.*14, 182.

26. Weber, *Legend of Freud,* 40–41.

27. Baines, 131; *S.E.*14, 182.

28. Ibid.

29. Just as the difference between two senses of an ambiguous term

may be only a matter of emphasis, so too can the issue of a representation's psychical location be more a matter of effective appearance than of objective existence. Thus, in section 2 of his essay "The Unconscious," Freud asks whether we are to suppose that the transposition of a representation "is linked to a new fixation of it, something like a second copy of it, which would be contained in a new psychical locality while the original unconscious copy would persist alongside or parallel to it. Or are we rather to believe that the transposition consists in a change of condition, an alteration of the same material occurring in the same locality?" (*S.E.* 14, 174). This question does not receive a response until the beginning of section 4 in a passage immediately following the various plays on the signifier *halt* discussed earlier. "We notice by the way," Freud says, "that we have unintentionally, as it were, grounded these reflections upon the assumption that the transition from the system Ucs to the system nearest to it is not effected through the making of a new copy, but through a change in condition, an alteration of cathexis. The functional hypothesis has here easily routed the topographical" (*S.E.* 14, 180).

30. Commenting on Lacan's formulation, Samuel Weber notes, "As signifier, language is 'intrinsically' substitutive, and hence, figurative. But since each figure always *gestures* toward another figure, the process of configuration is addressed at a destination it can never attain." *Return to Freud*, 115. It should also be noted that the Lacanian notion of a signifier that only takes its place by taking the place of another — *au lieu de l'Autre* — itself echoes Freud's tentative claim voiced in *Beyond the Pleasure Principle* that *"consciousness arises instead of [an Stelle der] a memory-trace"* (*S.E.* 18, 25). Interestingly enough, Walter Benjamin misquotes this passage in his essay "On Some Motifs in Baudelaire" when he writes, *"das Bewußtsein entstehe* an der Stelle der *Erinnerungsspur."* Harry Zohn passes on this apparent slip when he translates this phrase as "consciousness comes into being *at the site of* a memory trace" (160). While Benjamin's citation may be unfaithful to the original in the most literal sense, it nevertheless serves to tease out and highlight a crucial ambiguity at the core of Freud's thinking. What Benjamin draws attention to through his own apparent parapraxis, Lacan indicates through a pun on the phrase *au lieu de*. I argue in Chapter 5 that Benjamin draws out a similar ambiguity in the Freudian notion of *Angstbereitschaft*.

31. Baines, 131; *S.E.* 14, 182–83.

32. Baines, 131–32; *S.E.* 14, 183.

33. In this regard, it may be helpful to recall the distinction Freud draws between the "momentary impact" of an external stimulus and the "constant force" and "constant urgency" (*konstant drängende*) of a drive in "Drives and Their Vicissitudes" (*S.E.* 14, 118). This distinction seems to

translate into temporal terms the spatial contrast drawn here between a localized point of effraction (*Einbruchspforte*) and a more diffuse protective structure (*Vorbau*). Whereas the momentary impact of an external stimulus may be dealt with through a one-time response, the urgency (*Drang*) of the drive interacts with the process of repression (*Verdrängung*) in a more ongoing and compromising manner.

34. Baines, 132; *S.E.*14, 184; trans. mod.

35. Baines, 132; *S.E.*14, 184.

36. Thus, Freud returns to the question in the final section of "The Unconscious." Yet, as Samuel Weber has demonstrated, Freud's new contention that repression denies the translation of thing-representations into the "corresponding" word-representations itself raises more questions than it answers. For "there is the question of just how object-cathexes themselves come to be stabilized. Second, there is the question of the relation of the psychic to the social order, inasmuch as enduring and corresponding verbal associations imply the relation of the individual subject to a preexisting language-system, and hence to a social and cultural context. Third, in view of the overdetermined nature of words, manifest in dreams, jokes and other articulations of the unconscious, the notion of 'correspondence' raises the question of the intrapsychic mechanism that establishes verbal identity. If [as Freud claims] the verbal discourse of consciousness tends to be 'closed and exclusive,' how does closure and exclusion come about?" In pursuing these questions it is significant for our purposes that Weber goes on to underscore the dependency of the *"intrapsychic* mechanism of repression" on "interdictions that antedate and transcend the realm of the purely psychic." *"Repression,"* he insists, *"depends on systems of social constraints and sanctions.* Its power to exclude and hence to enclose—which is nothing short of its power to allow cathexes and, hence, the psychic, to take place—depends on a *place* that it does not constitute, but that is already structured by metapsychic forces and traditions" (Weber, *Legend of Freud,* 47–48; emphasis in original). It is this interrelationship of linguistic, psychical, and social forces that I endeavor to develop in Chapter 5 through a reading of texts by Freud, Benjamin, and Baudelaire.

37. Baines, 139; *S.E.*14, 192.

Chapter 5. *En Garde!*

1. These remarks on trauma are greatly indebted to Cathy Caruth's discussion of the subject in her introduction to "Psychoanalysis, Culture, and Trauma" (Special Issue), *American Imago* 48 (Spring 1991): 1–12, esp. 3.

2. This different mode of *arrival* in Benjamin is staged in Freud's writings on trauma as a problematic *act of leaving.* See in this regard Caruth's

reading of Freud's *Moses and Monotheism* in "Unclaimed Experience: Trauma and the Possibility of History," *Yale French Studies* 79 (January 1991): 190–92.

3. See Chapter 4, note 33. See also Harold Bloom, "Freud: Frontier Concepts, Jewishness, and Interpretation," *American Imago* 48 (Spring 1991): 135–52.

4. Compare in this regard Benjamin's description of aura in section 11 as "the associations which, at home in the *mémoire involontaire,* tend to cluster [*zu gruppieren streben*] around the object of perception"; "its analogue in the case of a utilitarian object is the experience [*Erfahrung*] which has left traces of the practiced hand" (186).

5. It might also be noted that Poe clusters a similar crowd of associations about the signifier "press" in "The Man of the Crowd."

6. In the deafening street that howled all around me,
   Tall, slender, in mourning dress, her grief majestic,
   A woman passed by, her elegant hand
   Raising and balancing the ceremonial hem;

   Agile and noble, and legs statuesque.
   And I there drank, clenched like a man in a fit,
   From her eyes, livid sky where storm is born,
   Drank the softness that charms and the pleasure that kills.

   A flash . . . then night! Beautiful fugitive,
   Whose look has suddenly made me feel reborn,
   Will I never see you again till eternity dawns?

7. Elsewhere, far from here! Too late! *Never* perhaps!
   For I don't know your course, and you don't know mine,
   O you I would have loved, o you who must have known it!

For more detailed readings of this poem in the context of Benjamin's essay, see Geoffrey H. Hartman, *Criticism in the Wilderness* (New Haven: Yale University Press, 1980), 67–71; and Elissa Marder's superb article "Flat Death: Snapshots of History," *Diacritics* 22, no. 3–4 (Fall–Winter 1992): 128–43.

8. As Benjamin comments, "This is the look . . . of the object of a love which only a city dweller experiences, which Baudelaire captured for poetry, and of which one might not infrequently say that *it was spared, rather than denied, fulfillment*" (170; emphasis added).

9. See in this regard Benjamin's simile of the tangent in his discussion of the importance of sense (*Sinn*) in the relationship between translation and original. "The Task of the Translator," in *Illuminations,* trans. Harry Zohn, ed. Hannah Arendt (New York: Schocken Books, 1969), 80.

10. See Ackbar Abbas's discussion of the attenuation of the power of the image as an effect of shock in "On Fascination: Walter Benjamin's Images," *New German Critique*, no. 48 (Fall 1989): 44.

11. Needless to say, the illusion of "moving pictures" is itself based on the optical effect of the after-image.

12.   One is even uglier and fouler than the rest,
       although the least flamboyant of the lot:
       this beast would gladly undermine the earth
       and swallow all creation in a yawn;

   I speak of Boredom which with ready tears
   dreams of hangings as it puffs its pipe.
   Reader, you know this squeamish monster well,
   —hypocrite reader,— my alias,— my twin!

13. See in this regard Siegfried Kracauer's *"Langeweile"* and *"Die War-tenden,"* in his *Schriften* (Frankfurt am Main: Suhrkamp, 1990), 5.1:160–70, 278–81, as well as Mann's meditations on tedium in his *"Zeitroman,"* *The Magic Mountain* (New York: Vintage Books, 1969).

14. Benjamin, *Das Passagen-Werk*, vol. 1, ed. Rolf Tiedemann (Frankfurt am Main: Suhrkamp, 1982), 161; translation mine.

15. In an excellent article, "Translating Freud," Jean Laplanche, Pierre Cotet, and André Bourguignon describe *Angstbereitschaft* as a "single compound word, both of whose terms are identical while the underlying connection is different. In the term *Angstbereitschaft,"* they explain, *"Angst* is sometimes that for which one prepares oneself ("preparedness for anxiety") and sometimes that which enables one to be ready for danger ("preparedness by anxiety").

"This means that the terminologist will have to respond to a double concern: to discern the relation or, more often, the multiple relations existing between two terms [or in this case, between the opposing senses of a single compound term] and also to opt for a translation that safeguards the polysemic, sometimes ambiguous value of the compositional link." Their article, which appears in *Translating Freud*, ed. Darius Gray Ornston, Jr. (New Haven: Yale University Press, 1992), is translated from the French by Maev de la Guardia and Bertrand Vichyn and is excerpted from the authors' *Traduire Freud* (Paris: Presses universitaires de France, 1989). See 181–82.

16. This latter conception comes closer to Freud's discussion in "The Unconscious" of anxiety's functioning as a quantitative signal of approaching danger and its relationship to the diffuse protective structure surrounding the substitute representation.

17. As Benjamin says, *"Beyond the Pleasure Principle* . . . presents a

correlation between memory (in the sense of the *mémoire involontaire*) and consciousness in the form of a hypothesis. The following remarks based on it [*die . . . an sie anschließen*] are not intended to confirm it" (160).

18. One might recall in this regard Aristophanes' story contained in Plato's *Symposium* which tells of the way Zeus and the other gods decided literally to divide and conquer a third, androgynous race that "in strength and power . . . were terrible . . . and had great ambitions" (*Symposium,* 190B). In chapter 6 of *Beyond,* Freud cites a portion of this story, which he says "deals not only with the origin of the sexual instinct but also with the most important of its variants in relation to its object" (69). Curiously, what he omits in his citation is precisely the gods' motivation for partitioning this race. He glosses over this element of conflict with the phrase, "Zeus let himself be persuaded to cut these men in two" (70; trans. mod.), whereas Aristophanes tells of how "they made an attempt on the gods, and Homer's story about Ephialtes and Otos was originally about them: how they tried to make an ascent to heaven so as to attack the gods. Then Zeus and the other gods met in council to discuss what to do, and they were sore perplexed. They couldn't wipe out the human race . . . because that would wipe out the worship they receive along with the sacrifices we humans give them. On the other hand, they couldn't let them run riot." Thus, Zeus decides to cut each of them in two. "At one stroke they will lose their strength and also become more profitable to us, owing to the increase in their number" (190C–D).

19. This notion of a "forebody" is taken from Elias Canetti's discussion of *Angst* in *Kafka's Other Trial.* There he writes, "Hypochondria is the small change of *Angst;* it is *Angst* which, for its distraction, seeks names and finds them. [Kafka's] sensitivity to noise is like a warning; it announces ancillary, as yet unarticulated dangers. One can evade these by avoiding noise like the devil: he has enough to do with the recognized dangers, whose concerted attacks he repulses, by naming them. His room is a shelter, it becomes an outer body, one can call it his 'forebody.'" Canetti, *Kafka's Other Trial,* trans. Christopher Middleton (New York: Schocken Books, 1974), 26–27. I return to these issues in Chapter 8 in the context of Benjamin's Kafka essay and the latter's story "The Metamorphosis."

20. Jacques Derrida, "Freud and the Scene of Writing," in *Writing and Difference,* trans. Alan Bass (Chicago: University of Chicago Press, 1978), 225; emphasis added.

21. It is not irrelevant to note in this regard that the word "trauma" derives from the cognate Greek term meaning "wound."

22. Obviously, in a modern, urban environment it is not merely or even primarily the individual subject who performs these operations but also

and perhaps above all the institution of the press. Compare in this regard Benjamin's brief discussion of newspapers (*Zeitungen*) in this essay: "If it were the intention of the press [*die Presse*] to have the reader assimilate the information it supplies as part of his own experience [*Erfahrung*], it would not achieve its purpose. But its intention is just the opposite, and it is achieved: to isolate what happens from the realm in which it could affect the experience of the reader [*die Ereignisse gegen den Bereich abzudichten, in dem sie die Erfahrung des Lesers betreffen könnten*]. The principles of journalistic information (freshness of the news, brevity, comprehensibility, and, above all, lack of connection between the individual news items) contribute as much to this as does the make-up of the pages and the paper's style" (158).

23. In this context in which consciousness of time appears to function as a supplementary "sixth sense," one might recall Freud's remark in *The Ego and the Id* that "the way we gain new knowledge of our organs during painful illnesses is perhaps a model of the way by which in general we arrive at the idea of our body. The ego is first and foremost a bodily ego; it is not merely a surface entity but is itself the projection of a surface" (*S.E.*19, 26).

24. For an extended discussion of the figure of the cross-coupler, see Joel Fineman's masterful essay "Shakespeare's *Will:* The Temporality of Rape," *Representations,* no. 20 (1987): 25–76.

25. Derrida, "Freud and the Scene of Writing," 226–27.

26. Rey Chow remarks, "The crowd represents an oppression that is nameless; it defies figural representation and yet is felt everywhere as effect." Rather than pursuing this insight, Chow merely adds, "However, unlike Baudrillard's, Benjamin's discourse remains modernist in the sense that, in spite of the amorphousness of the mass, he associates with it the element of shock which is attributed to the nature of Baudelaire's artistic process." Chow, "Benjamin's Love Affair with Death," *New German Critique* 48 (Fall 1989): 83–84.

27. The passage cited by Benjamin is from Baudelaire's *The Painter of Modern Life*.

28.   Along the old faubourg where the masonry is tented by
       Shutters, sheltering secret pleasures,
       When the cruel sun's redoubled beams
       Are lashing city and field, roofs and grain,
       I go, alone, to practice my curious fencing,
       In every corner smelling out the dodges of rhyme,
       Stumbling over words as over cobblestones,
       Colliding now and then with long-dreamed-of verses.

29. Here one might recall Derrida's discussion of "breaching" cited on page 5. The German term used by Freud is *Bahnungen.*

30. Gide is cited in Benjamin, 164.

31. Baudelaire's remarks are cited in *Das Passagen-Werk,* 1: 315; translation mine.

32. To this sentence Benjamin appends an important footnote in which he cites a passage from Poe's "Colloquy of Monos and Una." "There seems to have sprung up in the brain that of which no words could convey to the merely human intelligence even an indistinct conception. Let me term it a mental pendulous pulsation. It was the moral embodiment of man's abstract idea of Time. By the absolute equalization of this movement—or of such as this—had the cycles of the firmamental orbs themselves been adjusted. By its aid I measured the irregularities of the clock upon the mantel, and of the watches of the attendants. Their tickings came sonorously to my ears. The slightest deviation from the true proportion . . . affected me just as violations of abstract truth are wont, on earth, to affect the moral sense" (199–200). Here the subject no longer idly marks the passage of time but is instead subjected to it and marked by it as Time autonomizes itself in and as a movement of "absolute equalization."

33. See Georg Lukács's chapter "Reification and the Consciousness of the Proletariat," in *History and Class Consciousness,* trans. Rodney Livingstone (Cambridge: MIT Press, 1975), 83–223.

34. This lack of distance may explain Benjamin's description of the distracting element of film as "primarily tactile" (238).

35. Whereas Benjamin's notion of distraction represents a different mode of attention, Kracauer's essay "The Cult of Distraction" treats it as a hollow and inauthentic overstimulation of the senses. "The stimulations of the senses succeed each other with such rapidity that there is no room left for even the slightest contemplation to squeeze in between them. . . . The penchant for distraction demands and finds an answer in the display of pure externality." In *New German Critique* 40 (Winter 1987): 94, trans. Thomas Y. Levin.

Chapter 6. *Touche!*

1. Or rather, I should say that the main body of the essay concludes in this way. There is, of course, also the famous epilogue, which would require a separate, extended discussion.

2. One might recall in this regard Benjamin's reference to Freud's *Psychopathology of Everyday Life.*

3. Commenting on this move, Peter Gay remarks that "Freud's peroration, quoting *Faust,* is so felicitous that it is tempting to wonder whether he had not gone all this distance in order to close his text with Goethe's

famous line." *Freud: A Life for Our Time* (New York: Doubleday, 1989), 331.

4. The word "primitive" appears in quotation marks here and must be understood to be Freud's and not my own. The facile and problematic equation that he sometimes makes between children and so-called primitives will be discussed later.

5. Here, in spite of its awkwardness, I use the impersonal pronoun "it" in order to retain the gender neutrality of the German *es*. It is especially important to translate *es* as "it" when the noun it stands in for is *das Kind*. On the connection between *das Es* (the id) and *das Kind* (the child), see Bruno Bettelheim, *Freud and Man's Soul* (New York: Vintage Books, 1982), 57.

6. Emphasis in the original.

7. As we have had sufficient occasion to note, Freud implicitly associates the straightforwardly literal with what is physically most immediate — thus, for example, his equation of a literal sense of touch (*Berührung*) with the physical sense of direct bodily contact (*direkte Berührung mit dem Körper*).

8. Tylor's remark is cited in English in the original.

9. See in this regard Susan Derwin's fine essay "Mimesis in a Two-way Mirror: Freud's *Totem und Tabu*," in her book *The Ambivalence of Form* (Baltimore: Johns Hopkins University Press, 1992), 35–50.

10. See Shoshana Felman's excellent discussion of the practice and parapraxis of speech act theory in *The Literary Speech Act: Don Juan with J. L. Austin, or Seduction in Two Languages*, trans. Catherine Porter (Ithaca: Cornell University Press, 1983).

11. That examples in particular are fundamentally incontinent and in turn provoke acts of incontinence is suggested by Freud's discussion of taboo-breakers. "Anyone who has violated a taboo becomes taboo himself because he possesses the dangerous quality of tempting others to follow his example: why should *he* be allowed to do what is forbidden to others? He is thus truly *contagious* [*ansteckend*] insofar as every example infects one with a desire to imitate it [*jedes Beispiel zur Nachahmung ansteckt*]" (*S.E.* 13, 32; emphasis in original).

12. As is well known, the term "parasite" derives from the Greek *parasitos*, one who eats at the table of another; from *para*: beside and *sitos*: food, grain. For an extended discussion of this term and its historical vicissitudes, see Michel Serres, *The Parasite*, trans. Lawrence R. Schehr (Baltimore: Johns Hopkins University Press, 1982). See also Jacques Derrida, trans. Samuel Weber, "Limited Inc abc . . . ," *Glyph 2: Johns Hopkins Textual Studies* (Baltimore: Johns Hopkins University Press, 1977), 223–51.

13. See in this regard Lacan's revalorization of the bar in the Saussurean

algorithm of the sign in "The Agency of the Letter in the Unconscious," in *Ecrits: A Selection,* trans. Alan Sheridan (New York: Norton, 1977), 146–78. See also Jean-Luc Nancy and Philippe Lacoue-Labarthe's reading of this essay in *The Title of the Letter,* trans. François Raffoul and David Pettigrew (Albany: SUNY Press, 1992), esp. 35–36.

14. One might also recall in this regard his discussion of spacing in *The Interpretation of Dreams.*

15. It might be noted at this point that the question of weapons is also raised parenthetically at the beginning of Freud's description of the sons' collective murder of the primal father. There he remarks, "United, they had the courage to do and succeeded in doing what would have been impossible for them individually. (Some cultural advance, perhaps, command over some new weapon, had given them a sense of superior strength.)" (*S.E.* 14, 141–42); I return to this passage in Chapter 7.

16. That such compromises between isolation and contamination are precisely what interest Freud in the notion of taboo may be inferred from his claim that taboo's double sense of sacred and unclean belonged to it from the very first.

17. Harold Bloom, "Reading Freud: Transference, Taboo, and Truth," in *Center and Labyrinth: Festschrift for Northrop Frye,* ed. Eleanor Cook (Toronto: University of Toronto Press, 1983).

18. Thomas M. Greene suggestively links this passage to Freud's later essay "A Difficulty in Psychoanalysis," in his *Poésie et magie* (Paris: Julliard, 1991), 78–81.

19. The verb Freud uses to describe the coming together of the brothers in order to kill the primal father is *sich zusammentun,* a term which in this particular context could very well be translated literally as "getting their act together."

Chapter 7. Acknowledgments

1. R. Horatio Etchegoyen, "'On Narcissism: An Introduction': Text and Context" in *Freud's "On Narcissism: An Introduction,"* ed. Joseph Sandler, Ethel Person, and Peter Fonagy (New Haven: Yale University Press, 1991), 54.

2. Ibid., 66.

3. J. Laplanche and J.-B. Pontalis, *The Language of Psycho-Analysis,* trans. Donald Nicholson-Smith (New York: Norton, 1973), 337.

4. In *The Introductory Lectures on Psychoanalysis* Freud writes, "The picture of the blissful isolation of intra-uterine life which a sleeper conjures up once more before us every night is in this way completed on its psychical side as well. In a sleeper the primal state of distribution of the libido is restored—total narcissism, in which libido and ego-interest, still

united and indistinguishable, dwell in the self-sufficing ego" (*S.E.*16, 417).

5. Gérard Genette defines free indirect style as those moments "when the narrator takes on the speech of the character or, if one prefers, the character speaks through the voice of the narrator, and the two instances are then merged." Elsewhere he adds that "the remarkable advantage . . . derived from this ambiguity [is that it] permits [the author] to make his own language speak this both loathsome and fascinating idiom of the 'other' without being wholly compromised or wholly innocent." *Narrative Discourse: An Essay in Method,* trans. Jane E. Lewin (Ithaca: Cornell University Press, 1980), 174, 172. Freud slips into free indirect style in the passage beginning, "The child shall have things better." I return to this narrative "mood" in Chapter 8.

6. Mikkel Borch-Jacobsen draws attention to the pivotal significance of this passage: "The whole theory of narcissism . . . depends on this paragraph, especially since this is the only passage in the essay in which Freud answers (so to speak) the question he had left open in the first section, namely, the question of the *origin* of primary narcissism." *The Freudian Subject,* trans. Catherine Porter (Stanford: Stanford University Press, 1988), 114.

7. Recall in this regard Freud's discussion of a magical recathexis of the seemingly neutral space isolating the "represented" from the "representation." Once again the contamination of this space dislocates the temporal relationship of a model or body that presumably "stands *before*" to an image or copy that allegedly "takes *after*." Here nothing can be said to stand before the image that does not in effect come *after* it—at least insofar as the image "itself" will never have been either an image of identity or a self-identical image. Instead, its primacy will have always already been double, split, and out of sync: phase one and a half and/or one in half.

8. For an excellent discussion of Lacan's theory of the "mirror stage," see Samuel Weber, *Return to Freud: Jacques Lacan's Dislocation of Psychoanalysis,* trans. Michael G. Levine (Cambridge: Cambridge University Press, 1991), 7–20.

9. Or as Lacan says in his seminar on the *"idéal du moi-moi idéal,"* "a human being can only see himself as a fully formed totality in and as a mirage of the self, outside of the self. [*L'être humain ne voit sa forme réalisée totale, le mirage de lui-même, que hors de lui-même.*]" It is significant that Lacan returns to the mirror stage in his "Remarque sur le rapport de Daniel Lagache: 'Psychanalyse et la structure de la personalité'" and in "De nos antécédants," precisely in order to (re-)introduce the question of "the glance of the other" into his discussion. Lacan, *Ecrits* (Paris: Editions du Seuil, 1966), 647–84, 65–72.

10. Here one might recall Freud's reference to Kant in the preface to

Totem and Taboo, where he states that "taboos still exist among us. Though expressed in a negative form and directed towards another subject-matter, they do not differ in their psychological nature from Kant's 'categorical imperative,' which operates in a compulsive fashion [*zwangsartig*] and rejects any conscious motives" (*S.E.* 13, xiv). On the relationship of Freud and Kant developed through a reading of *Totem and Taboo,* see Mikkel Borch-Jacobsen, "The Law of Psychoanalysis," trans. Gina Michelle Collins, *Diacritics* (Summer 1985): 26–36. Also see Jacques Derrida, *"Devant la Loi,"* trans. Avital Ronell, in *Kafka and the Contemporary Critical Performance,* ed. Alan Udoff (Bloomington: Indiana University Press, 1987), 128–49.

11. Needless to say, the Lacanian "mirror phase," like the Freudian notion of primary narcissism, is defined not so much as a genetic moment or stage of development but as a turning point or trope destined to be repeated incessantly.

12. A comparison of my translation of this sentence to that of James Strachey reveals an interesting ambiguity in Freud's use of the verb *erscheinen.* Strachey writes, "The subject's narcissism *makes its appearance* [*erscheint*] displaced on to this new ideal ego . . ."

13. Baines, 75. Strachey, by contrast, translates the same passage as follows: "It would not surprise us if we were to find a special psychical agency which performs the task of seeing that narcissistic satisfaction from the ego-ideal is ensured and which, with this end in view, constantly watches the actual ego and measures it by that ideal. If such an agency does exist, we cannot possibly come upon it as a *discovery*—we can only *recognize* it; for we may reflect that what we call our 'conscience' has the required characteristics. Recognition of this agency enables us to understand the so-called 'delusions of being noticed' or more correctly, of being *watched,* which are such striking symptoms in the paranoid diseases" (*S.E.* 14, 95).

14. As Freud says, the real ego is "constantly watched [*unausgesetzt beobachtet*]" by conscience, which "is appointed watchman [*Wächter*] over the ego-ideal" (*S.E.* 14, 96; trans. mod.).

15. According to Freud, "The institution of conscience was at bottom an embodiment first of parental criticism" (*S.E.* 14, 96).

16. Patrick Mahoney, *Freud as a Writer* (New York: International Universities Press, 1982), 40.

17. Not only does Freud introduce this scene as "a fantastic sounding hypothesis [*Hypothese, die phantastisch erscheinen mag*]," but he concludes it with a long footnote, which begins, "This hypothesis, which has such a monstrous air . . . [*Die ungeheuerlich erscheinende Annahme* . . .]" (*S.E.* 13, 142). While this term is used primarily to signal Freud's

debt to the "hypotheses of Robertson Smith," one might also interpret it as an attempt to situate his own version of the primal scene in a speculative dimension more along the lines of the "hypothesis of primary narcissism."

18. In his polemic with Freud, René Girard asserts, "The work was published in 1913, when ethnology was still a fledgling science. The theories drawn on by Freud—Frazer's, in particular Robertson Smith's—have long been superseded. The concept of totemism is virtually obsolete; and above all, Freud's main thesis is patently false." *Violence and the Sacred,* trans. Patrick Gregory (Baltimore: Johns Hopkins University Press, 1977), 194–95.

19. Freud sums up all these connections in his concluding citation of Faust's famous line, "In the beginning was the Deed."

20. Claude Lévi-Strauss, *The Elementary Structures of Kinship,* trans. James Harle Bell, John Richard von Sturmer, and Rodney Needman (Boston: Beacon Press, 1969), 491; Derrida, *"Devant la Loi,"* 138.

21. Lévi-Strauss argues that "the failure of *Totem and Taboo,* far from being inherent in the author's proposed design, results rather from his hesitation to avail himself of the ultimate consequences implied in his premises. He ought to have seen that phenomena involving the most fundamental structure of the human mind could not have appeared once and for all. . . . One can speak of explanations only when the past of the species constantly recurs in the indefinitely multiplied drama of each individual thought, because it is itself only the retrospective projection of a transition which has occurred, because it occurs continually" (491). Derrida says, "The structure of this event is such that one is compelled neither to believe nor disbelieve it. Like the question of belief, that of the reality of its historic referent is, if not annulled, at least irremediably fissured. Demanding and defying the récit-telling, this quasi-event bears the mark of fictive narrativity. . . . This is the origin of literature and of the law at once—like the dead father, a story told, a spreading rumor, without author or term, but an ineluctible and unforgettable récit" (138).

22. In light of the fact that the essay "The Dynamics of the Transference" was published *before* the final two sections of *Totem and Taboo*—a fact of which Bloom is undoubtedly aware—his use of the term "crossing" in this passage should be understood not in the sense of a temporal movement from one text to another but rather in the sense of a *chiasmatic* movement of reading in which *Totem and Taboo* and the essay on transference would be shown to inform—and displace—each other; this indeed seems to be his strategy in "Reading Freud," 322.

Chapter 8. The Sense of an *Unding*

1. The letter is in Franz Kafka, *Letters to Friends, Family, and Editors,* trans. Richard Winston and Clara Winston (New York: Schocken Books, 1977), 286–89. This volume is based on the collection of Kafka's *Briefe (1902–1924),* ed. Max Brod (New York: Schocken Books, 1958). See also Gilles Deleuze and Félix Guattari's discussion of this letter in their chapter "What Is a Minor Literature?" in *Kafka: Toward a Minor Literature,* ed. and trans. Dana Polan (Minneapolis: University of Minnesota Press, 1986), 16–27.

2. Kafka, *Letters to Friends,* 288; trans. mod.

3. For a book-length discussion of this essay, see Sven Kramer's *Rätselfragen und wolkige Stellen: Zu Benjamins Kafka-Essay* (Lüneburg: zu Klampen, 1991).

4. All further page references, which appear in parentheses in the body of the text, are to Benjamin's "Franz Kafka: On the Tenth Anniversary of His Death," in his *Illuminations,* trans. Harry Zohn, ed. Hannah Arendt (New York: Schocken Books, 1969).

5. The following discussion of the "cloudy spot [*wolkige Stelle*]" in Benjamin is greatly indebted to Werner Hamacher's unpublished essay "Failing Literature: (Benjamin's Reading of Kafka's Example)." See also his reading of "The Word *Wolke*—If It Is One," in *Benjamin's Ground,* ed. Rainer Nägele (Detroit: Wayne State University Press, 1988), 147-76.

6. Such structures, I would suggest, may also include the stress of an accent, the -phor of metaphor, or the *tragende* -fer of transference (*Übertragung*).

7. The notion of orbital paths such as those traced by the rings of Saturn also resonates in the German term used by Benjamin.

8. More generally, I would suggest that there is a certain structural affinity between the "cloudy spots" of the Kafka essay and the "crowded passages" of Benjamin's essay on Baudelaire discussed in Chapter 5. In both, a language of positing, positioning, and *Stellung* gives way at certain crucial points to more diffuse movements of displacement, disfiguration, and *Entstellung.*

9. It is no accident that the passages dealt with here belong to a section of Benjamin's essay whose introductory paragraph sets the tone for what follows. In it, Benjamin relates Knut Hamsun's reaction to the trial of a maid in a nearby town who had killed her infant child. "She was sentenced to a prison term. Soon thereafter the local paper printed a letter from Hamsun in which he announced his intention of leaving a town which did not visit the supreme punishment on a mother who killed her newborn child — the gallows, or at least a life term of hard labor. A few years passed.

Growth of the Soil appeared, and it contained the story of a maid who committed the same crime, suffered the same punishment, and, as is made clear to the reader, surely deserved no more severe one" (127). Introduced by this story, the section never quite leaves the question of infanticide, which returns in various guises in the following pages.

10. See in this regard Derrida's essay *"Devant la loi,"* trans. Avital Ronell, in *Kafka and the Contemporary Critical Performance,* ed. Alan Udoff (Bloomington: Indiana University Press, 1987), 128–49.

11. Walter Benjamin, "A Berlin Chronicle," in his *Reflections,* ed. Peter Demetz, trans. Edmund Jephcott (New York: Schocken Books, 1978), 8.

12. References are to Corngold's translation of *The Metamorphosis* (New York: Bantam Books, 1972) and appear henceforth in parentheses in the body of the text.

13. Commenting on the fact that Kafka's text reaches its climax by the end of the first line (whose last word is indeed the past participle of the verb *verwandeln*), Martin Greenberg notes, "a climax that occurs in the first sentence is no real climax." Greenberg, *The Terror of Art: Kafka and Modern Literature* (New York: Basic Books, 1968), 84.

14. In a letter of October 25, 1915, Kafka implores his publisher to allow the text of *The Metamorphosis* to appear without any depiction of the "insect" Gregor has become. "It struck me," he writes, "that Starke, as an illustrator, might want to draw the insect itself. Not that, please not that! I do not want to restrict him, but only to make this plea out of my deeper knowledge of the story, as is natural. The insect itself cannot be depicted. It cannot even be shown from a distance." *Letters to Friends, Family, and Editors,* 114–15.

15. That is, the adjective *geheuer* is employed only with the prefix *un-* or is preceded by the negation *nicht,* as in the phrase *"mir ist das nicht geheuer."* Similarly, the noun *Geziefer,* which is in fact still to be found in the dictionary, is now employed primarily as a synonym for the term *Ungeziefer,* to which it was initially opposed.

16. In a provocative essay on labyrinths, Philip West notes that in the symbolism of the High Middle Ages a clean beast was one who knew how to interpret the Bible, whereas an unclean beast could not transcend the most mundane literalism. Philip West, "Redundant Labyrinths," *Salmagundi* 46 (Fall 1979): 78.

17. Willa and Edwin Muir translate the phrase *ungeheures Ungeziefer* as "gigantic insect" in *Kafka: The Complete Stories,* ed. Nahum N. Glatzer (New York: Schocken Books, 1976) 89, while Corngold renders it as "monstrous vermin" in *The Metamorphosis* (3). Reflecting on the problems involved in translating these terms, Corngold says, "what is remarkable in *The Metamorphosis* is that "the immortal part" [Adorno] of the

writer accomplishes itself odiously, in the quality of an indeterminacy sheerly negative. The exact sense of his intention is captured in the *Ungeziefer*, a word that cannot be expressed by the English words 'bug' or 'vermin.'" Stanley Corngold, *Franz Kafka: The Necessity of Form* (Ithaca: Cornell University Press, 1988), 57.

18. Here one might wish to return to Kafka's letter to Brod and his discussion of *mauscheln*. "What we have here," he says, "is the product of a sensitive feeling for language which has recognized that in German only the dialects are really alive, and except for them, only the most individual High German, while all the rest, the linguistic middle ground, is nothing but embers which can only be brought to a semblance of life when excessively lively Jewish hands rummage through them. That is a fact, funny or terrible as you like." Such rummaging, I would suggest, is evident in the linguistic distortions of *The Metamorphosis*. For a further discussion of this famous passage, see Hannah Arendt's introduction to the English translation of Benjamin's *Illuminations*, 31–35.

19. That Gregor is always in need of an interpreter is confirmed not only "intratextually" by Kafka's use of free indirect style, in which the narrator's voice supplements that of the character, or, if one prefers, the character speaks through the voice of the narrator, but also "extratextually" by the enormous body of secondary literature which the text continues to elicit. See in this regard Stanley Corngold, *The Commentators' Despair: The Interpretation of Kafka's "Metamorphosis"* (Port Washington, N.Y.: Kennikat Press, 1973). In many ways the reading I propose here is an attempt to identify the structure of supplementarity and belatedness which will have been set in motion by *The Metamorphosis*.

20. *The Diaries of Franz Kafka (1910–1913)*, trans. Joseph Kresh, ed. Max Brod (New York: Schocken Books, 1948), 211.

21. I would further suggest that the blurry scene of *Vereinigung* described here be related to the vision of parental union recounted at the end of section 2, in which Gregor sees his mother force "herself onto his father, and embracing him, in complete union [*in gänzlicher Vereinigung*] with him—but now Gregor's sight went dim [*nun versagte aber Gregors Sehkraft schon*]—her hands clasping his father's neck, begged for Gregor's life" (39).

22. In contrast to Walter Sokel, who sees in this situation evidence that Gregor is now no longer treated as an adult or even as a man, since people talk through him rather than to or with him, I would argue that the scene draws attention both to Gregor's centrality in the family dynamic and in more literal and ironic terms to the strange capaciousness of his "regular human room, a little on the small side." Cf. Sokel, *Franz Kafka—Tragik und Ironie: Zur Struktur seiner Kunst* (Munich: A. Langen, 1964), 77.

23. In a superb discussion of *The Metamorphosis,* to which my own reading is greatly indebted, Heinz Politzer observes that as space closes in on Gregor, time also seems to dissolve. See his *Parable and Paradox* (Ithaca: Cornell University Press, 1962), 69.

24. As Adorno observes, "Gestures often serve as counterpoints to words [in Kafka]: the pre-linguistic that eludes all intention upsets the ambiguity, which like a disease, has eaten into all signification in Kafka. . . . Such gestures are the traces of experience covered over by signification. The most recent state of a language that wells up in the mouths of those who speak it, the second Babylonian confusion, which Kafka's sober diction tirelessly opposes, compels him to invert the historical relation of concept and gesture." Theodor W. Adorno, "Notes on Kafka," in his *Prisms,* trans. Samuel Weber and Shierry Weber (Cambridge: MIT Press, 1992), 249.

25. Despite appearances, Gregor's prostration is not altogether a bad thing. As Kafka writes in a letter to Felice Bauer, "Just as when lying on the floor one cannot fall, so, when alone, nothing can happen to one." Kafka, *Letters to Felice,* trans. James Stern and Elizabeth Duckworth (New York: Schocken Books, 1973), 176. This letter was written between January 29 and January 30, 1913. Kafka worked on *The Metamorphosis* from November 17 to December 7, 1912.

26. One might consider in this regard the following passage from Kafka's *Letter to His Father:* "My writing was all about you. All I did there, after all, was to bemoan what I could not bemoan upon your breast. It was an intentionally long-drawn-out leave-taking from you, yet, although it was brought about by force on your part, *it did take its course in the direction determined by me"* (emphasis added). *Dearest Father: Stories and Other Writings,* trans. Ernst Kaiser and Eithne Wilkins (New York: Schocken Books, 1954), 177.

27. See in this regard Politzer's illuminating discussion of the ensuing scene in which father and son do a kind of circle dance about one another. Politzer sees in the image of the circle a symbol of "the inextricable self-involvement of Gregor's fate." He continues, "With the consistency that characterizes Kafka's inspiration at its best, he now chooses a round object [an apple] to put an end once and for all to Gregor's aimless circular wanderings." *Parable and Paradox,* 73.

28. While Frederick Ahl unfortunately does not discuss the sections of book 8 devoted to the story of the Minotaur, one may infer from his brilliant study of *The Metamorphoses* that the seemingly frivolous attempt to sound out the resonant *Wand* in the midst of Kafka's *Ver-wand-lung* is in fact very much in keeping with Ovidian metamorphic tradition. Ahl's reading of *The Metamorphoses* is based on a hypothesis—which is carefully

documented and, to my mind, persuasively proven in the course of his book—that Ovid "accompanies his descriptions of change in physical shape with changes in the shape of the words with which he describes those changes" (51). He argues that "for Ovid, as for Plato, the letters within words are the substrate, the shifting reality which establishes, undermines, redefines meaning at the verbal level. A sentence is a movable configuration of letters and syllables rather than of words" (54). Taking one example among many, Ahl observes how in "the first line of Ovid the Greek METaMORPHosis is itself changed into the Latin MUTatas . . . FORMas. FORMa is a cross-language anagram of MORPHe and MUTatas even echoes the consonant patterns of the Greek." Frederick Ahl, *Metaformations* (Ithaca: Cornell University Press, 1985), 59.

29. Ovid, *The Metamorphoses,* trans. Mary M. Innes (London: Penguin Books, 1955), 179. Further references appear in parentheses in the body of the text.

30. See Hermann Pongs, "Franz Kafka—'Die Verwandlung' zwischen West und Ost," in *Dichtung im gespaltenen Deutschland* (Stuttgart: Union, 1966), 262–85.

31. Friedrich Nietzsche, *On the Advantage and Disadvantage of History for Life,* trans. Peter Preuss (Indianapolis: Hackett Publishing, 1980), 8.

32. Mark Anderson makes a compelling argument for reading this picture "as a coded reference to Kafka's own appropriation of Sacher-Masoch's narrative," *Venus in Furs.* See his fascinating book, *Kafka's Clothes* (Oxford: Oxford University Press, 1992), 136; see also his "Kafka and Sacher-Masoch," in *Franz Kafka's "The Metamorphosis": Modern Critical Interpretations,* ed. Harold Bloom (New York: Chelsea House, 1988). In order to make this argument, however, Anderson must treat the fifth side of the frame, the glass against which Gregor presses himself and which holds him fast, as a transparent medium that effaces itself and its own significance in order to allow one to see through it to the depths of the framed contents of the picture. This kind of approach, while certainly fruitful, nevertheless tends to *look through* rather than *at* the glass and by extension through a signifying surface that parasitically draws attention to itself as a sonorous and semi-opaque becoming-wall of metamorphosis. To observe this all too conspicuous foreground of *Die Ver-wand-lung,* I have argued that it is necessary to read in a pointedly myopic fashion, pressing oneself against the text's glassy surface as it in turn holds one fast.

33. As though to stress the importance not only of the frame but of the activity of framing, Gregor's mother explains to the chief clerk that "it's already a distraction for [her son] when he's busy working with his fretsaw. For instance, in the span of two or three evenings he carved a little

frame. You'll be amazed how pretty it is" (10). Later on, when Gregor's room is being cleared out, it is said that the mother and sister were "depriving him of everything that he loved; they had already carried away the chest of drawers, in which he kept the fretsaw and other tools" (35). Even the first mention of the picture in the second paragraph of the text emphasizes the way in which Gregor "had recently cut [it] out of a glossy magazine and lodged [it] in a pretty gilt frame" (3).

34. Corngold, *Kafka,* 49.

35. Here I follow with slight modifications Corngold's translation of a passage from Anders's superb *Kafka, pro und contra* (Munich: Beck, 1951) rather than that of A. Steer and A. K. Thorlby, *Franz Kafka* (London: Bowes & Bowes, 1960). Cf. Corngold, *Franz Kafka,* 49. For a detailed discussion of the way Anders's hypothesis has been taken up and modified by Kafka criticism, see Corngold's chapter *"The Metamorphosis:* Metamorphosis of the Metaphor," 47–89.

36. Among the more notable exceptions to this approach are Werner Hamacher's "Failing Literature (Benjamin's Reading of Kafka's Example)," and Clayton Koelb's *Kafka's Rhetoric: The Passion of Reading* (Ithaca: Cornell University Press, 1989).

37. It is perhaps no coincidence that this process of defamiliarization reaches its uncanniest extreme in the scene in which Gregor mounts the picture on the wall. Finally tearing himself loose from the glass "to which he firmly adhered," he begins to crawl frantically "to and fro, over everything, walls, furniture, and ceiling" until the room itself seems to come unhinged: "the whole room," Kafka writes, "began to reel around him [*als sich das ganze Zimmer schon um ihn zu drehen anfing*]" (37; trans. mod.).

38. Corngold, *Kafka,* 85.

39. For an extended discussion of the relationship of narrator and protagonist in *The Metamorphosis,* see Roy Pascal, *Kafka's Narrators: A Study of His Stories and Sketches* (Cambridge: Cambridge University Press, 1982).

INDEX

Works are indexed under authors' names.

stincts, 80; and jokes, 82–83; and
language, 182n26; and pain, 80; and
phobia, 117; and pleasure, 80; and
representation, 82–85, 87; and resistance, 47; and substitution, 85; and
taboo, 126; and translation, 12; and
writing, 4–5, 24–25, 42
Resistance, 2, 50; in dreams, 51; of psychoanalysis, 47; and repression, 47;
and transference, 127
Reversal, in dreams, 34, 35
Revolution of 1848, and Heine, 1
Rey, Jean-Michel, 188n21
Rieff, Philip, 193n9
Rituals, and Freud, 124–25
Roustang, François, 11, 191n2
Rulers, social and political, 124–26,
186n15; and taboo, 124, 125–26, 135

Sadism, 7
Sammons, Jeffrey, 51–53, 69–70
Saussure, Ferdinand de, and Lacan, 17,
20, 202–3n13
Scheherazade, *Tales of the Thousand
and One Nights,* 62; and Kafka, 154
Schorske, Carl, 40–41
Screen memories, 16, 183n31, 192n6;
and Freud's language, 75
Secondary revision, 76; and dreams, 11,
12, 37–40, 81; and Freud's text, 137,
187n20; and Heine, 45; and narcis-
sism, 146
Self: and shock, 109; and generations,
139. *See also* Ego
Self-censorship, 29; and Freud, 26–28;
in Heine, 3, 28, 43–46, 54, 72,
187n20, 190n18; and Lacan, 26; and
writing, 41–42
Serres, Michel, 189n15, 202n12
Shakespeare, William, *Hamlet,* and
Heine, 43–44, 187n20
Shelley, Mary, 62
Shock: and Baudelaire, 93–94, 105–6;
and consciousness, 101–2; and experience, 106; and film, 110, 112,

113; and self, 109. *See also* Shock
defense
Shock defense, 102–3, 113; and Walter
Benjamin, 74, 90, 93, 98, 100,
198n10; and distraction, 113; and
interception, 99–100; and temporal-
ity, 109. *See also* Shock
Signorelli, Luca, 75, 192n7
Smith, Robertson, 142, 206n18
Sokel, Walter, 209n22
Space, in Kafka, 162–67, 170–71, 173–
78, 209n19
Spleen (Baudelaire's concept), 102, 109
Strachey, James, 11–12, 77, 79, 82, 97,
116, 136, 142, 183n31; and Baines,
193n9, 205n13; his commentary,
187n20; 205n12
Strauss, Leo, 179n4
Stuttering, in Heine, 3, 45, 52, 66–67
Subject: and censorship, 38; as dreaming, 36–37; and Heine, 67; and psy-
choanalysis, 8–9. *See also* Ego; Self

Taboo, 202n11; its etymology, 119; and
neurotics, 116; and rulers, 124, 125–
26, 135; and temporality, 140; and
transference, 145
Temporality. *See* Time
Time: and censorship, 31–32, 78–83,
90; and conscience, 140; and
dreams, 33, 124; and film, 111–12;
and Freud, 100–103, 193–94n12; and
interception, 103; and Kafka, 163;
and narcissism, 131–32, 134, 137, 139;
and shock, 91, 109; and taboo, 140;
and writing, 151, 154, 194n19
Touch: and aggression, 123–24, 126;
and Benjamin, 114; and Freud, 115;
and love, 123–24; and taboo, 123–24,
126; in *Totem and Taboo,* 115–16,
121–22
Transference, 146; and analysis,
127–28; Freud's understanding of,
126–28, 193n6; and Lacan, 18; and
narcissism, 130, 132–34, 136; and